• • • • • • •

GETTING IT RIGHT

THE **SECOND** TIME

• • • • • • •

Getting It Right the Second Time

HOW **AMERICAN**

INGENUITY TRANSFORMED

FORTY-NINE **MARKETING**

FAILURES INTO SOME OF

OUR MOST **SUCCESSFUL**

PRODUCTS

Michael Gershman

▲ Addison-Wesley
Publishing Company, Inc.

Reading, Massachusetts   Menlo Park, California
New York   Don Mills, Ontario   Wokingham, England
Amsterdam   Bonn   Sydney   Singapore
Tokyo   Madrid   San Juan

Many of the designations used by manufacturers and sellers to distinguish their products are claimed as trademarks. Where those designations appear in this book and Addison-Wesley was aware of a trademark claim, the designations have been printed in initial capital letters (e.g., Green Giant).

Amana is a registered trademark of Raytheon Corp. Aunt Jemima, Puffed Rice, and Quaker Oats are trademarks of Quaker Oats Corp. Barbasol is a registered trademark of Pfizer, Inc. Birds Eye, Jell-O, and Postum are registered trademarks of General Foods Corp. Borden's and Cracker Jack are registered trademarks of Borden Co. Budweiser is a registered trademark of Anheuser-Busch, Inc. Burma Shave and Marlboro are registered trademarks of Philip Morris. Coleman is a registered trademark of MacAndrews & Forbes Holdings, Inc. Culligan is a registered trademark of Culligan International. Dixie Cups is a registered trademark of James River Corp. Gerber is a registered trademark of Gerber Products Company. Green Giant is a registered trademark of Green Giant Corp. Hires Root Beer is a registered trademark of Cadbury Schweppes, Inc. Hoover is a registered trademark of Chicago Pacific Corp. Kleenex and Kotex are registered trademarks of Kimberly-Clark Corp. Kraft is a registered trademark of Kraft Inc. L'eggs is a registered trademark of Consolidated Foods. Life Savers is a registered trademark of RJR Nabisco. Lite Beer is a registered trademark of Miller Brewing Co. NCR is a registered trademark of NCR Corp. Pampers is a registered trademark of Procter & Gamble. Paper Mate and Toni are registered trademarks of Gillette. Pepsi-Cola is a registered trademark of Pepsico. Post-it is a registered trademark of 3M Corp. Quaker State is a registered trademark of Quaker State Motor Oil. Seven-Up is a registered trademark of Dr Pepper/Seven-Up. Sherwin-Williams is a registered trademark of SWP Co. Singer is a registered trademark of Singer Corp. Smirnoff is a registered trademark of Heublein, Inc. Softsoap is a registered trademark of Colgate-Palmolive. Timex is a registered trademark of Timex, Inc. Tupperware is a registered trademark of Tupperware Home Parties. Vaseline is a registered trademark of Chesebrough-Pond's. Vicks is a registered trademark of Richardson-Vicks. Welch's is a registered trademark of Welch's Inc. Wheaties and Yoplait are registered trademarks of General Mills. Wisk is a registered trademark of Unilever. Wrigley's is a registered trademark of Wrigley Co.

Library of Congress Cataloging-in-Publication Data

Gershman, Michael.
    Getting it right the second time : how American ingenuity transformed forty-nine marketing failures into some of our most successful products / Michael Gershman.
        p.   cm.
    Includes bibliographical references.
    ISBN 0-201-55082-2
    1. Consumer goods—United States—Marketing—Case studies.
    2. Brand name products—United States—Marketing—Case studies.
    I. Title.
    HF5415.G424   1990
    658.8'00973—dc20   90-35428

Jacket design by Steve Snider
Text design by Barbara Werden
Set in 11-point Sabon by Shepard Poorman, Indianapolis, IN

ABCDEFGHIJ-MW-9543210
First printing, August 1990

• • • • • •

This book is dedicated to my mother, Ann Lobell Gershman, and to Michael Powers, who always told me to try, try again.

• • • • • •

CONTENTS

• • • • • • •

ACKNOWLEDGMENTS

• • • • • •

MANY of the companies whose products are profiled in *Getting It Right the Second Time* were helpful in providing background material, verifying dates, and arranging interviews with the principals involved. I am grateful for the cooperation of Borden, Inc.; Chesebrough-Pond's; Coleman Corporation; Culligan International; Dixie Cups; General Foods; General Mills; Green Giant Foods; Hanes Corporation; Heublein, Inc.; Kimberly-Clark; Miller Brewing Company; 3M Corporation; Minnetonka Corporation; National Cash Register; Philip Morris; Procter & Gamble; Richardson-Vicks; 7-Up Company; Sherwin-Williams Corporation; Timex Corporation; and Tupperware Home Parties.

I would also like to personally thank Bob Bernstein, Bob Bertini, Dave Fogleson, Jo Ellen Helmlinger, Don Hintz, Jack Lewis, Jim Lovejoy, Mike Komives, Ellen Lubell, Betsy Russo, Peter Seremet, Bob Taylor, Cathy Taylor, and Grant Wood for the time they so graciously contributed to this project. I must also thank my agent, Betsy Nolan, for her wisdom and support over the long haul and Nancy Miller and Jane Isay for their enthusiasm and the finishing touches they provided.

Finally, this book could never have been written without the help of my wife and best friend, Suzy Kalter Gershman.

Michael Gershman

· · · · · · ·

INTRODUCTION

· · · · · · ·

This is a book about the American Dream, the happy knowledge that it is possible to start with nothing and to end up with something, sometimes a Very Big Something.

Dixie Cups, Life Savers, the microwave oven—these are the kinds of products entrepreneurs *dream* of creating. Each is worth millions today, but that wasn't always the case. In fact, each was originally an abject failure. Dixie Cups were part of an elaborate water fountain no one would buy, Life Savers were the laughing stock of the candy business, and microwaves didn't sell originally because consumers worried that radiation might make them sterile.

These products and forty-six others like them were conceived, failed, and reborn in the U. S. A., thanks to Yankee ingenuity and the enthusiasm and determination (some would say pigheadedness) of their creators. When their original dreams fizzled, these entrepreneurs wouldn't accept failure. They analyzed the reasons for their setbacks, came up with new marketing strategies, and successfully remarketed their products.

Marlboro cigarettes, the quintessence of symbolic masculinity, were born with red and white "beauty-tip" filters to attract female smokers. Kleenex was originally touted as a glamour product, complete with endorsements from Hollywood stars. Sales of Smirnoff vodka were so small at first that they were tallied along with "liqueurs and miscellaneous" by the Internal Revenue Service. The originators of Quaker Oats, Aunt Jemima pancake mix, and Pepsi-Cola all went bankrupt *several times* before their successors took the very same brands and made them successful.

Older products have been given new life (Jell-O, Welch's, Barbasol). Whole categories once considered unsalable (ballpoint pens, low-calorie beer, premixed paint) have been turned around and have become enormously profitable.

When the creators of these products realized that no one was buying what they had to sell, they had two choices:

- walk away and lose everything, or
- start over with a remarketing plan.

I first heard the phrase "remarketing" while researching a book about the barter business. Moreton Binn, the self-styled "Baron of Barter," used it to talk about how he found alternative distribution for discontinued merchandise—bicycles, lawn mowers, and cosmetics—and "remarketed" them in company stores, army PX's, or South American supermarkets.

I began thinking about Binn's clients, the manufacturers who saw their products being sold for ten cents on the dollar. Curious about how other entrepreneurs had handled less-than-successful launches, I began reading company histories and was fascinated to discover that many of the giant brands of today—Welch's, Wheaties, Vaseline—had, at one time, nearly disappeared. Then, with a new marketing approach, they not only had been reborn but had also become worldwide successes.

Of course, some products become immediate successes—Kodak, Reynolds Wrap, Slice. But, the truth is, with few exceptions, marketers generally stub their toes with new product introductions, which is why New Products Marketing has become its own specialty in business school.

New products can be *very* expensive. Depending on the category, product introductions can cost anywhere from $10 million to $100 million with no guarantee of success. Ron Peterson of Peterson & Blyth, a New York packaging firm, says, "These days, it's going to cost you $25 million to launch a regional brand of beer." With a perfume sold internationally and introduced lavishly, the tab can even reach as high as $70 million.

What's more, new products are enormously chancy. In the 1950s, the rule of thumb was that six out of every seven new products failed, but this percentage has become seriously outdated. Consultant Edward M. Tauber, formerly the chairman of the marketing department at the University of Southern California, evaluated the success of 6,695 new food products introduced between 1970 and 1979. He found that only *ninety-three*, not much better than one out of a hundred, eventually achieved sales of $15 million or more a year and had cost an average of $7. 4 million each to launch.

Given the high cost of product introductions, the likeliness of failure, and the fight for retail space (there are 228,000 branded products for sale in the U.S.), remarketing an existing brand becomes extremely attractive.

Why do products fail? Michael Komives, a marketing consultant who advises clients like General Foods and Anheuser-Busch, lays part of the blame on faulty reasoning. He says, "Marketers feel that if X is good, then twice as much X has to be twice as good, but that's just not so."

As an example, he mentions Baybry's, Anheuser-Busch's attempt to cash in on the wine-cooler craze with a champagne cooler. "If a wine cooler is good, a champagne cooler should be great, right? It turns out, however, that people consider champagne a special-occasion drink, not an everyday drink, which means they consume it less often. Even worse, champagne often has *negative* associations, like the wedding celebration that ended in a messy divorce."

Pollster A. C. Nielsen, Jr., who's got numbers for everything, cites thirteen reasons for the failure of new products, including "failure to create an integrated marketing plan." Marketing failures can also include overpricing, underadvertising, missing the right target au-

dience, or downplaying ethnic factors that figure in the buying
decision.

Rosser Reeves, the driving force behind Ted Bates's advertising
agency, listed six reasons for product failure. He said (among other
things), "Your competition might be outspending you three to one or
dealing you to death with one-cent sales, co-op advertising allowances,
and special discounts to retailers."

Some reasons for failure are more basic. For instance:

1. *The name may be wrong.* Elijah's Manna, Little Short Cake
   Fingers, and I Scream were the original names of Post Toasties, Twinkies, and Eskimo Pie. And Frisbees were once
   called Salad Plates, Bucket Tops, and Pluto Platters. A new
   name can be the key to a total change in marketing emphasis. When a customer told Dr. George Bunting, "Doc, your
   sunburn cream sure knocked out my eczema," Dr. Bunting's
   Sunburn Remedy became Noxzema (knocks eczema) and
   was used for a much broader range of ailments.
2. *The distribution may be wrong.* When Henry Ford noticed
   that some of his employees were cooking their lunches over
   wood left over from dashboards, he forced his dealers to
   take a carload of charred wood with every carload of cars; it
   was an abysmal failure. Then a friend of Ford's, E. G. Kingsford, bought up the charcoal and began selling it in supermarkets, along with lighter fluid and a tiny grill—the first
   home-barbecue kit. Kingsford briquets have been a market
   leader ever since.
3. *The timing may be off.* Instant coffee was a bomb at Buf-
   falo's Pan American Exposition in 1901. People had grown
   used to drinking brewed coffee and had the time to make it.
   During World War II, though, defense workers wanted coffee more quickly, and instant caught on as an easy-to-make,
   wartime drink.
4. *The competition may be killing you in the press.* Thomas Edison, who championed the use of direct current (DC), suggested that his direct competitor, alternating current (AC),

backed by George Westinghouse, would be the perfect alternative to hanging for capital offenses. Consumers equated alternating current with certain death until Westinghouse turned things around by using AC to light Chicago's Columbian Exposition in 1893. When six months passed without an accident, AC became safe in the mind of the public and was eventually adopted as standard around the world.

5. *The product may need new packaging.* Coca-Cola lost customers to Pepsi-Cola after World War II, because consumers preferred Pepsi in cans to Coke in glass bottles. In 1894, Psyche, "the White Rock girl," was five foot four, weighed 140 pounds, and measured 37-27-38. By 1983, she had grown four inches, shed 22 pounds, and taped out at 35-24-34.

6. *The product may be in the wrong department.* Carnation Instant Breakfast was a bomb when it was launched in the low-calorie food section of the supermarket. Shelved with breakfast foods, it took off immediately.

Whatever the causes of failure, the cost of new product introductions is staggering, the competition is tough, and the marketing environment grows increasingly complex. Given this ever-more-crowded marketplace, the numerous ways in which products can fail, and the high cost of product launches and buy-outs, trying again with a product that didn't succeed the first time becomes good business.

Over the past five years, I have read numerous company histories and newspaper and magazine articles (cited in the bibliography) and have conducted more than two hundred personal interviews with entrepreneurs and marketing professionals on the subject of how to turn products around. Out of the many possible candidates, I have selected forty-nine well-known products that might have died if their champions hadn't believed in their dreams. The case histories of their remarketed brands are the basis of this book.

My research also led me to conclude that the standard "four *P*'s" of marketing—product, place, price, and promotion—are seriously out of date. No fewer than *twelve P's* now figure in the marketing process. They are:

PERCEPTION	PIGGYBACKING
PITCH	POSITIONING
PACKAGING	PLACEMENT
PRICE	PREMIUMS
PROMOTION	PUBLICITY
PROMISES	PERSEVERANCE

This book examines how each of these *P*'s played a vital part in remarketing a product. A marketer using this list can discover not only what's wrong with his or her product, but also what to do about it.

It's rare that any product has a one-*P* problem; there is usually tremendous overlap, and several may work together to either sink or re-float a problem product. The case histories in this book are classified by what I call the Pivotal *P*—the one overriding factor on which success or failure turned. I've also ranked the other two, three, even four Primary *P*'s that figured in the product's turnaround.

This book details forty-nine products you might never have heard of if their creators hadn't had the faith to follow their dreams, to "go the distance." They overcame the conventional wisdom and lived to see the products of their imagination thrive when they got it right the second time!

Chapter One

DON'T **PITCH** IT

THE WRONG WAY

• • • • • •

EVERY salesperson has a pitch, an approach, a selling proposition, the "sizzle" he or she provides, along with the steak. The pitch achieved such importance in advertising that, for years, the Ted Bates agency based its business solely on its ability to find a "unique selling proposition" (USP), then pound it into the heads of potential consumers.

The pitch is the bridge between producer and consumer, the platform (like a politician's platform) that provides common ground for buyer and seller. That's why it's so important that the pitch be the right one, to establish that common ground. When the pitch doesn't ring true, potential buyers are immediately turned off.

What Would You Do If I Sang Out of Tune? Not every pitch is perfect, God knows. As we'll see later, the microwave oven and low-calorie beer originally relied on technological razzle-dazzle at a time when people were looking for quicker cooking and less filling beer.

And pitches become outdated. Pepsi's 1940s claim that it offered "twice as much for a nickel, too" had to be dropped quickly when the price changed to a dime. Likewise, Schlitz's claim that it had "gusto" evaporated when chemicals were substituted for natural flavoring.

There are also only a few basic appeals from which to choose. Like the six basic plots of fiction, marketing pitches eventually rest on a small number of factors: price (four rolls of Kodak for the price of three), convenience (new easy-to-use Johnson's Wax), speed (fast-acting Bayer Aspirin), performance (Maxwell House tastes better than Folger's), and status (The American Express Gold Card).

Pitched Battles   The most persuasive pitches always take the competition into account and often include several of the other *P*'s:

1. "7-Up—The Uncola." The pitch positions 7-Up as lighter, more refreshing than heavy, sugary colas. And, since colas are popular, uncola drinkers get the benefit of being just a wee bit unconventional.
2. "Anacin is recommended by eight out of ten doctors." This is a piggyback pitch, relying on the authority of doctors to make Anacin more attractive.
3. "Get Quaker State in the handy new plastic bottle." Clearly, this pitch is based on the packaging, which promises to be less messy than the old cans.

Wild Pitch   Much of the pitch has to do with the product's nature and its target audience. Marketing a perfume on the basis of price would cheapen a product that depends on imagery, mood, packaging. Conversely, stressing the low-calorie nature of Gablinger's Beer made it sound like a drink for sissies.

One-Two Pitch   Occasionally, a pitch rests on two elements. Lite beer is the classic example, with its "Tastes Great, Less Filling" appeal. Less obvious is the basic appeal of life insurance. The overt reason to buy is "protecting one's family." But, part of the appeal rests on "watching your estate grow."

Payoff Pitch   The pitch is the cornerstone of advertising. Martin Revson once said, "In the factories we make cosmetics. In the stores we sell hope." The right pitch makes the consumer feel that, yes, this perfume (or toothpaste) can make a difference in my life. In one case, an adman pitched a product by linking it to a common household problem.

WISK   Ring-a-Ding-Ding

A good example of an innovative product that got off on the wrong foot is Unilever's Wisk, the first liquid detergent. Introduced in 1956 as the "liquid miracle for family wash," it was unfamiliar to consumers and cost twice as much per washload as powders. Moreover, its sales pitch wasn't terribly credible.

The pitch, as it turns out, was a prime example of a technique that the public has chosen to reject on many levels and with many products: the old new-technology-gee-whiz pitcheroo. In the case of Wisk, the pitch was something like "Hey, look what the white coats in the lab have come up with now, ladies, a brand new chemical that makes miracles in the washing machine."

As it turns out, all detergents (including All) involve chemical trade-offs during the manufacturing process; that means no single brand can clean all kinds of stains and soil marks equally well, because all these soiling agents are made of different chemicals themselves. In other words, no detergent could actually be a miracle worker because of its built-in limitations; the pitch for Wisk—implying that this was a miracle product that did it all—was based on a faulty premise with wishful thinking substituted for honest fact. That's bad business, because sooner or later someone will catch on.

After a while, the advantage that Wisk legitimately had—the novelty of being a liquid—wore off, and consumers inevitably discovered that it had drawbacks like the other brands; the liquid miracle plummeted from 4.2 percent to 2.8 percent of detergent sales in 1967.

Then James Jordan, who worked on Wisk at the time for Batten, Barton, Durstine & Osborne, read research indicating that housewives considered dirty shirt collars their single biggest laundry headache. Now a principal in his own agency, Jordan, McGrath, Case, & Taylor, Jordan decided to adopt a niche strategy for his brand; he made this single stain problem the basis of a campaign that used the housewives' own testimony to sell them.

Jordan's jujitsu strategy took advantage of the fact that housewives had already admitted that collar stains were hard to remove and used it as a weapon against them. He decided that a sizable percentage of housewives would try Wisk if they could be made to feel guilty about *not* trying it. He used "ring-around-the-collar" as an all-purpose villain that could create tension with neighbors, produce migraine headaches, prevent promotions for hubby, upset stable marriages, and generally screw up relations between washer and washee.

The subtext of the pitch was the very specific information that Wisk worked best on one kind of stain. Please notice that, rather than being all things to all stains as in the past, Wisk was now lowering consumer expectations. Instead of being a "miracle," it now merely promised to solve one specific and irritating problem. (That it chose to do so in an equally specific and irritating way is beside the point.)

Jordan's pitch lowered consumer expectations and focused them on a subject that already interested them. The new approach made Wisk the housewife's partner in getting rid of those potentially upsetting collar stains and created a perfect bridge between product and consumer. Sales tripled between 1967 and 1974.

• • • • • • •

PRODUCT   LIQUID DETERGENT

Pivotal *P*: Pitch

When the sales pitch about wash day miracles began to pall, Wisk changed its tune and focused on one irritating problem.

Primary *P*: Positioning

Building ring-around-the-collar into a problem that might affect marriages or family income made buying Wisk a practical purchase.

• • • • • • •

NATIONAL CASH REGISTER   Intercepted Passes

Sometimes the pitch is great, but it never reaches its ultimate target. One entrepreneur found a direct way to deliver his message and really cashed in.

John H. Patterson, the founder of National Cash Register (now known as NCR) fought to make the adding machine a success with retailers—even as their clerks were sabotaging his efforts. He couldn't get ahead because some of the very people he had to sell to had the most to lose by buying his product. (They weren't dumb.)

Neither was Patterson. After a lot of trial and error, he learned to deliver his pitch on neutral grounds.

In the 1880s, retail clerks and bartenders routinely rifled the till they were supposed to be guarding. For one thing, there was as yet no mechanical way of overcoming this human predilection toward petty larceny; for another, retailers and saloonkeepers would have been initially skeptical about any invention that purported to keep clerks honest. Back then a "taste of the till" was as much a part of a clerk's income as a waiter's tips, and no one had yet created a way to curb this wretched excess.

What was needed was a new system, and Patterson had already shown some promise with systems shortly after graduating from Dartmouth College. While working as a toll-taker on the Miami and Erie Canal, he had invented a way to verify collections and thus avoid the disputes which figured so prominently along the canal. Each time a boat passed through his station and paid the toll, Patterson gave the canal boat captain a receipt; the receipt graphically showed the next toll-taker along the canal that the boat had paid the previous toll, eliminating any problems with payment.

When he and his brother Frank started the Southern Coal and Iron Company in Coalton, Ohio, Patterson's natural feel for administration helped make the company an immediate success. Shortly after he had opened a company store for his employees, he was dismayed to see it effectively drain away the profits from his coal company; his clerks, like clerks everywhere else, were looting the cash drawer.

Consequently, when Patterson heard about a crude type of sales register that had been created by a Dayton saloonkeeper, he was all ears. James Ritty, the owner of a local bar, had gotten the idea from watching a tachometer-like device count the revolutions of a steamship's propeller. While his contraption did work, it was just about as unwieldy as the name he had given it—Ritty's Incorruptible Cashier.

This primitive adding machine combined: (1) a keyboard with

which one could record various amounts; (2) a bell, which clanged whenever cash was changing hands; and (3) a clock dial, instead of the more familiar tin pop-up shields, which would indicate the amount of each purchase. The shortcomings of the dial were overshadowed by one very important plus: A paper tape inside the machine was automatically punched whenever a sale was recorded, and it was tamper-proof. At the close of each business day, the proprietor could count the holes, translate them into cash terms, and know—to the penny—the actual receipts for that day. Armed with the receipts and a copy of the day's inventory, the proprietor could know if a clerk had under-rung any amount and pocketed the difference.

Such a machine had great potential, but Ritty and his brother had yet to realize it. They had patented it in 1879, and had sold just nineteen in their first two years in business. When Patterson heard about the Cashier, he ordered two of them sight unseen despite the $100 price tag and ordered another two after he'd seen the first pair in action. With the Cashiers in place, Patterson's company store turned a $1,000-a-month loss into a $1,000-a-month profit. The forty-one-year-old entrepreneur became convinced that selling the machine would make him rich and impulsively paid $6,500 for Ritty's company. Derided by friends, Patterson tried to void the deal the next day by offering Ritty $2,000, but Ritty turned him down.

Forced to work with a machine that amounted to a corporate impulse buy, Patterson quickly figured out ways to improve it. He added a printer to the machine so retailers didn't have to interpret paper tapes to find out their daily receipts, and he changed both the product and company names to National Cash Register. Next, he decided to shake up the advertising business which, up to that time, had mostly consisted of announcements of goods on hand. Deciding that his target market was every sizable retailer in the Midwest, Patterson dubbed them "Probable Purchasers" and kicked things off by sending NCR circulars to 5,000 "PP's" every day for eighteen days straight, 90,000 pieces of mail, an unfathomable number in those days.

This first concentrated direct-mail campaign was a total bust. Patterson soon learned that the bulk of his sales material had been intercepted and destroyed by retail clerks who opposed even the idea of a cash register. The honest ones staged walk-outs, offended at the idea that their morals had been impugned; the dishonest ones informed NCR salesmen who came to follow up that the boss was always "out" or "too busy."

Patterson's marketing force was even met with strong-arm tactics, and clerks sabotaged several registers in protest. When the first NCR salesmen (they were all male in those days) encountered resistance, Patterson went so far as to provide them with miniature, three-key machines that could be concealed in boxes; however, surly clerks and burly bartenders quickly caught on and gave the bum's rush to any salesman innocently carrying a display case.

If there were ever a classic case of the sales message not reaching the target, it was this one. Even seeing, much less selling, the bosses was doubtful in this hostile environment. Yet, even if the NCR salesman got in to see the storekeeper, there was no assurance that he would make a sale. For one thing, many owners were not unaware of the thievery but did little to prevent it. When a hotel bartender working for ten dollars a week bought a diamond stickpin after six months on the job, an NCR salesman asked the owner why he didn't simply discharge the bounder. The tavern owner replied that he would just "lose another thousand dollars on the next man, because he would do the same thing."

In addition to doubting their ability to prevent thievery through different hiring practices, most retailers remained unconvinced that any mere mechanical device could detect and prevent thievery, which they conceived of as a basic human flaw. The attitude was that a clerk bent on stealing would figure out a way to do it, machine or no machine.

There was a third drawback to the cash register—the expense of the machines. While small stores might benefit from one register, large ones with a number of separate departments might have to spend six hundred dollars to become fully equipped, an enormous sum for an unproven product.

Forced to confront this powerful trio of negatives, Patterson decided on several inducements to overcome them. To defuse the price issue, he updated the installment plan (see Chapter 7) and offered lenient credit terms to storekeepers. He also hired private detectives—

at his own expense—to prove conclusively to retailers that pilferage was a major problem and that they couldn't afford to be without his machines.

Of course, he couldn't use either of these powerful arguments until an NCR salesman could actually speak with a retailer in a calm, nonthreatening atmosphere, particularly one in which clerks couldn't influence their bosses. He had the product, but he didn't have the right pitch or the ear of the prospect.

After his first hard-sell, direct-mail campaign failed, Patterson refined his approach, worked from lists of new business owners, and sent hand-addressed envelopes marked "Highly Confidential." Clerks didn't dispose of these as quickly, and when the owner opened one, he found that he had been invited to a suite at the best hotel in town. The occasion was a private demonstration of a machine that could save him money; as a further inducement, merely keeping the appointment often earned the owner a small prize, such as a good-quality letter opener.

Now NCR had created the product and identified the prospect; all it needed was the right sales pitch, and Patterson's analysis resulted in his landmark achievement, a creation that shaped America as surely as the railroad, the telephone, or the computer; he created the canned sales presentation.

In true systematic fashion, Patterson began poring over order forms to find out which of his salesmen had the single best sales record and was startled to discover that it was his brother-in-law, Joseph H. Crane. Patterson called Crane into his office, questioned him about the reasons for his success, and discovered that the conscientious Crane had "memorized his sales talk" as the result of a memorable failure.

On that occasion, Crane had had three Prospective Purchasers cornered in Findlay, Ohio; after his talk, all three declined to buy. Reflecting on his failure a bit later, Crane decided that he had neglected to mention a number of important selling points to all three potential customers. Chastened, he memorized his sales pitch word for word so that he would never again blow a sale by omitting a selling point or key feature.

The religious Patterson was at least as impressed with the parable as he was with the pitch itself. After Crane had recited all four hundred and fifty words of it several times, the boss's secretary took it down word for word. Once she had the basic pitch on paper, Crane and Patterson played the roles of salesman and customer and wrote down every conceivable objection as well as a host of appropriate responses to each one. After his secretary had recorded the entire conversation, Patterson had it printed and distributed to every sales office.

The talk became the NCR Primer, the first canned sales presentation in American history. A 1916 version said, "It is the same primer, in substance, that was used twenty-five years ago, and if it is rewritten twenty-five years hence, it will still be the same." To underline its importance, there were specific orders under Patterson's signature that the talk be memorized. Later, the founder would drop in on his agents without warning and give quick quizzes on the primer; those who failed were fired immediately.

After Crane's approach had been fully field tested, Patterson lured ten full-time sales agents away from other companies by offering them exclusive territories—another radical idea for the time—and deliberately overpaid them. He felt that high commissions, which were maintained even when sales increased, gave his men motivation to sell all the harder.

Patterson also came up with nine commandments for dealing with Prospective Purchasers:

1. Don't fail to seat the prospect properly.
2. Don't point your finger or pencil at him.
3. Don't sit awkwardly in your chair.
4. Don't have a calendar on the walls. It may remind him of an appointment or a note falling due.
5. Don't put your feet on the chair.
6. Don't smoke.
7. Don't slap him on the knee or poke him with your finger.
8. Don't chew gum or tobacco.
9. Don't tell funny stories.

Armed with The Commandments, The Speech, and The Responses to Objections, his messianic marketers turned hotel rooms into tabernacles and sold, sold, sold. An 1883 ad extolled the virtues of the cash register and showed a cartoon of Uncle Sam looking longingly at an NCR register and saying, "B'Gosh! I wish I had one of them over to the Treasury."

That year, NCR sold 1,050 machines; by 1892, it had sold 15,000. When the panic of 1893 hit, Patterson didn't retrench like the copycat manufacturers his success had attracted. Instead, he doubled his advertising and hit fifty towns in fifty-one days to keep morale high.

Then NCR loaned cash registers to 650 businesses at the Columbian Exposition, the 1893 Chicago World's Fair. A high percentage quickly bought the machines, and many of them even became foreign sales agents for NCR. While business dropped to nothing in many other areas of the economy, NCR had a record year, selling 15,487 units and establishing itself as the nation's leading provider of cash registers.

Historian Daniel Boorstin noted Patterson's contribution in *The Decline of American Radicalism*. He wrote, "The cash register . . . helped make a revolution in accounting among small merchants and . . . promoted efficiency in department stores, chain stores, and supermarkets. . . . For the first time, reliable statistics about an individual business enabled the merchant to figure precisely his annual profit or loss."

By the time he had finished showing American business how to get things done, Patterson had also created the national sales convention and the first "spiff program," an incentive vacation trip to Europe—by steamer, no less. His methods were later spread by former employee-disciples like young Thomas Watson, the founder of IBM, and dozens of other high-level managers. *Fortune* once estimated that fully one-sixth of America's big-time corporate executives and sales managers from 1910 to 1939 had been trained by NCR. The company didn't slow down in the 1980s either; in the last ten years, NCR's revenues from the sale of business information processing systems have nearly tripled from $2.1 billion to $6 billion.

• • • • • • •

PRODUCT   CASH REGISTER

Pivotal P: Pitch

NCR's pitch was sabotaged by retail clerks until Patterson shifted his presentation to neutral ground and talked to owners one-on-one.

Primary P: Perception

Being able to hear a complete presentation reassured retailers about what was originally an unfamiliar and possibly threatening new machine.

• • • • • • •

WHEATIES   Kid Stuff

In 1921, a Minneapolis health clinician stirred a batch of bran gruel a tad too vigorously, scattering drops of it onto a hot stove. After he scraped the thin wafers off, he discovered that cooking had transformed them into tasty flakes. The Breakfast of Champions was born. Sort of.

Washburn Crosby Company, the forerunner of General Mills, tried to make a breakfast cereal of the bran, but the flakes kept crumbling until the company's head miller succeeded with his thirty-sixth variety of wheat. Jane Bausman, the wife of a Washburn Crosby executive, won a company-sponsored contest by calling the cereal Wheaties, because "there's nothing as endearing as a nickname." Eventually what became endearing about Wheaties was its pitch and the ability that pitch had to target a specific audience.

Wheaties went on sale late in 1924, and according to company literature, "Wheaties was on its way, but not very far, and not very fast . . . it was apparent that something was needed."

Two years later, in an effort to give the brand some life, Minneapolis radio station WCCO (for Washburn Crosby Company) took a municipal court bailiff, a printer, a businessman, and an undertaker and formed them into a male quartet called The Gold Medal Four.

Christmas Eve 1926 was made even more special in the Twin Cities by the quartet's rendition of the world's first singing commercial. It went something like this:

> Have you tried Wheaties?
> They're whole wheat with all of the bran
> Won't you try Wheaties?
> For wheat is the best food of man.

The company says the commercial "literally saved the life of Wheaties," but sales were still not much to brag about. In 1928, a year after Washburn Crosby and three other millers had formed General Mills, 53,000 cases of Wheaties had been shipped nationally, 30,000 of them in the Minneapolis–St. Paul area where the commercials were being broadcast. The jingles were fine, but the somewhat stilted, spoken copy told parents, "Make Your Child Love Whole Wheat" and "Eat Whole Wheat This Alluring Way." The choice was clear: kill the brand or change the campaign.

In 1931, General Mills decided to bypass parents and appeal directly to children. In line with this strategy, the company agreed to sponsor a children's show in what historian James Gray called "the first well-planned effort to speak directly to the child as the ultimate consumer of a ready-to-eat cereal."

Target your audience and pitch it.

The star of the show was Skippy, the hero of a popular comic strip by Percy Crosby and a movie star to boot. Skippy had already made his radio debut on WMAQ in Chicago, but General Mills sponsored his first network broadcast. Piggybacking onto Skippy's popularity, General Mills created one of the first "radio clubs"—the "Skippy Secret Service Society." Youngsters sending in two Wheaties boxtops became members, received certificates, buttons, and a secret code and handshake; more than half a million responded. The response validated the pitch to youth, and by 1932, the Gold Medal Four were off the air.

At this point, radio had saved Wheaties on two separate occasions with campaigns based on different appeals to different groups— first parents and then children aged six to ten. Now what was needed was a campaign that could appeal to a broader audience than either small children or adults. Beginning in 1933, General Mills made a promise to Wheaties eaters and then fulfilled it by creating a Wheaties-eating role model to which groups of all ages could respond.

A few days before the 1933 baseball season started, WCCO paid $10,000 for the rights to broadcast the games of the Minneapolis Millers of the minor league American Association. As a bonus, they also got the sponsorship of a signboard on the centerfield fence of the Millers' ballpark. When a Millers' executive asked what to put on the signboard, Knox Reeves, the head of Wheaties' ad agency, quickly drew the phrase "Breakfast of Champions" across a Wheaties box, and that became the signboard message; every time a Miller hit a home run, the company would give a case of Wheaties to charity.

As luck would have it, that year Joe Hauser of the Millers set a then-minor league record by hitting sixty-nine homers. Young would-be Joe Hausers around Minneapolis began calling any well-hit ball "a case of Wheaties," and the "Breakfast of Champions" slogan began taking on richer and richer meaning. While it hadn't been planned, the slogan became one of the slickest pieces of positioning strategy ever created; when commercials identifying Wheaties as the "Breakfast of Champions" were broadcast on stations outside Minneapolis, impressionable young boys, convinced of Wheaties' sympathetic magic, ate it by the carload.

As Jim Murray of the *Los Angeles Times* points out, "There was no evidence that, as part of the daily diet, Wheaties contributed one way or the other to athletic prowess, but the kids of America were taking no chances."

The broadcasts reached baseball lovers, and Skippy appealed to the very young (six-to-ten-year-olds); however, there were still other audiences to reach. The company decided to create a radio "champion," an adventure hero who could sell Wheaties to a broader age range.

"Jack Armstrong, the All-American Boy" was destined for great things. The show went on the air in July 1933, ran away with the Saturday morning ratings, and stayed on for eighteen years. The hero of Hudson High and his pals Billy and Betty Fairfield traveled the world in search of adventure and found it within the allotted twenty-four minutes of each half-hour broadcast. Moreover, Jack Armstrong was the vehicle for bringing the "radio premium" to life.

As we will see, Henry Crowell turned around Quaker Oats (see Chapter 5) by creating the "in-pack" and "on-pack" cereal premiums, which are either inside the package or attached to the outside. General Mills revived the premium idea and gave it a whole new dimension by combining it directly with radio. One of the first Jack Armstrong shows mentioned a "shooting plane" in the script and offered it to the public for a boxtop and ten cents. The resultant flood of orders depleted stocks of Wheaties around the country; it would be nearly six months before Wheaties was readily available again.

This happy combination of radio and premium enabled General Mills to create an annual promotion called the "Spring Deal." Consumers who bought two packages of Wheaties in a participating grocery store got special "near-pack premiums" (because the premiums were located near the Wheaties display). Stores were pre-stocked to meet the demand, and railroad cars filled with the Breakfast of Champions were strategically placed to replenish them. These precautions were proven necessary by the first Spring Deal in 1936, a blue glass cereal bowl with a picture of Shirley Temple on the bottom. Five million went quickly, along with 10 million boxes of Wheaties. Jack Armstrong proved equally powerful, moving 5 million explorer telescopes in 1938 and 6.6 million torpedo flashlights in 1939 in less than two weeks.

Meanwhile, the Breakfast of Champions theme closely associated Wheaties with sports, and billboards in major league parks such as Boston's Fenway Park and Yankee Stadium got the message across, as did broadcasts over ninety-five radio stations covering major and minor league games. General Mills never did find a major league Joe Hauser, but subsequent endorsement deals with Babe Ruth, Jack Dempsey, Red Grange, Babe Didrickson, and forty-six of the fifty-one members selected for the 1939 All-Star Game served the same purpose.

The slogan became so ingrained that endorsers of competing products couldn't unremember it. When Lou Gehrig was supposed to push Huskies, a competing brand, in a live radio broadcast, he told a national audience that the key to his slugging success was "Wheaties."

Wheaties' one-two punch of sports heroes and fictional derring-do reached its height of effectiveness at the end of the 1940s when radio had peaked in popularity and television was increasingly a factor. A company brochure says General Mills was unable to sponsor television play-by-play because "the margin in the food business does not provide an advertising budget of sufficient size to meet the tremendous rights and time costs." TV sports had become big business, and the rights fees and salaries General Mills had paid for radio were a thing of the past.

Jack Armstrong left the air in 1951, and General Mills turned away from the mass appeal of the Breakfast of Champions to pursue the children's cereal market. Trading in Mickey Mantle for Mickey Mouse, the brass in Minneapolis changed Wheaties' package and brand image in an effort to get in on the heavy per-capita consumption that characterizes children's dry cereals. In this unfortunate replay of the Skippy experience, General Mills got the six-to-ten-year-olds back but lost the boys and men who had identified with the Breakfast of Champions theme. Sales slumped immediately, as much as 10 percent in a single year.

In the end, pitch came to shove and the old slogan saved Wheaties. Even though the line hadn't been used for five years, Wheaties was still the Breakfast of Champions, not just a kiddie cereal. In 1956, Wheaties recanted and decided to capitalize on its equity with a single athlete, settling on Olympic pole vaulter Bob Richards after reviewing five hundred possible candidates. Ever since, Wheaties has stayed with the sports theme, aligning itself with two other Olympic spokespersons—Bruce Jenner in the 1970s and Mary Lou Retton in the 1980s. All three appeared on the front of the Wheaties box, along with Pete Rose, Chris Evert, Walter Payton, and Michael Jordan.

Viewed from a certain perspective, Wheaties' situation is analogous to a magazine like *Seventeen*, which is actually read by twelve-year-old girls who aspire to be "sophisticated." In the same vein, Wheaties can best attract young boys by using successful, older athletes as role models. General Mills has faced this issue recently by using older role models like Payton and Rose and using the theme line, "Now go tell your mama what the big boys eat."

• • • • • • •

PRODUCT   WHEATIES

Pivotal P: Pitch

Wheaties' success has been based on a pitch most young cereal eaters find irresistible and the close tie to well-known sports figures.

Primary P's: Promotion, Premiums

Tying premium offers to its radio shows gave Wheaties a way to delight young consumers and increase store traffic.

• • • • • • •

KLEENEX TISSUES   Imperfect Pitch

The next time you blow your nose with a Kleenex tissue, you might pause to reflect on the fact that what you're using is a gas-mask filter originally touted as an upscale beauty aid.

As noted in Chapter 2, Kimberly-Clark was stuck with huge amounts of Cellucotton when World War I ended and introduced the sanitary napkin with its Kotex brand. Since the Roaring Twenties had created demand for makeup on a national scale, it stood to reason that there would eventually be a market for makeup remover—cold cream—and a neat way to dispose of it. Management saw an opportunity, and Kimberly-Clark produced thin sheets of Cellucotton, called them Kleenex Kerchiefs, and introduced them in 1924 as a cold-cream remover, a disposable substitute for face towels.

To glamorize the product and justify its premium price (a hundred Kleenex tissues cost 65 cents), the company used Helen Hayes, Ronald Colman, Gertrude Lawrence, and other reigning Hollywood stars in endorsement ads. By 1926, the product was limping along, and Kimberly-Clark was hedging its bets on Kleenex as a glamour product, leading to a change in marketing direction.

Renamed Kleenex Absorbent Kerchiefs, they were offered in the new, less expensive "boudoir" size, which only cost about half as much (35 cents) as the "professional size." When down-pricing alone still didn't make the product popular, marketers worked to develop a new, more convenient delivery system for the individual tissues. The dramatic Serv-A-Tissue pop-up box was introduced in 1929, but, according to company literature, sales were still "encouraging, but by no means sensational."

At this juncture, it looked as if Kimberly-Clark had bitten off more than it could chew; the switch from industrial to consumer marketing was a daunting one for such a conservative company. Kimberly-Clark had had to undergo a disorienting change from selling to a steady group of long-standing, high-paying industrial clients to dealing with millions of disloyal and unpredictable consumers buying a low-priced, unfamiliar item. In addition, the company had made a questionable decision in entering the image-conscious and highly competitive field of health and beauty aids with its first consumer product. Worst of all, the company still didn't have a handle on what it was selling, a fact that became evident when the product was renamed Kleenex Cleansing Tissues, its third name in six years.

But, if Kimberly-Clark didn't know precisely how to sell Kleenex at the time, it did have a long and illustrious history of listening to its customers and heeding their complaints. When a given machine began to produce paper that customers considered inferior, it was immediately replaced. Once a fire destroyed the company's entire stock of newsprint and three paper-making machines. Rather than disappoint its customers, Kimberly-Clark put every employee on overtime, and four weeks later a makeshift mill had produced its first carload of newsprint.

This long-standing attitude may explain the company's sensitivity to the steady stream of letters from consumers who used Kleenex in a very unglamorous way—for blowing their noses.

In February 1930, Kimberly-Clark decided to test the two appeals—makeup removal and nose blowing—in a predecessor of the Pepsi Challenge, more formally known as a split-run copy test. Full-page ads were created for two competing newspapers in Peoria, Illinois. The ads were identical in size and layout, and both offered respondents a free box of Kleenex; the only difference was in the headlines.

The first said, "We pay to prove there is no way like Kleenex to remove cold cream." The second stated, "We pay to prove Kleenex is wonderful for handkerchiefs."

When 61 percent of the readers said they were using Kleenex as handkerchiefs, Kimberly-Clark quickly changed its advertising to reflect the more popular sales appeal, the more perfect pitch. Once the image of Kleenex as a nasal tissue took hold, it became easier to sell sub-markets the same pitch.

Full-page ads appeared, telling mothers to send the kids off to school with Kleenex lest they spread germs; the same message was adapted to the workplace (creating yet another niche market), and the eventual headline "Don't put a cold in your pocket" doubled sales the first year it was used.

Given this kind of foothold in the market, Kimberly-Clark was now free to promote secondary uses, and a 1936 package insert listed no less than forty-eight, including the tissues' ability to clean tools and drain fried foods. Eventually the company offered $5 for each new use of what had then become known as Kleenex Disposable Tissues. The multiple-usage campaign peaked between September and December 1939 with the classic "Kleenex True Confessions" ad campaign— 24,000 readers "confessed" to other uses they'd found for the tissues.

Fifteen years after it was introduced, Kleenex had become an established product and had helped turn Kimberly-Clark, once exclusively an industrial paper supplier, into a $3 billion consumer-goods company. From 1924, when the brand was introduced, to 1989, when the combined sales figures for Kimberly-Clark tissues exceeded $450 million (Kleenex taking the lion's share), Kleenex Tissues has undergone three name changes, four major packaging changes, and numerous revisions of both its pricing and its advertising philosophies. All of this stemmed from discovering the product's main benefit, embodying a pitch for that benefit, and highlighting it in successive marketing efforts.

• • • • • • •

PRODUCT KLEENEX

Pivotal *P*: Pitch

Switching from a borderline beauty pitch to a down-to-earth appeal to nose-blowers broadened Kleenex's potential market.

Primary *P*'s: Price, Package

Lowering the price and adopting a convenient, innovative pop-up box allowed consumers to discover other uses for Kleenex.

• • • • • • •

Chapter Two

DON'T RULE OUT

A RIDE VIA

PIGGYBACK

• • • • • •

T HE road to success is not necessarily a glamorous one.

In the early 1970s, meat prices rose and products appeared that extended meat dishes with noodles or rice. General Mills entered the market first with Hamburger Helper, a name nearly impossible to forget. According to publicist Barry Wegener, it became "as important to General Mills as Wheaties or Cheerios."

By taking a backseat to the lowly hamburger, General Mills found a great way to sell noodles. In marketing circles, such a strategy is known as piggybacking, coattailing, or hitchhiking.

These terms eloquently suggest attaching one new element onto one already established. When your product runs into stubborn consumer resistance, one solution is to mate it with an already accepted product, service, or idea; if you choose wisely, you get a chance to use the built-in acceptance of the latter to lower resistance to the former.

Using an established product (yours or someone else's) to promote a new one is essentially the same thing as using a brand name, rather than a celebrity, to endorse a product. Endorsement campaigns depend on the not entirely unreasonable notion that some of the popularity of the endorser will rub off on the product itself.

The basic piggybacking idea works like a magician's sleight-of-hand: Get consumers to focus on something familiar and distract them from the strangeness of your own brainchild. With the right marriage of new and old, the old standby product generates good feelings so that the consumer focuses on the newcomer's novelty (a plus), rather than dwelling on its strangeness (a minus).

Inside Story The manufacturers of established products are usually wary of letting a newcomer mess with their hard-won franchises, but in one classic case, a magazine publisher gracefully introduced a potential competitor for advertising dollars. Clay Felker, then publisher of *New York*, introduced *Ms.* magazine by binding it inside the December 20, 1971, issue of his magazine and distributing it in New York City. Back then, the notion of a magazine devoted to women's equality might have been daunting to advertising agencies and their clients. Piggybacking onto Felker's already accepted magazine dispelled the newness of the magazine started by Pat Carbine and Gloria Steinem. It also gave *Ms.* mainstream acceptability, plus the imprint of publishing honcho Felker (which spoke loudly to potential advertisers). It told New Yorkers who considered themselves hip that *Ms.* was important.

Piggybacking has worked in publishing and hosts of other product categories. Consider:

- *Soft drinks and condiments.* Where would tonic water be without gin?
- *Side dishes.* In the latest incarnation of the Hamburger Helper idea, Birds Eye's Custom Cuisine makes no bones about what is the main event and offers microwavable vegetables and sauces to go with chicken, beef, pork, fish, or tofu—whatever entrée the consumer desires.
- *Cosmetics.* By this time, the "gift-with-purchase" idea has become so ingrained in the cosmetics industry that buyers of lotions and fragrances expect a "freebie" whenever they buy something. This expectation has often led manufacturers to

test new products by giving them away as "gifts." Those that test well become products on their own.

- *Fast foods.* McDonald's reworked the way Cracker Jack piggybacked toys onto candy (see Chapter 8) with its Happy Meals, which contain small, inexpensive toys, along with a drink, french fries, hamburgers, or chicken. In turn, Binney & Smith, the makers of Crayolas, piggybacked onto McDonald's audience. The company put its crayons in Happy Meals and, essentially, was able to offer samples of its products nationally at no cost. B & S focused national attention on a mature product competing with magic markers, finger paints, and felt-tip pens by getting a tantamount endorsement from McDonald's as well as access to millions of consumers in its target market.

In all these categories, the piggyback works like a marriage: Two parts of the whole provide the synergy to become a bigger and better whole new thing, or the weaker partner simply rides the coattails of the successful partner into the limelight.

Mixed Marriages Sometimes you are having trouble selling Product A, but you know that the public has accepted Product B, a product mentally or physically connected with your turkey. Through a joint promotion, you can marry these two items and hope that the loser will piggyback its way into the hearts and minds of consumers. Thus Warner Books once tried to sell a "summer" novel with suntan lotion, and Kraft tries to sell more caramels each fall by providing a coupon good for a free bag of apples.

The mixed marriage is often a leveraged promotion that uses the popularity of one item to enhance another product. Take, for example, the 1985 nuptials of Teddy Ruxpin and Quaker Oats.

Quaker Oats Instant Oatmeal was trying to establish itself as a microwavable, cold-weather breakfast cereal for children. The brand asked Marketing Equities International (MEI) of New York to create a sales program that would heighten dealer interest and consumer awareness.

Since Teddy Ruxpin was already popular, MEI came up with a

series of Teddy Ruxpin story booklets, which were "flagged" on the brand package front and inserted as a premium. A second element was added when a 900 telephone number was introduced so that children could talk to Teddy. To lighten the bite on parents' wallets, all proceeds from the calls were given to the National Association for the Protection of Children. Then Worlds of Wonder, Teddy's maker, which later became bankrupt, manufactured products for supermarkets that were unavailable in toy stores; store managers used the toys in aisle-end displays to draw traffic, and sales of Quaker Oats Instant Oatmeal rose a significant 13.4 percent.

Flash Piggybacking You don't even need a product to piggyback; trends or attitudes often serve the same end. You just have to be in the right place at the right time.

Fashion has piggybacked onto the movies since the 1920s. People wore cut-up, sleeveless sweatshirts for years, but when Jennifer Beals wore them in *Flashdance*, ready-to-wear manufacturers piggybacked onto their popularity and made millions. Ditto the *Annie Hall* look. Similarly, by piggybacking onto legitimate fears about the spread of AIDS, the condom business was able to make a monumental turnaround in the late 1980s.

Extending the Franchise Many manufacturers even hitchhike onto their own brand names to create new products in unrelated areas. Consultant Edward Tauber, a former marketing professor at the University of Southern California, calls the practice "franchise extension." He says it allows a company to enter a new business using "the leverage of its most valuable asset—the consumer awareness, goodwill, and impressions conveyed by the brand name." Successful hitchhiking products would include Vaseline Intensive Care skin lotion, Arm & Hammer laundry detergent, Minolta copiers, and Jell-O Pudding Pops (see page 46).

DIXIE CUPS   Deep Cover

Every once in a very long while, a piggybacking product must become completely invisible to succeed. Invisibility gained visibility for Dixie Cups when the product piggybacked onto ice cream and came of age as a container before it would be accepted by the public as a drinking device—an example of backdoor piggybacking at its finest.

It happened like this.

Hugh Moore came to New York from Kansas armed only with $3,000, his father's gold watch, and the notion that Americans could be made to pay for something they had been happily getting for free. Since the 1850s, Americans had been drinking water from tin dippers on trains, in railway stations and in barrels outside general stores. The water was free, but the cup was hardly free from germs. Public cups were never washed and, inevitably, became tainted with all manner of water-borne diseases.

Moore was scandalized by the ramifications for public health and was convinced that, once educated, people would gladly pay for a sanitary drink of water to avoid disease. He had dropped out of Harvard to start the American Water Supply Company of New England with fellow Kansan Lawrence Luellen. Searching for financial support, the two men had gravitated to New York City, taking rooms at the Waldorf-Astoria "to impress people," and opened an account at the Title Guarantee & Trust Company. Though most New Yorkers scoffed at the idea of making a business out of selling water, Arthur Terry, the bank's treasurer, said one of the bank's directors "at times went into far-fetched schemes."

Terry introduced Moore to investment banker Edgar Marston, a partner of Blair & Company, and Marston was horrified by Moore's account of the way drinking from a public dipper could lead to a quick and agonizing death from communicable diseases such as diphtheria. Marston passed Moore along to William T. Graham, the president of American Can Company, and he agreed to finance Moore's Public Cup Vendor Company in 1908 to the tune of $200,000.

The company leased 6,000 square feet of space in New York City and began producing expensive porcelain vending machines, which were divided into four sections: The uppermost section held ice, the next highest dispensed cups, the next drained off waste water, and the consumer put discarded cups in the bottom.

The original marketing concept was to sell five ounces of water in individual, disposable paper cups at a penny apiece using a five-gallon bottle of spring water, a column of a hundred cups, and the elaborate machine. The contraption had its drawbacks, and the cups did too—rough brims, flat bottoms, and a tendency to tip over. On the other hand, once dispensed, they could not be forced back up into the machine, assuring each purchaser of a clean, unused cup of water every time.

Early advertising was as grandiose as all of Moore's other plans. The public was cordially invited to "quaff Nature's Nectar from this chalice." Although the chalices were usually located on trains or at transfer points for New York's trolleys, most New Yorkers had little interest in paying for water they could get for free.

Doctors and health officers looked at the machine differently, however, and praised one when it was exhibited at the World Tuberculosis Congress in Washington. While selling the machine to health professionals, Luellen ran into a hospital-supply representative who contributed to a key change in marketing direction.

Hearing that hospitals were looking for small cups to use in gathering sputum samples, Luellen realized that it would be a lot easier to sell the cup than it had been to sell the water. In a repositioning effort reminiscent of Gail Borden's switch from meat to milk (see Chapter 12), the young Kansans decided to sell the cup in simple vending machines rather than in the cumbersome water machine. The way to do that was by making the sanitary paper cup an acceptable alternative to the dreaded dipper. Moore later recalled, "We had to sell the idea that drinking out of dirty glasses was dangerous."

That this had to be proven as late as 1908 is nearly inconceivable to us; after all, decades earlier, in 1860, Louis Pasteur had proven just how deadly liquid-borne germs could be. Lamentably, however, the message hadn't gotten through where water was concerned. When Professor Alvin Davidson of Lafayette College released his report of the germs found with the aid of a microscope on public drinking cups in Easton, Pennsylvania, some people were horrified, but most ignored the study.

The paper cup got its initial boost of public support only because it made water more available than whiskey: The Anti-Saloon League endorsed Moore's cup as a device that offered a soul-saving drink of fresh water as opposed to demon spirits.

The support of teetotalers was gratifying, but Moore needed another push from a fellow Kansan to make his point. When he wasn't patching up gunfighters in Dodge City, Dr. Samuel Crumbine had done a series of experiments that proved conclusively that common dippers and glasses spread disease. For five years, he waged a lonely war against such vessels and watched helplessly as healthy children drank from the same cups used by tubercular patients traveling through Kansas to neighboring Colorado for "the altitude."

Then, in 1909, he became the state's Health Officer and immediately ordered common drinking cups abolished throughout Kansas. Railroad managers howled and resisted, because their lines passed through Kansas. A Pullman Company vice president summed up their feelings by shouting, "This damn little Health Officer in Kansas has ordered us to take out the glasses we have always used. We have nothing to take their place."

Moore was delighted to point out that this was no longer true, but Pullman still didn't buy. Most railroad executives reacted like the general manager of the Chicago Northwestern, who said, "Look here, son. I have drunk out of unwashed glasses in railway cars and saloons as my father did before me for sixty years. Pick up your little cups and run along so I can get back to work."

One exception was the Lackawanna Railroad, which had tried to expand its market by appealing to women (a case of franchise extension by gender). As the lure, the line had invented a fictional spokesperson named Phoebe Snow (a name also adopted by a pop singer in the 1970s). Phoebe loved to travel on the Lackawanna because the railroad used only anthracite coal, which burned cleaner than other varieties, leaving no soot on dainty Phoebe's clothes.

A series of print ads set to the rhyme scheme of "The House That Jack Built" advertised the Lackawanna. This one was typical:

> Says Phoebe Snow
> About to go
> Upon a trip
> To Buffalo:
> "My gown stays white

> Both day and night
> Upon the Road of Anthracite."

When Moore plumped for Lackawanna's cup business, he submitted:

> Phoebe dear
> You need not fear
> To drink from cups
> That you find here
> With cups of white
> No bugs will bite
> Upon the Road of Anthracite.

He won that battle but kept on losing the larger war against apathy concerning public drinking cups. He had installed his cups in some railroad stations as well as aboard the Lackawanna, but the public still didn't want to spend a penny for a cup of water. When Luellen tried to move the crusade into soda fountains, which were growing in number as public gathering places, he discovered, much to his regret, that a dishwasher's weekly wages cost less than a thousand of his cups did.

Ten years had passed since the beginning of his crusade. Moore had already changed the company name to the Individual Drinking Cup Company (1910) and Health Kup (1912), but he still needed something less clinical sounding. One day, while pondering how to sell his cups, he looked at the door of his office neighbor—the Dixie Doll Company. He remembered that, back when banks issued their own money, one New Orleans bank featured dix, the French word for ten, on its ten-dollar notes. When the bank subsequently became known for the strength of its currency, riverboat men began to refer to the notes as "dixies," and Dixie came to mean any southern territory in which dix notes were held in high esteem.

The name was short, looked well in print, and was easy to pronounce. Moore asked his neighbor's permission, got it, and began marketing his product in 1919 as Dixie Cups. A snappy new name didn't translate into increased sales, and four more lean years passed as

Moore and Luellen wondered when they were going to get a break. It finally came, but to capitalize on the opportunity, they had to make the ultimate piggybacking sacrifice—disguising their product as a package.

Early in the 1920s, improved refrigeration and manufacturing made candy cheaper and easier to carry and store than ever before. Competing snack foods suddenly saw this development as a threat to their market share. One of them—the ice cream industry—was even more concerned, feeling that its own sales had reached a saturation point. At the time, ice cream was sold only in bulk, and worried manufacturers saw children increasingly switching to the much handier candy bar as a way of satisfying their need for sweets. Interested in cutting the size of portions (and raising the unit price, of course), production people who knew of Moore's Dixie Cup saw it as a convenient way of packaging ice cream in smaller amounts, and, they hoped, increasing sales as well.

The first few experiments in packing ice cream into small paper cups were disastrous. One five-ounce Dixie Cup disintegrated after being filled with ice cream and closed with a lid; the second used a special filling machine, which resulted in crushed cups and wasted ice cream. It was only when Moore committed every resource of his company that a new way to use existing machinery and technology was discovered. By cutting the size in half—to two and a half ounces—Dixie was able to create an entirely satisfactory way of neatly packaging ice cream in small sizes.

Moore and Luellen were thrilled to be selling their cups in quantity to somebody, anybody. What neither foresaw was that by packaging ice cream in a neat, convenient container, they were also popularizing small, disposable paper cups. Just as institutions later familiarized masses of people with frozen foods, consumers subconsciously began to accept the paper cup as a disposable container for solids, semisolids, and liquids. It is not overstating the case to say that, for the first time in marketing history, a package became synonymous with the product it contained. The generic name for any kind of ice cream in any kind of handy little cup became known as a "Dixie Cup."

Given national name recognition in its incarnation as an ice cream container, the handy Dixie Cup began selling well on its own. Inevitably, increased public awareness of sanitation made Dixie Cups even more popular for drinking in the home and public places. After fourteen years of marketing trials and errors, Moore and Luellen lived to see the death of the public dipper and the total acceptance of the disposable drinking cup. By 1990, Dixie Cups had become so popular that the James River Corporation, which now produces them, estimates that 42 million are used every day.

•   •   •   •   •   •   •

PRODUCT   PAPER CUPS

Pivotal P: Piggybacking

Since there was no market for paper drinking cups, Dixie Cups hitchhiked onto ice cream's popularity as an indirect way of gaining acceptance.

Primary P's: Perception, Positioning

Moore had to change public perception of the tin dipper and show the paper cup to be a healthier alternative. Positioned as a container, the cup sold well on its own.

•   •   •   •   •   •   •

KOTEX   Rags to Riches

"You shouldn't take baths then."
    "Pickles will sour then, and cream won't whip."
    "If a dentist fills a tooth then, the filling will fall out."
    "Then" was the 1920s code word for menstruation, and this is a small sampling of the dozens of myths that surrounded the process in that era. With attitudes like this, it's no wonder that sanitary napkins were not an easy item to bring to market. In fact, the only way Kimberly-Clark could introduce Kotex was to hitchhike onto medical authority.
    Remember that the very subject of menstruation was taboo; many women didn't even discuss it with their own daughters. As a

result, some young girls experiencing their first period needlessly thought they might be hemorrhaging internally.

Women dealt with menstruation then by using (and reusing) felt or linen cloths, which they washed out as best they could and used month after month, giving rise to the expression "dirty linen" (as in "let's not air our dirty linen in public"). Women who could not afford linen used rags. The system was certainly unclean, possibly unhealthy, and ultimately unsatisfactory.

A huge potential market existed for a disposable napkin, but no consumer-goods company had yet seen fit to make one. Instead, Kimberly-Clark, a conservative supplier of paper to a variety of industries, assumed the unlikely (and uncomfortable) role of trailblazer in 1921.

At that point in its forty-nine-year history, Kimberly-Clark had exclusively supplied wrapping paper, newsprint, ledger paper, and wallpaper stock to American industry; however, shortly after World War I broke out, top management had become convinced that the company's future lay in two ways of processing wood chemically. One made bleached paper, ideal for quality reproduction of photographs in magazines and catalogs; the other produced a cellulose product as fluffy as cotton.

Early in 1914, this absorbent wadding was developed commercially as Cellucotton dressing, and during World War I, Kimberly-Clark was able to demonstrate its usefulness to hospitals, the Red Cross, and the War Department. Cellucotton offered absorbency five times that of cotton, was more resistant to infection, and cost only about half as much. Kimberly-Clark agreed to provide it to the War Department at cost, refusing to make a profit, and Cellucotton was immediately accepted for medical use in Europe.

By 1917, when America entered the war, Cellucotton was used widely to bandage wounds, and demand for it had quadrupled. The company continued to add to its production capacity, built two new mills to produce more of it, and had three plants turning out nothing but Cellucotton on a full-time basis. When the war ended in 1919, Kimberly-Clark decided to cancel all military contracts, again out of patriotic motives. Thanks to this magnanimous gesture, the paper company found itself with huge amounts of Cellucotton and no ready market for it.

In 1921, its board held an emergency meeting to discuss the situation and, after much debate, decided to make a full-scale entry into the consumer market with a variety of products made from Cellucotton.

One strong possibility was a sanitary napkin. On their own, nurses in France during the war had used Cellucotton in that way. This disposable method of dealing with menstruation caught on so quickly with women that the American Fund for the French Wounded, which had benefited from Kimberly-Clark's generosity during the war, suggested that the company market Cellucotton commercially as pads.

Given the taboos surrounding menstruation at the time, Kimberly-Clark was understandably ambivalent about marketing sanitary napkins. The idea was eventually accepted, but with some careful distancing between the product and the corporation. For one thing, another company, International Cellucotton Corporation, was formed to market the napkins, and it remained separate for thirty years before being merged back into Kimberly-Clark. For another, the product name, Cellunap—a contraction for Cellucotton napkins--was picked because "an article of this nature should carry a trade name which in no way would reflect its purpose."

At this stage, the sanitary napkin was a product half the people in the world needed but nobody wanted to talk about—least of all the company that was manufacturing it. Nevertheless, the company got encouragement from hospitals, which had used Cellucotton to bandage wounds. This positive feedback convinced executives to advertise the pads.

The first ad agency, Charles F. W. Nichols Company, immediately suggested changing the name to Kotex (for cotton textile). A Nichols memo states, "It sounds clean, and it is logical. More than that, it more than satisfies the niceties in that it is not suggestive per se of the uses to which the article is put."

The agency decided to rely on what would not be called until later the "high-tech approach," as embodied in this headline:

To Save Men's Lives Science Discovered
Kotex

(Cotton Textile)
A Wonderful, Sanitary Absorbent

A Wonderful, Sanitary Absorbent What? Right. Despite the bow to Science and satisfying "the niceties," Kotex never really does tell us just what is being advertised.

Despite these major problems and the ad's melancholy tone, Kimberly-Clark executives wanted to run it in a number of medical trade magazines. But Nichols concluded that ads targeted toward druggists, doctors, nurses, and hospital administrators "would not justify the expenditure." Instead, he counted on an intensive campaign in women's service magazines, because, as he said in a letter, "This is the first time magazines have ever printed sanitary-napkin advertisements."

There was merit in his "advertising-as-news" idea. At the time, women's service magazines had an even greater hold on their audience than TV soap operas did in the 1990s. In particular, *Ladies' Home Journal* was such a dominant force that druggists habitually asked the magazine for advance proofs of ads so they might better gauge the demand for advertised products. Nichols wrote in his campaign outline, "To make the wholesaler and jobber stock up on Kotex, to give our salesmen and the jobbing salesmen in the trade the most effective weapon, we urge eight full pages in the *Ladies' Home Journal.*"

There was just one hitch.

The magazine refused to carry the ads.

Ads that did run in other magazines were as vague as the first one and only hinted at what the product could do. After the first campaign proved ineffective, a second campaign showed two nurses on either side of a man in a wheelchair and another woman, presumably his wife or sweetheart, nearby. Nebulously headlined, "At stores and shops that cater to women," the ad stressed Kotex's war service, yet didn't mention the medical tie-in to nurses. At the bottom left, in type small enough to make a used-car salesman blush, the ad offered twelve napkins postpaid for sixty-five cents as well as a (small) list of shops that sold Kotex.

Naturally, such tentative marketing didn't do much to embolden women who were too embarrassed to ask for Kotex in the first place. Most dealers wouldn't stock it, and those that did hid it in a back room. Stores were loath to display it; when a Woolworth's on Market Street in San Francisco displayed Kotex in the window, a men's organization lobbied successfully to have it removed.

The upshot was that Kimberly-Clark was trying to change customer habits about a taboo product that magazines wouldn't advertise, retailers wouldn't stock, and women—the natural target market—refused to discuss. Sampling could only be done discreetly by mail, and then only through women who had responded to the ads. The advertising was tentative, the media selection was completely off-target for the times, and in-store merchandising was nonexistent. A company memo understates matters by stating, "sales were discouragingly slow."

If ever there were a product that needed to piggyback onto something old, new, borrowed, or blue, it was Kotex in 1923. At this important juncture in Kimberly-Clark's history, the company enlisted the aid of two advertising legends—Albert D. Lasker, president of Lord & Thomas (forerunner of Foote, Cone & Belding), and copywriter Claude Hopkins. After becoming successful hawking mail-order products separately, the two joined forces to establish a host of brands, including Palmolive soap and Goodyear tires, and also resuscitated Puffed Rice (see Chapter 8).

Since both had served their apprenticeships selling patent medicines, Lasker and Hopkins were aware that matters of health carried great weight with the public. The savvy Hopkins quickly saw that by recasting menstruation, a natural function, as a hygiene problem, he could hitch a ride on the always high esteem in which the medical profession was held.

His very first ad was headlined "The Safe Solution of Women's Greatest Hygiene Problem." The copy earnestly discussed problems associated with menstruation and was signed by "Ellen J. Buckland, Registered Nurse."

As you may have guessed, Buckland was a fictitious character, much like Betty Crocker (who was created around the same time). Buckland gave some measure of comfort to women who had painful periods but couldn't discuss them with even their closest friends. As an added benefit, nursehood endowed her with the medical authority of a health professional. Female Kimberly-Clark staffers used her name to respond to personal letters and offered booklets signed by her to women in need of the most basic information.

Inventing Nurse Buckland paid immediate dividends in another way. Women who had previously been too embarrassed to write for sample pads suddenly felt more at ease, because they were writing to a woman and a "real live nurse." Hopkins had also suspected that women would take a hint from the magazine ads and turn to real nurses for advice and samples of Kotex; when nurses began to get such requests, Kimberly-Clark followed up with a massive sampling program, with nurses acting as intermediaries and giving the pads their medical blessing.

Lasker's greatest contribution to Kotex was a merchandising brainstorm. To make it psychologically easier for women to purchase the product, he devised a novel "wrapped package plan." A series of ads in druggists' trade magazines told retailers to display Kotex in large, easily spotted, unmarked packages that would give no clue as to the contents; any woman wanting to buy one could simply deposit fifty cents in a box near the pile of packages, take one, and leave without saying a word. Along similar lines, Lasker got Kimberly-Clark to make the product available through nonthreatening distribution outlets—pharmacies that offered home delivery and ladies' room vending machines in public places.

Meanwhile, the sales force began a three-pronged effort aimed at dealers:

- *Free goods*—retailers ordering a gross of packages got twenty-two free.
- *In-store visibility*—trade ads headlined "Kotex, Don't hide it" urged dealers to display the pads openly in their stores.
- *Display incentives*—Kimberly-Clark paid dealers for every photograph that showed Kotex in a store window and even awarded prizes for the most inventive displays.

Kotex's push philosophy bore fruit in 1925, when Carson Pirie

Scott, the large Chicago department store, began to promote Kotex heavily throughout the store and in their advertising. Once Kimberly-Clark had attracted this kind of retail support, the *Ladies' Home Journal* could no longer avoid Kotex; when several months of Kotex ads produced no visible aftershocks from readers, the magazine even ran a feature story about menstruation, which helped alleviate some of the taboos surrounding the use of sanitary napkins.

Montgomery Ward gave sanitary napkins the final imprimatur by featuring Kotex prominently in its 1926 mail-order catalog. A mere five years after pads had made the quietest entrance in new product history, women were buying sanitary napkins by the millions and choosing among no fewer than three hundred competing brands.

By 1928, Ellen J. Buckland was looking a bit shopworn and wisely opted for early retirement. Her place was taken by that quintessential '20s creature, the advice columnist. "Mary Pauline Callender" dispensed chatty advice typical of the sobsister journalists of the day and offered still-reticent women a new reason to try Kotex: "80 percent of better-class women have discarded ordinary ways for Kotex."

Clearly, in the space of seven years, the reigning female authority figure had changed from nurse to socialite; dainty drawings of high-toned Kotex users spoke volumes about the strides made since Nichols's wheelchair ads.

It's interesting to note that when Tampax introduced tampons in 1936, it used a fashion-oriented pitch from the very beginning. Illustrations and photographs showed attractive women doing something active—skating, swimming, dancing; moreover, the models were always dressed in white—to make the point that tampons removed the fear of staining. Despite this second commercially available form of feminine protection, over 20 percent of American women were still using homemade pads as late as 1939; however, as more women joined the wartime work force, defense plants began to feature vending machines for Kotex, Tampax, and their competitors. By 1945, nearly all American women were using commercially made pads and tampons.

In hindsight, it's difficult to figure out what all the fuss was about. Drugstores, convenience stores, and supermarkets are now jam-packed with row upon row of feminine-protection products, which are available in a bewildering assortment of sizes, shapes, and formulations. Package fronts contain vivid four-color variations on the fashion/activewear motif, which has changed little in the fifty years since Tampax came on the scene. And where is the medical information that was so crucial to Kotex's success sixty years ago? You'll find it in small type squeezed onto the back of the package near the UPC symbol.

Even though Ellen J. Buckland keeps to herself these days in a quiet corner of the Home for No Longer Living Trademarks, her presence in the early Kotex ads was a major factor in making sanitary pads acceptable. By creating a fictional third party to act as a go-between, Lasker and Hopkins gave women an easily accessible, authoritative source for reliable information on a sensitive subject and free samples of a taboo product. And, by positioning menstruation as a "unique problem," they were able to use serious, informative advertising about their potent product, which could help provide the solution.

• • • • • • •

PRODUCT   SANITARY NAPKINS

Pivotal P: Piggybacking

Kotex hitched a ride on the coattails of the medical profession to add authority to its marketing efforts.

Primary P's: Positioning, Promotion

Positioning menstruation as a problem allowed women to consult health professionals about a slightly taboo product and made it easier to buy with the silent-purchase plan.

• • • • • • •

SMIRNOFF VODKA   Dampened Spirits

Pablo Picasso once said that the three greatest discoveries of the postwar Western world were Brigitte Bardot, modern jazz, and vodka.

If so, the discovery went unnoticed in the United States for quite a while. In fact, until the mid-1950s vodka sales in the United States were so unimpressive that they were reported to the Internal Revenue Service under a miscellaneous category that also included liqueurs. Smirnoff couldn't get Americans to drink volumes of vodka, no matter what they did—until they invented the Moscow Mule and piggybacked onto a trend.

Vodka has been the national drink in Russia for nearly four centuries. In the sixteenth century, Ivan the Terrible established Czar's Bars (public drinking establishments) so the general populace could enjoy it straight, or flavored with herbs, fruits, and nuts. (Pertzovka, reportedly Joseph Stalin's favorite, is infused with hot red peppers.)

In 1886, Peter Smirnoff displayed his family's vodka at Russia's largest trade fair; when Czar Alexander III tasted it, the Smirnoff family became Purveyors to the Imperial Russian Court. By 1917, however, imperialism was on the way out in Russia, and so were the Smirnoffs. Vladimir Smirnoff took the secret of the Smirnoff process with him to France and finally sold the American rights for $2,500 to Rudolph Kunett, whose family had supplied the grain for the Smirnoffs in Russia.

Kunett worked in sales for Standard Oil and Helena Rubinstein during the Depression and saved his pennies in hopes of establishing Smirnoff in America. In January 1934, he set up America's first vodka distillery in Bethel, Connecticut. He had only one problem: No one wanted to drink the stuff. There was absolutely no demand for Smirnoff whatsoever. Vodka was considered a fiery drink from a politically suspect country; sales were a mere 6,000 cases a year at $6 a case.

But $36,000 was nothing to sneeze at during the Depression, particularly to the president of a one-product company. John G. Martin, the head of Heublein, Inc., was trying to survive the Depression solely on the sales of A-1 Sauce, a relative luxury.

In 1934, Martin had helped Kunett by agreeing to sell Smirnoff under his company's name to save Kunett the $1,600 licensing fee required by Uncle Sam. By 1939, Kunett was ready to give up and remembered Martin's gesture. He told Martin, "I'm willing to sell the U. S. rights to Smirnoff to anyone who'll give me $14,000 and a job." Martin accepted the offer, gave Kunett a small royalty on sales of Smirnoff, and made him director of advertising. Some colleagues denounced the transaction as "Martin's folly."

All the criticism stopped the day Martin received an order from his South Carolina distributor, Ed Smith, for five hundred cases. This order was of particular interest, since Martin had had to twist Smith's arm to take only twenty-five cases a few months earlier.

The mystery was solved when Martin traveled to Smith's warehouse and discovered that the corks in all the vodka bottles were labeled Smirnoff whiskey. It turned out that the bottles were part of a final shipment of 2,000 cases that had been produced by Kunett's distillery just before it closed down in Bethel. With his stock of vodka corks depleted, a foreman had decided to use the corks left over from an ill-fated attempt to market Smirnoff whiskey. The foreman reasoned that no one would know the difference, since the bottles were labeled Smirnoff Vodka and corks would be covered by tax stamps.

That expedient solution might have gone undetected except for the curiosity of Ed Wooten, Heublein's only salesman in the South. Eager to sample the new whiskey, Wooten uncorked the bottle and found it had no smell, sipped it, and found it had no taste. He was baffled but nevertheless felt a warm glow of relaxation and decided to make the most of the liquor's unwhiskeylike properties. Wooten made up signs that said "Smirnoff's White Whiskey. No Taste. No Smell." The "White Whiskey" moved like crazy.

Wooten said, "People liked the feeling of relaxation associated with drinking whiskey, but they didn't really like its taste or smell. The White Whiskey eliminated both of those problems."

Martin had his own theory. He said, "When I got there, I found out that they were drinking Smirnoff and milk, Smirnoff and Coca-Cola, Smirnoff and almost anything. That gave us an idea, the first glimmer of where we were going."

Unfortunately, Martin had to file his theory away for four years. World War II broke out shortly thereafter, and the grain used in manufacturing vodka was diverted to more essential uses. Although the war didn't help Smirnoff directly, it did expose Americans to sake in Japan, a variety of wines in France, and ale and stout in Great Britain, heightening American tolerance for spirits other than Scotch, rye, gin, and bourbon.

After the war, Martin concentrated on finding a way to undermine consumer resistance to Smirnoff as "that fiery stuff." Aware that vodka mixed well with fruits and vegetables, he hit on the notion of promoting Smirnoff by piggybacking onto mixers—like Scotch and soda or gin and tonic. Such an approach would dilute the vodka and make it more palatable to American tastes.

Circumstances later inspired him to create a unique, three-way promotion.

On a spring night in 1946, he ran into an old acquaintance named Jack Morgan and his friend Susan Brownell at the Cock 'n' Bull, Morgan's Beverly Hills restaurant, which catered to transplanted Brits in the movie business. When Martin brought up his problems marketing vodka, Morgan related his own difficulties getting Americans to sample Cock 'n Bull Ginger Beer, long a favorite with British drinkers. Then Brownell chimed in with *her* marketing problem; she had recently inherited a copper factory and was having difficulty finding buyers for the bowls and mugs it produced.

Martin came up with an ingenious way to turn three white elephants into a mule. He asked the bartender for some Smirnoff, some ginger beer, and a copper mug, mixed the liquids, added a squeeze of lime, and, after huddling with Morgan and Brownell, christened the drink the Moscow Mule.

The name was a masterstroke. It suggested the strength that Americans associated with vodka; however, diluted with ginger beer, the drink itself produced "a relaxed feeling" without making people drunk. The effect was that drinkers began to view vodka not as "fiery stuff" but as "mellow stuff." As a bonus, due to its invention at a movie-industry hangout, the Moscow Mule became fodder for syndicated Hollywood gossip columnists, and, buoyed by the publicity, trendy hostesses began serving the drink with the funny name.

Martin knew the Mule would soon become "last year's drink" if he didn't capitalize on its trendiness quickly. Instead of putting his efforts behind influencing consumers to buy Smirnoff, he decided to establish it initially by influencing bartenders to mix it with ginger beer and other potables; taking a cue from Morgan and his other movie friends, he decided the best way to win friends and influence bartenders was to put them in pictures.

He went from bar to bar in Beverly Hills, dropped off a free bottle of Smirnoff, and explained how to mix the Mule to each barkeep. At the end of his visit, Morgan generously offered to take an instant picture of the bartender with one of the new Polaroid cameras and give it to him—if he'd take a sip of the Mule. No bartender refused when Martin put a Moscow Mule in his hands and a bottle of Smirnoff in a prominent place behind the bar and told him to smile.

In all the excitement, the bartenders didn't notice that Martin always took two pictures, giving one to the bartender and saving the other to show the bartender at the next saloon what his competitor was up to. After Martin had finished his photographic tour of Beverly Hills, bartenders were convinced that Smirnoff was becoming more popular and began ordering it in larger quantities.

By the mid-1950s, Americans were learning to mix Smirnoff with other liquids, often at Martin's sole suggestion or in joint campaigns planned with fruit and vegetable trade organizations or soft drink manufacturers.

Smirnoff had even generated enough sales by 1955 to justify an advertising campaign. One ad pictured comedian George Jessel with the headline, "I, George Jessel, invented the Bloody Mary." Even though the drink had been invented in Paris in 1921 by Fernand Petiot of Harry's New York Bar, the Jessel ad made it the most discussed drink in the country, ironically, just about the time Kunett retired.

Almost thrown away at the bottom left was the line "it leaves you breathless." This coy reminder that one could drink vodka without having "drinker's breath" offered a powerful benefit. Used more prominently as a headline (and mated with photographs of exotic locations like Egypt's Great Pyramid), the line became an advertising classic and was the final element in establishing Smirnoff. Every "breathless" ad talked about a mixed drink like the Bullshot, Vodka Martini, Harvey Wallbanger, Gimlet, Black Russian, and Screwdriver, which became the most popular mixed drink in America.

Mixed drinks like the Screwdriver and Bloody Mary established vodka in the United States, and for some time vodka has been the most popular distilled spirit in America, accounting for nearly one out of every five bottles sold. Americans can now choose among five hundred foreign and domestic brands like Rimski and Korsikoff or less exotic brands like Bernards Surf and Go Big Red.

Heublein has headed the list from the beginning, is now a $2 billion company, and sells more than 6 million cases of Smirnoff every year in the U. S. alone. John Martin learned from the Smirnoff whiskey incident that vodka had to be disguised or piggybacked onto other liquids to become palatable to Americans. Recent research conducted by the Vodka Information Bureau indicates just how crucial a factor piggybacking was in the success of vodka. Only 15 percent of vodka purchasers ever drink it straight, and none of these purists takes it neat exclusively. That keeps Heublein researchers coming up with drinks like vodka mixed with sugar and powdered lemon-lime drink mix— The Big Chill.

•   •   •   •   •   •   •

PRODUCT   VODKA

Pivotal *P*: Piggybacking

Smirnoff used the popularity and consumer acceptance of fruit juices and carbonated beverages to defuse vodka's image as "fiery stuff."

Primary *P*: Positioning

"It leaves you breathless" gave imbibers a way to avoid "whiskey breath" and positioned other liquors as unsophisticated and old-fashioned.

•   •   •   •   •   •   •

JELL-O   The Big Shake-Up

Before Sara Lee, before Klondike Bars, before Frozen Juicy Light 'n' Creamy, there was Jell-O, the ultimate convenience dessert. Jell-O is also the ultimate piggyback story over the long haul. The firm was able to keep on keeping on, first by instituting a home-sampling program aimed at ethnic audiences, then by relying on its name value when sales started slipping, and then, using the revivified name, by extending its product line.

All consumers had to do to make great desserts with Jell-O was boil water, add powdered gelatin, and refrigerate the mixture in a bowl or mold for four hours. To jazz it up you could throw in some fruit for added flavor and texture. It was quick, easy, didn't require any cooking prowess, and kids grinned when they saw it wobble and wiggle.

Jell-O appeared in the marketplace in 1897, although the first patent for a gelatin dessert was given to Peter Cooper, inventor of the Tom Thumb locomotive, in 1845. Cooper never manufactured it; that fell instead to Pearl B. Wait, a cough-syrup maker in Le Roy, New York, who started producing a gelatin his wife May named Jell-O.

After trying to market Jell-O for two years without success, Wait sold the brand for $450 to a neighbor named Orator Frank Woodward (his real name).

Jell-O was a dud.

Woodward had already had success selling such home remedies as Kemp's Laxative, Raccoon Corn Plasters, and Grain-O, a coffee substitute like C. W. Post's Postum; however, food products were tougher to sell than medicine, and Jell-O was a tougher sell than most foods. People understood that it was supposed to be easier to digest than heavy cakes and pies, but the rich-dessert habit died hard, and Jell-O was new and unfamiliar. At one point, Woodward got so disgusted that he offered to sell Jell-O lock, stock, and barrel for thirty-five dollars to his plant superintendent, A. S. Nico. Nico politely declined.

What made Jell-O finally catch on was giving away samples of the ten-cent dessert door-to-door, along with a brochure that described how to make and use it. Moreover, Woodward made sure he was able to communicate directly with a nation of immigrants; he published the brochure in French, German, Spanish, Swedish, and Hebrew. RFD routes were obtained with the cooperation of postal authorities, and even though they bore no names and addresses, the booklets were left at every home by postal delivery. Once an area had been sampled, sales staff could convincingly tell grocers to order stock to meet the demand; in 1902, sales shot up from almost nothing to $250,000.

Sales of Jell-O neared $1 million in 1906, and by 1909, Woodward was sure enough about its continued success to make the last shipment of Grain-O.

By the 1920s, Jell-O had become a $10 million annual grosser, had introduced D-Zerta, a sugar-free gelatin dessert for diabetics, and had distributed its 250 millionth recipe book. Jell-O, made in the same factory as Grain-O, merged with its arch-rival, the Postum Cereal Company, on December 31, 1925. Once unable to command a buyout price of $35, Jell-O was exchanged for 570,000 shares of Postum stock; at $77 a share, that gave Jell-O a theoretical value of $43.8 million. The Postum Cereal Company acquired all of Clarence Birds-eye's subsidiaries in 1929 (see Chapter 12), including the name General Foods, and adopted it as the new corporate name.

Jell-O only got bigger in the next thirty years. The brand began a decade of sponsoring Jack Benny's radio show in 1934 and expanded its original six flavors of gelatin with six different puddings. Sales of packaged desserts doubled from 1941 to 1950, and at mid-century Jell-O had 70 percent of the $100 million gelatin dessert market and outsold all other brands of packaged desserts combined.

To its credit, the dessert foods division of General Foods was constantly looking for ways to increase sales of Jell-O beyond the sales of the original six fruit flavors of gelatin. Among other things, the division:

- increased the number of flavors and configurations of Jell-O to include fruit- and chocolate-flavored pie fillings;
- created vegetable flavors of Jell-O Salad Gelatin (for example, celery, which could be used in salads and for parts of the meal other than dessert);
- pitched the product to weight-conscious Americans who wouldn't buy D-Zerta because they didn't want to admit they were dieting; and
- produced flavorless Jell-O for women who could use it supposedly to strengthen their fingernails.

In 1968, American families bought an average of sixteen boxes of Jell-O products in a year, an all-time high. Then Jell-O began slowly declining in popularity (some would say, inevitably). By 1970, consumption had slid to 15.6 packs and fell below 15 packs by 1972. In hindsight, the decline was caused by several interrelated factors. The huge increase in the number of working women had already begun, which left less time for meal preparation in traditional households, leading to a corresponding increase in the use of convenience foods. Second, Americans freed of societal restraints "did their thing" by entering second childhood. Cookies, potato chips, ice cream sandwiches, and other "munchies," formerly regarded solely as children's fare, became acceptable for adults, foreshadowing the future explosion of Häagen-Dazs, Famous Amos, DoveBars, and "gourmet" popcorn.

General Foods tried to fight back by stressing the economic value of Jell-O. A major remarketing effort was undertaken, with price as the pivotal P and the theme "To make exciting desserts on a budget, start with Jell-O gelatin." The theme was less than compelling, and the strategy behind it was questionable. In urging consumers to mix Jell-O with other foods, General Foods was embracing a view of the product as an add-on, a sort of Hamburger Helper for desserts, after years of being a star on its own. The campaign was a failed attempt at piggybacking, and Jell-O's stock sank even lower when ready-to-serve cakes and pies, miniature ice cream sandwiches, and frozen-juice bars came on the market. By 1979, the average American family was buying only 11.4 packs a year of Jell-O products.

An entirely fresh approach was called for, and it came early in 1979, when Peter Rosow, general manager of General Foods' desserts division, suggested looking at Jell-O as if it were a brand-new product. The first step was creating brand-new research, and Young & Rubicam, Jell-O's agency for fifty-one years, began interviewing consumers in focus groups and in-home interviews. The results showed that Jell-O's main appeal lay not in its versatility as a cooking staple nor in its value as an economical dessert. Instead, consumers reminded General Foods that Jell-O had symbolic value and a unique emotional appeal. Jell-O reminded consumers of happy family gatherings.

Alexander Kroll, president of Young & Rubicam, told *Forbes*, "There's a lot of affection for Jell-O. It's the name. It's Jack Benny. It's your mother serving it."

Given these results, Rosow admitted that Jell-O's recent marketing "may have been too intellectual. We were too focused on product attributes, not on experience." This sense of Jell-O as a family experience was captured in a series of television commercials. People of all ages were shown enjoying Jell-O at family events like weddings and reunions. Moreover, the commercials were aired not with soap operas and other daytime television, which cater mostly to housewives, but with primetime shows, greatly expanding the potential audience.

Sales increased with the first campaign, and a second set of commercials used a playful approach, "Watch that wobble, see that wiggle, taste that jiggle," echoing soft-drink advertising and appealing to young people. Sales of Jell-O products rose 1 percent by 1980, and sales of 576 million packs of Jell-O upped its share of the gelatin-dessert market from 70 percent to 71.4 percent.

While the campaign was successful, it wasn't the end of the remarketing of Jell-O, but rather a new beginning for an eighty-year-old brand. The revival of Jell-O gelatin, which capitalized on the value of the Jell-O name, later led General Foods product managers to find new products to identify as part of the Jell-O family.

In one case, marketers remembered a 1960s experiment with frozen, ready-to-eat pudding, which wasn't even tested, because it was "hard as a rock." By the mid-'70s, however, General Foods was using an emulsifying process to keep products like its Birds Eye Cool Whip soft. The idea evolved from frozen pudding in a dish to frozen pudding on a stick, and, eventually, this little piggyback went to market.

Jell-O Pudding Pops were tested in 1979 and introduced nationally in 1982. A $25 million ad campaign, some rub-off popularity from spokesman Bill Cosby, and the Jell-O name produced sales of $65 million in the first eight months of the brand's availability and hit nearly $100 million the first year; five years after entering the frozen-novelties market (anything on a stick), General Foods was grossing $300 million with seven flavors of Pudding Pops, six varieties of Gelatin Pops, and four kinds of frozen Fruit Bars.

In addition to the seventeen frozen novelties, as of 1987, the Jell-O name was on nine dessert mixes, twenty-six gelatin desserts (ten of them sugar-free), eighteen instant puddings and pie fillings (including pistachio), nine not-so-instant puddings and pie fillings, and two sugar-free puddings and pie fillings. The eighty-one Jell-O products can be found in from four to eight sections of the average super-market.

General Foods asserts that the Jell-O trademark now has "virtu-ally 100 percent awareness," and *Forbes* would agree. In February 1987, the magazine rated it as one of the top ten consumer franchises, along with Levi's, Pepsi-Cola, Coca-Cola, Campbell, Budweiser, Mc-Donald's, Johnson & Johnson, Marlboro, and Kraft.

•   •   •   •   •   •   •

PRODUCT   JELL-O

Pivotal *P*: Piggybacking

General Foods leveraged the equity the Jell-O name enjoyed with consumers to remarket an eighty-three-year-old product and piggybacked on it to enter frozen desserts.

Primary *P*: Promotion

Jell-O scored originally by giving immigrants recipe booklets in their native tongue, which lessened its unfamiliarity and gave consumers a free additional benefit.

•   •   •   •   •   •   •

Chapter Three

DON'T

UNDERESTIMATE

PUBLIC **PERCEPTION**

. . . . . .

REMEMBER when smoking and fur coats were glamorous? Smoking has become anti-social (even illegal), and, with the animal rights movement picking up steam, more and more women are pondering a different answer to the question, "What becomes a legend most?"

Cigarettes and mink coats have experienced severe declines in their "perceived value," a term likely to surface in most marketing meetings. Perceived value is the public's collective answer to the marketer's question, "How much is this product worth to you?"

Clearly, the line between perception and reality is a thin one. Is Imperial margarine really better because it's "the high-priced spread"? Will drinking Pepsi make me "think young"?

Marketers try to enhance what are, ultimately, boxes on shelves with every kind of image-making magic they can find; however—and, I personally believe, fortunately—the public has the final say and makes up its own collective mind as to the perceived value of a given product.

Yet, it is equally true, as we shall see, that consumers often have strong, preconceived notions of what a product is or does and can be dead wrong. Worse yet, from a marketer's viewpoint, telling the consumer he or she is wrong is an excellent way to lose a customer.

Public Perception   It's hard to know how to educate an entire country or even a targeted mass of prospective purchasers. It's hard to know whom you have to reach: the store buyers who will stock your product or the consumers who must demand it in order for you to have a success. Moreover, public perception has its own energy, its own force, and if the force isn't with you—good luck to you and yours.

Public perception can ride on a crest of news events, trends, social fashions, and/or subtle "in's" and "out's." Perception can change quickly in some fields and slowly in others; perception varies with age groups, ethnic groups, and various demographic configurations. Yet, over all, public perception is the subtext of the times, the sociology of the moment. In order to sell your product, you may need a reading from the men and women in the street.

Irrational Attitudes   Theodore Levitt, Harvard University's esteemed marketing professor, points out that corporations often lay their own marketing failures at the feet of "that old bugbear, consumer irrationality."

While it's true that blaming consumer behavior can be a cop-out for misguided marketers, it is also true that the public is very slow to accept product changes in the areas of personal hygiene and food preparation, for instance. As we shall see, such reluctance slowed acceptance of the microwave oven at one end of the temperature spectrum, and frozen foods at the other end. Birds Eye had to contend with nutritional concerns about the healthfulness of frozen foods, which the public constantly confused with inferior, cold-storage foods. When such institutions as schools and hospitals endorsed frozen foods, however, these genuine concerns gradually vanished. Ironically, becoming institutionalized nearly killed the microwave oven.

AMANA   Making Waves

The microwave oven was originally a consumer product trapped inside a company (Raytheon Corporation) that had never been successful selling consumer products. With that background, it's not hard to understand why this revolutionary product—that statistics now show is owned by one out of every four American homes—bombed. Raytheon didn't realize that what it was really fighting was a battle of public perception. Once the company stopped selling new-fangled machinery and began to sell quicker, easier cooking, it was able to turn around a turkey.

Raytheon had been responsible for developing much of America's radar capability before and during World War II. The company had created both the Hawk and Sparrow missiles and had become the world's leader in providing navigational equipment for every kind of sea-going vessel, from dinghies to aircraft carriers.

A charter member of America's military-industrial complex, Raytheon starred on the battlefield but just couldn't get it together on the home front. The company had mismarketed every consumer product it had ever developed, including television sets, record players, and transistor radios—when each was at its peak as a consumer item.

Yet none of these failures was as galling as Raytheon's inability to market the microwave oven. By the 1960s Raytheon had lost $5 million on the microwave, making it the biggest consumer failure in company history.

The discovery that electromagnetic waves could be absorbed into food and become heat energy, causing the food to cook, had grown out of Raytheon's wartime research into radar. That effort had been led by engineer Percy Spencer, the American most responsible for the development of radar for use in World War II.

British scientists H. A. H. Boot and J. T. Randall had devised the pulse-type microwave magnetron for radar use in 1939, and John D. Cockroft, who led the British radar effort, had shown it to Spencer on a Friday afternoon in 1940. Spencer later said he had thought it was "awkward and impractical" and had asked whether he could take it home over the weekend. Working on Britain's greatest wartime secret in his garage, Spencer made improvements in the design, which made it easier to turn out radar units in large quantities.

The effort took years, during which time Spencer and other Raytheon engineers noticed that pulsing magnetrons didn't generate a continuous flow of microwaves; they pulsed on and off, generating a few hundred watts of power—just enough to warm one's hands in the midst of a New England winter.

Spencer first associated the heat that microwaves generated with cooking in 1942. According to company legend, a candy bar melted in his pocket while he was testing a magnetron in a radar experiment. The day after the armistice was signed, he made the first experiment in microwave cooking history by holding a bag of unpopped popcorn next to a power tube that generated from three hundred to five hundred watts. After several other experiments, Spencer cooked an egg for the board of directors; although the egg exploded, the board agreed to fund further experiments.

Spencer got his first microwave-cooking patent in 1949, and by 1953, Raytheon had a Radarange on the market and had also licensed its technology to Tappan and Litton. But the microwave ovens of the 1950s were far different from those of the 1980s in that they:

- had to be installed by electricians, because they operated at 220 volts.
- had to be serviced by plumbers, because the power tube was water-cooled to prevent it from overheating.
- were as large as refrigerators, standing five feet high.
- were outrageously expensive, costing around $1,295 (nearly as much as a stripped-down, 1955 two-door Chevrolet sedan, which cost $1,535). Given these drawbacks, fewer than 10,000 microwaves were sold in the United States.

Between 1953 and 1967, microwaves were literally made by hand in Hooksett, New Hampshire, for restaurants and airlines. In a curious turnabout from Clarence Birdseye's experience (see Chapter 12), selling microwaves to institutions didn't make microwaves attractive to consumers; instead, they became "industrial" in the public's mind, which slowed acceptance even more.

In *Breakthroughs*, his own history of how it happened, Raytheon physicist John M. Osepchuk is quoted as saying, "We didn't have the foggiest idea of how to market them [microwave ovens] and we knew it."

They got help from a most unexpected source. In 1960 Raytheon demonstrated a Radarange at an international trade show in Japan, and such companies as Sanyo and Toshiba immediately saw a market. The leading Japanese firm in magnetrons was the New Japan Radio Company (NJRC). Banned from working on military applications, NJRC had concentrated on communications applications, and shortages of key materials had forced it to make magnetrons from cheaper elements. In the wake of the trade show, Sanyo agreed to fund further research to come up with an even smaller magnetron, and Toshiba sold 2,500 microwaves to the Japanese National Railroad—each of which used an NJRC magnetron.

When word filtered back to Massachusetts, Raytheon bought a one-third interest in NJRC, gave the Japanese company access to all its designs, and eventually capitalized on the genius of engineer Keishi Ogura. Ogura's work made microwaves easier to manufacture and service, increased their energy efficiency, and enabled them to run on electrical voltage used in the average home in Japan and the United States.

Raytheon had bought engineering expertise by looking East; now it turned West and got marketing savvy from a religious sect.

The Amanas were, until 1931, a community entirely controlled by their church. Settled in Iowa, members of the Amana Colonies belonged to the Society of True Inspiration, a religious group born in the seventeenth century as a splinter group of Lutherans. By 1931, the Colonies were surviving mostly on a line of hand-built beer coolers designed by master marketer George Foerstner. Foerstner transformed that product into Amana Refrigeration, which Raytheon bought in 1965 for $25 million.

Amana had not built the market for home freezers by selling freezers directly. Instead, George Foerstner shrewdly sold wholesale food door-to-door and, eventually, broached the subject of freezers. Raytheon had bought Amana for Foerstner's expertise, hoping that he would help market the microwave. Chairman Charles F. Adams said, "We'd give it one shot, and if it didn't work, we'd put an end to it once and for all."

At first, Foerstner wasn't interested. After listening to how technologically advanced the product was, the normally religious Foerstner fulminated, "I don't give a goddam how exciting a thing is that you've got technologically. It's not going to sell in the marketplace until you can convince the consumer that he needs it."

What would convince a consumer—he was sure—was smaller size, easier installation, and lower price. Using only his instincts, Foerstner decided that the microwave should be about as big as an air conditioner, weigh about the same, and sell for $499. Commenting in *The Creative Ordeal*, Otto J. Scott says, "In several terse sentences, Foerstner had taken microwave radar, one of the great military secrets of World War II . . . and reduced it to the level of an air conditioner."

But that was Foerstner's genius, because he made everyone at Raytheon understand that for fourteen years they'd been trying to sell strange machines when they should have been marketing a valuable service—faster cooking. Once the perception of the product changes, so does its place in the market. Just as he had sold food as a means to promote the home freezer, George Foerstner used the microwave as a waystation to easier meal preparation.

He began his educational campaign with a pitch to Chicago's leading appliance wholesalers and retailers. He said, "Anyone who sells a microwave oven has to be able to demonstrate it." Amana educated every interested dealer and showed him or her how to work the machine; once they'd finished basic training, each dealer got, as a graduation present, several free bags of popcorn.

Amana's president Andre Meyer has often said, "The Radarange would not have succeeded without popcorn." Every dealer learned to demonstrate the microwave making popcorn, which may help explain the rise of gourmet popcorn in the 1970s. Meyer says, "They would smell the popcorn popping. They would hear the popcorn popping. Then we'd give them some and they'd say, 'Gosh, this really does work.' "

Such demonstrations were fine for retail stores but impractical for large groups. Searching for a way to educate many consumers at one time, Amana borrowed a page from politics and set up whistle-stop tours for the microwave. For several weeks, a special train wound westward from Chicago, complete with balloons and bands; at each stop, heavily recruited housewives and press people got on board and were given microwaved food to sample, beverages, and cooking demonstrations of foods more sophisticated than popcorn.

The barnstorming tour planted the seed for the need of a microwave, but there were still hurdles to overcome. People were afraid of chromosome damage from excessive radiation and afraid that the microwave would become so accessible that young children would operate it—with adverse consequences. One appliance dealer says, "They used to be afraid that some kid was going to take the family cat and put it in the microwave and cook it."

To make sure that such fears didn't derail his bandwagon, Foerstner added the ultimate service contract to every Radarange sold in Chicago. An Amana home economist would visit every purchaser, help with the installation, explain the three buttons on the front and how they worked, and walk the cook through his or her first microwave meal. As an added service, the home economist stayed on twenty-four-hour call, and service personnel were ready to answer any emergencies within a few hours. The service was so successful that Amana made it mandatory for distributors to have home economists on staff whom Amana trained to give cooking demonstrations in retail stores.

It is safe to say that microwaves became accepted hesitantly in the 1960s, were greeted eagerly in the 1970s, and became necessities in the 1980s. Worldwide sales increased exponentially from 30,000 in 1968, to 790,000 in 1975, to 15.4 million in 1989. By lowering the price, quieting irrational consumer fears, and demonstrating the convenience and versatility they offered, George Foerstner eventually made millions of people want microwave ovens. And by buying his sales expertise and the technical excellence of NJRC, Raytheon finally achieved its first success in consumer products.

• • • • • • •

PRODUCT   MICROWAVE OVEN

Pivotal *P*: Perception

Raytheon had to: (1) sell the concept of quicker cooking—not new, improved technology; (2) consumers had to learn that microwave ovens were not dangerous.

Primary *P*'s: Promotion, Promise

Demonstration (with the popcorn giveaway) was an important teaching technique; in-home instructors and back-up assistance sold the promise of success.

• • • • • • •

GREEN GIANT   Pea Nuts

You don't have to be hawking a forbidding new machine for the public to misperceive your product. Even something as innocuous as a tiny garden pea can face irrational resistance.

Ward Cosgrove, a member of the board of the Minnesota Valley Canning Company, discovered the "Prince of Wales" garden pea on a trip to Europe in 1926. It was wrinkled, oblong, and, as peas go . . . huge. In those days, Americans much preferred "Early Junes," which were smooth, round, and small. Consumers thought peas with a bumpy skin like "Prince of Wales" would be "tough" and hard to chew. Cosgrove had his employees taste "Prince of Wales" anyway. When they agreed that the pea had a sweetness and tenderness "Early Junes" couldn't match, he decided to bring the big pea home.

Unfortunately, Minnesota Valley's most important customers weren't consumers. Instead, they were large grocery stores, which sold Cosgrove products under their store name. These "private label" customers refused to stock the peas. Their attitude was, "You're banging your head against the wall, Ward. There's no market for these peas; big peas never sell."

Undeterred (mostly because the peas tasted so good), Cosgrove decided to end-run the food chains temporarily and market the pea directly to consumers. When people began asking for the peas, food chains would have no choice but to order them. The key had to be finding a way to turn the pea's size into something more attractive—to change the perception of big peas from negative to positive.

Cosgrove felt strongly about "Prince of Wales." He said, "We weren't going to apologize for it." Instead, he took the product's biggest possible drawback and boldly put it right on the can. "We made it a marketing feature by calling the brand 'Green Giant.'"

The idea was terrific, but attorney Warwick Keegin pointed out that the two words were descriptive and therefore could not be trade-marked under existing U. S. law. Instead, he suggested using a "real" giant on the label as a symbol. Furthermore, Keegin argued that the giant had to be green, to which Minnesota Valley's former president Bill Dietrich said, "That's ridiculous, Warwick. Whoever heard of a green giant?"

Indeed.

Keegin won the battle, and a young Chicago ad executive made a bit of advertising history with Minnesota Valley, his first account. Leo Burnett, later the father of the Marlboro Man and other advertising successes, worked over the Giant concept in 1935 and conjured up a giant with a winning smile, created a valley for him to roam, a memorable slogan for him to speak ("Ho, ho, ho"), and, finally, made him noticeably taller. Burnett was so pleased with his creation that he decided the new, improved trademark should be known as the "Jolly Green Giant."

Jolly Green Giant peas became a success, and, by the 1940s, the small, smooth pea went the way of the brontosaurus. In 1950, Minnesota Valley Canning adopted the name of its formerly unfashionable product and officially became the Green Giant Company.

•   •   •   •   •   •   •

PRODUCT   "PRINCE OF WALES" PEAS

Pivotal *P*: Perception

Brokers, grocers, and consumers needed a reason to try big peas when they were happy with small garden peas; the Green Giant name and logo gave them one.

•   •   •   •   •   •   •

POSTUM   Coffee Nerves

The Boston Tea Party in 1774 may have made America a coffee-drinking country, but there were more than a few unsettled stomachs in the intervening one hundred years. Coffee made from fruit or grains began appearing as early as the 1850s in response to a national problem—dyspepsia. The *Encyclopedia Americana* said at the time, "Few are so happy as to pass through a life of ordinary duration, without undergoing a protracted struggle with this malady."

Postum, an alternative to coffee made from coffee beans, was able to enter the market successfully by focusing on curing dyspepsia. By changing public perceptions about both coffee itself and previous bad-tasting coffee substitutes, C. W. Post succeeded where dozens of others had failed.

When vegetarianism took hold in the mid-1800s, through the teachings of Samuel Graham (creator of the Graham cracker), literally dozens of coffee substitutes had been marketed. No brand—whether cereal-based, bread-based, molasses-based, or based on any combination thereof—had ever become successful with consumers.

Coffee was known to cause stomach upsets, yet people were unsure how to prevent distress and even less sure of what else to drink in the morning.

In fact, the public had greater faith in methods that ran the gamut from folk medicine to outright quackery. Some of the favored remedies for stomach discomfort then included prolonged starving, *drinking* Epsom salts, applying flaxseed poultices to the stomach, hydrotherapy, and drowning food in cayenne pepper or horseradish (to wake up the stomach's soothing juices, of course).

One of the many Americans who suffered from chronic stomach troubles was Charles W. Post, who had invented a bicycle, a suspender, and a mechanical piano, done woodworking, sold blankets, run a paint shop, and hammered iron on an anvil. The only thing he'd never done was cure his stomach—although he had tried patent medicines like No. 2 Cassia Bitters, Scott's Emulsion, and Peruvian Balm, sea voyages, mineral baths, massage, dieting, gymnastics, and even enemas. Nothing had helped.

Then Post began hearing of the miraculous results patients with similar problems were having at "The San"—the Battle Creek Sanitarium in Battle Creek, Michigan. While it had been founded by Seventh Day Adventists, under the direction of Dr. John Harvey Kellogg, The San had also attracted repeat visitors, such as Theodore Roosevelt, William Jennings Bryan, and John Patterson, the dynamic president of National Cash Register. Impressed by it all, Post left a failing cottonseed mill in Fort Worth, Texas, and arrived at The San a sick, middle-aged man in a wheelchair.

Ten months later, he had lost forty pounds and was, if anything, sicker than before.

His wife, Ella, took him out of the San to study Christian Science with Mrs. Elizabeth Gregory, and, in a matter of weeks, he was greatly improved. The cure was so dramatic that Post began thinking of providing similar cures as a business proposition.

Although Post couldn't offer personal testimonials to the health care provided at The San, he had been impressed with many of the vegetarian foods served there—as much for their marketing potential as for their taste. He approached Dr. Kellogg about the possibility of jointly promoting a bran-and-molasses health coffee called Monk's Brew, a product that, like caffeine-free bread and molasses-based coffee, was served at The San. Dr. Kellogg declined, although he'd been promoting grain- and nut-based products since 1881; Post decided to sell his own brand of grain-based coffee anyway.

The conventional wisdom was that grain-based coffee would

never succeed, because the coffee habit was so . . . ingrained. But coffee had once before yielded its position as the leading breakfast drink. In 1869, George Gilman and George Hartford had reduced tea prices by 70 percent with their Great Atlantic and Pacific Tea Company, and tea was the national morning drink until coffee makers counterattacked with price cuts and promotion. Post thought he had a chance to sneak in and win over a few million coffee drinkers.

Post knew that coffee was also vulnerable on health grounds. When he started his own medical boardinghouse in Battle Creek, the La Vita Inn, he served what was still called Monk's Brew at every meal. Informal market research helped him come up with a combination of wheat, bran, and molasses that people enjoyed. When they took some home in bags after their cures were complete, he was convinced he had beaten the bad-taste rap with his recipe.

By December 1894, Post felt confident enough to lay out $21.91 for two bushels of wheat, 200 pounds of bran, and ten jugs of molasses, and spent another $46.85 on a gas stove, a peanut roaster, a coffee grinder, and several mixers. The result was Postum Cereal Food Coffee, first produced in January 1895 and hawked around Battle Creek in a handcart pushed by its creator.

Given the bad reputation coffee substitutes had with retailers, Post had no choice but to adopt a "push" strategy for his product, one that focused on convincing store owners to stock it. He pushed the pushcart; he pushed the product, fighting public perception all the way. Needing advertising space but not having the money to pay for it, he traveled to nearby Grand Rapids. While the editor of the *Grand Rapids Evening News* watched, Post brewed some coffee; the editor tasted it, liked it, and Post left with an advertising credit for $1,000.

Then he approached a Grand Rapids grocery jobber about his product, and the man contemptuously showed Post sacks of a similar product called Caramel Coffee. He said, "Mister, that stuff has been laying around unsold for eight years. People just won't drink it." But Post gave him a sample cup, sweet-talked him, and eventually beat down his objections with a two-pronged strategy. Post offered him (1) the local advertising he'd already negotiated, and (2) a consignment billing policy, which meant that the jobber only paid for what he sold—after it was sold.

Yet, all of Post's cleverness in removing negatives from the dealer's side of the marketing equation might have gone for naught if he hadn't also come up with a way to make cereal-based coffee acceptable to a mass audience. He decided that the only way to get large groups of people interested in cereal-based coffee was to scare the living daylights out of them.

Post foreshadowed the advertising-inspired maladies of the twentieth century—body odor, halitosis, and psoriasis—by creating his very own set of coffee-related diseases: coffee nerves and coffee heart. He told the story of one poor devil who lost his eyesight from drinking coffee and invoked the power of suggestion and the Chinese water torture in another ad:

> Constant dripping wears away the stone. Perhaps a hole has
> been started in you . . . .Try leaving off coffee for ten days.

Post believed in the efficacy of patent medicines and borrowed liberally from their "scare" methods of advertising. But he also pioneered in that sophisticated, ultramodern marketing technique known as positioning (see Chapter 4). By labeling coffee as unhealthful and the cause of a mysterious but serious disease, he created the perfect amount of doubt in a potential customer's mind. Reading the ads, the unsophisticated consumers of the time might muse, "Maybe that's why I'm so nervous in the office. Maybe that's why I can't sleep at night."

Having created an atmosphere of uncertainty, Post followed up by warning consumers that coffee was full of "poisonous alkaloids," a source of rheumatism, and also a direct cause of "Coffee Heart," Post's terrifying substitute phrase for palpitations. Post didn't stop at implying that coffee caused physical disease; he suggested that drinking it was the root of all evil.

Consider this excerpt:

> Is your yellow streak the coffee habit? Does it reduce your
> working force, kill your energy, push you into the big crowd of
> mongrels, deaden what thoroughbred blood you may have, and
> neutralize all of your efforts to make money and fame?

If you weren't getting ahead at work, coffee was the villain. If you squabbled with your spouse or were less than the perfect parent, coffee deserved the blame. If you had problems with arthritis, rheumatism, nerves, an uneven heartbeat—coffee, coffee, coffee was your problem.

By contrast, Postum drinkers were pictured as vigorous, energetic, successful doers. To reinforce the consumer's impression that he or she had done the right thing by buying Postum, Post included a brochure, "The Road to Wellville," in every package.

After the ads had drawn well in Michigan, Post arranged credit with a Chicago advertising agency and began buying space in national magazines like *Scribner's* and *Harper's Weekly*. Postum's sales doubled, tripled, then quintupled. By 1898, Post was netting $3 million annually.

Of course such a strategy couldn't have worked unless there was good reason to doubt the healthfulness of coffee in the first place. And, while Post laid out the evils of coffee with a trowel, as medicine, nutrition, and chemistry have evolved, much of what he suspected has been proven to a certainty; caffeinated coffee is now routinely denied to patients with severe stomach, heart, and nerve disorders, and decaffeinated coffee products do a thriving business.

•   •   •   •   •   •   •

PRODUCT   CEREAL-BASED COFFEE

Pivotal *P*: Perception

The public had to be convinced that regular coffee was bad for them and that a substitute would better their digestion and, perhaps, their lives.

Primary *P*'s: Promotion, Promise

Through advertising and sampling, Post was able to reach his market; with the promise of nothing to lose, he was able to rally the grocery trade behind his product.

•   •   •   •   •   •   •

LITE BEER   Athletic Supporters

Most endorsement campaigns use glamorous figures to influence consumers. To introduce Lite Beer and to overcome the perception problems inherent in a lower-calorie "man's drink," the best shot Miller had was to go with a glamorous/un-glamorous endorsement campaign.

Since we don't have real royalty or an acknowledged aristocracy in America, we have to make do with aviators, athletes, authors, and actresses as the leaders of the pack. Athletes were used commercially as early as 1886, when their pictures appeared on trading cards inserted into cigarette packs, and they remained true-blue heroes through two world wars, the Depression, and the Cold War.

Things changed in the 1960s.

For one thing, television had made athletes familiar visitors in the American home, undercutting the historical view of them as unapproachable heroes. For another, they were no longer being paid peanuts and used agents to negotiate bigger and bigger contracts. Finally, labor disputes, such as the furor over baseball's reserve clause and clashes between football players and owners over drug treatment, made even the most starry-eyed sports fans acutely aware that their heroes were being paid large amounts of money to do their jobs. Like accountants, stevedores, and scientists, athletes were just working stiffs. Exit the glamour considered essential in an endorsement campaign.

On the plus side, however, athletes began to be perceived more as human beings than as idealized figures, and this change enabled them to endorse many categories of products for the first time. In the 1930s, the "aw shucks, folks" pose ballplayers had been forced to adopt had limited them to appearing on cereal boxes. World War II brought a bit more realism, and athletes began to promote adult products like cigarettes. By the 1960s, Frank Gifford was modeling Jantzen bathing suits, Sonny Liston was pushing Braniff Airlines, and Wilt Chamberlain was squeezing into a Volkswagen.

In the 1960s, hair dryer manufacturers employed athlete macho as a hook to get men to use hair dryers, formerly considered the sissiest of products (yet another perception problem that was success-fully tackled). When Joe Namath was paid $10,000 to shave his Fu Manchu mustache with a Schick electric razor, and when he later appeared on national television wearing pantyhose, more and more advertisers and agencies realized that athletes could add a unique ele-ment to any product in the context of an endorsement campaign, particularly where male consumers were concerned.

The prospect of instant credibility and a close identification with the product eventually led the Miller Brewing Company to combine high-visibility athletes with low-calorie beer. Miller used all-time win-ners to sell a category that was a three-time loser.

Piels, Rheingold, and Meister Brau had all tried to make low-calorie beer palatable to the American male, and all had failed.

Trommer's Red Letter, the first low-cal beer, was also the most short-lived. Marketed by the Piels Brewing Company of Brooklyn, New York, and originally touted in 1964 as a low-calorie beer for women, Trommer's was withdrawn after a paltry six weeks on the market. Sales were slow for a very good reason. Pitching beer to women is an anomaly when the market is dominated by young men aged 21–40 who make up only a third of the population but drink 80 percent of the beer.

Three years later, Rheingold tried low-calorie Gablinger's and also failed. In a fiasco often lumped with Corfam and the Edsel, Rhein-gold presented its diet beer as a technological breakthrough that would help beer drinkers keep slim. Trying to cash in on the trend toward lighter foods, Gablinger's stressed moderation, when most beer drinkers down two or more at a sitting, a luxury consumers of hard liquor can't afford without sacrificing coherence and large motor skills.

On top of these perception problems, Gablinger's had one of the most difficult problems a product can be faced with. It was lousy.

Diet beer had bombed when touted to women and bombed again when presented as a way for appearance-conscious males to stay slim. Undaunted, the Peter Hand Brewing Company of Chicago intro-duced Meister Brau Lite in 1967. Meister Brau Lite was also initially marketed to weight-conscious male beer drinkers and, even though it tasted better than the first two low-cal beers, it didn't do much better in the marketplace. After promising initial sales, the brand failed to generate significant reorders and hobbled along until June 1972, when Peter Hand was acquired by the Miller Brewing Company.

By this time, however, the fitness craze had hit full-force, and Miller's marketers thought the timing might now be ideal for a low-calorie beer. Even if that were so, Miller understood that there were still obstacles—taste for one thing, and the image of low-cal beer for another.

Beverly Jurkowski of Miller says, "Beer is an image-related product in a highly regulated industry. Once you've made it taste good, the rest of the marketing is in the mind of the consumer."

Miller did indeed reformulate Meister Brau Lite, change its name to Miller Lite, and improve its taste; more important, it figured out a way to make low-calorie beer attractive to men, who made up the bulk of the market. Meister Brau Lite was no longer low in calories; it was "less filling." Preliminary research showed that alluding to beer as low-calorie gave it a "diet" image. Using the more ambiguous "less filling" adroitly sidestepped the issue and didn't sissify Miller Lite.

To test this approach, a long-term research project was done in Anderson, Indiana, a hard-working, blue-collar manufacturing town. The beer drinkers exposed to Meister Brau Lite there didn't like the taste of reduced-calorie beers, which were for "diet" drinkers, not real beer drinkers. But Miller Lite was different: They drank it because it tasted good and also because it didn't fill them up as much as regular beers. Follow-up research confirmed that Anderson men were not unique. Other male beer drinkers would also welcome a beer that didn't give them the bloated feeling they sometimes got from regular beers. Of course, this new beer could not be perceived as a reduced-calorie beer and it had to taste good.

Since Miller already knew how to produce good-tasting, low-calorie beer, the key to remarketing the category depended on changing the perception that such beverages were aimed only at women or wimps.

This stance could be dramatized by using "regular guys" to remove the aura of femininity, and, simultaneously, Miller could offer consumers a unique benefit—a beer that was less filling.

Beer drinkers interpreted the statement that Lite contained "one-third fewer calories" to mean that they could drink three beers with the "penalty" of only two beers. In other words, one beer was "free," a unique benefit indeed. Miller had stumbled on a way to put a new face on Schaefer beer's slogan—"the one beer to have when you're having more than one." You could drink more Schaefer, because it tasted great, but you could drink even more Lite, because it was less filling.

To illustrate this "heavy-user" argument, Miller adopted the slogan suggested by the McCann-Erickson agency—"Everything you ever wanted in a beer . . . and less."

Then client and agency settled on advertising Miller Lite (the unsuccessful Meister Brau name had been dropped) with an athlete-spokesman format that offered both endorsement value and unquestioned masculinity. Just as hair dryers became mainstream when endorsed by athletes, low-calorie beer would use athletes to remove the stigma of sissiness from low-calorie beer.

Commercials were set in "unquestionably beery environments" to "reinforce the regular beer positioning." The chosen endorsers were not leading men in the classic Hollywood or Madison Avenue sense but, rather, character actors chosen to reinforce Lite's appeal to the average beer-drinking American. And they were macho guys to boot.

McCann-Erickson creative director Bob Lenz had originally intended to kick off the series of ads with Eddie Egan, a colorful New York cop and the real-life model for Popeye Doyle in *The French Connection*; unfortunately, Egan was under indictment at the time for bribery, and Lenz's second choice, newspaper columnist Jimmy Breslin, wasn't interested in doing commercials. Then Lenz saw an ad featuring New York Jets star Matt Snell on a New York bus and put "beer" and "athletes" together in his mind.

Snell had appeared on camera for Rheingold beer, and when the brewery began to promote Gablinger's, he got a complimentary case. In the book *Lite Reading*, he told sportswriter Frank Deford, "It tasted like frozen ice water." In contrast, when McCann-Erickson considered Snell for the first Miller Lite commercial, the agency sent

Snell a case to get his reaction. Snell liked it, agreed to a screen test, and starred in the first Lite beer commercial, which was taped in July 1973. Lenz told *Esquire*, "Once we saw the result, we knew we were onto something."

Snell set the pattern, and although standard pretty boys Mickey Mantle and Paul Hornung were used once apiece, the "stars" of the Lite commercials turned out to be "regular guys"—former jocks Tom Heinsohn, John Madden, Bob Uecker, Boog Powell, and Dick Butkus. Butkus starred in the commercial shot in May 1975, just as Lite was going national. The tenth of the series, it featured Butkus bowling badly; the idea of an athlete laughing at himself or herself got tremendous public reaction. The commercials already had made an impact on sales, but this one set the style for much of what was to follow.

This key change in attitude proved to be an important element when Schlitz entered the light beer market. Schlitz had also used athletes as the focal point of its commercials, but in the standard, humorless way. When Anheuser-Busch later introduced Natural Light beer and used former Lite spokesmen like Mantle, Joe Frazier, and Nick Buoniconti, Lite began its Tastes Great/Less Filling debates with Tommy Heinsohn and referee Mendy Rudolph. Anheuser-Busch recycled Lite's old stars with unconvincing copy. The attitude each athlete was forced to adopt was "Gee whiz, I thought Lite was a great beer but now I've found something better." In contrast to this contrivance, Lite was making millions of Americans laugh with mock arguments and lines like Rudolph's "All right, Heinsohn, you're out of the bar."

Miller Lite sold well right from the start; unfortunately, surveys showed that it "cannibalized" the flagship Miller High Life brand without increasing Miller's overall market share. Thereafter, the brand was designated as Lite beer from Miller, but the damage had already been done; the brand had grown so quickly that the U. S. Supreme Court ruled that Miller could not enjoin other beers from identifying themselves as "light" beers. Although Miller had created the category of light beer, it couldn't keep the name to itself, because the term had become generic.

Nevertheless, the commercials have become an institution, and the All-Stars have become, individually and collectively, an important promotional vehicle for Lite. Off-camera, several of the All-Stars give motivational speeches and make personal appearances for the company. Commenting on the phenomenon, broadcaster Al McGuire says, "The most popular team in the United States today isn't playing anybody. It's the Lite All-Stars."

While Miller was once concerned that Lite was cannibalizing sales of its High Life brand, the positions have been reversed, and Lite beer is now America's second best-selling beer, behind only Budweiser.

• • • • • • •

PRODUCT   LOW-CALORIE BEER

Pivotal P: Perception

Using believable former athletes made low-calorie beer more desirable and more acceptable to male beer drinkers.

Primary P: Positioning

Unsuccessful light beers appealed to wimps and weight-watchers. Lite's "less-filling" position allowed beer drinkers to consume more of it.

• • • • • • •

Chapter Four

I N the mid-1950s, McCann-Erickson was fired as the advertising agency for Brunswick, the bowling ball manufacturer.

Marion Harper, the agency's driving force, asked to meet with Brunswick's top management and saved the account by selling the idea that Brunswick could become the General Motors of recreation. Asked how he accomplished this task, saving the account against all odds, Harper said, "I merely changed the battlefield. It's all spelled out in Clausewitz's *On War*. 'If you can't win the battle, change the battlefield.'"

Changing the Battlefield   Changing the battlefield, in marketing terms, is repositioning the product. The phrase was used as early as 1928, when the trade magazine *Printers' Ink* complimented Lucky Strike for "positioning of a product for a certain kind of customer." In the 1930s, Plymouth, a three-year-old competitor of Ford and Chevrolet, told car-shopping consumers to "Compare All Three." The slogan suggested equality for a brand that was really a newcomer and had much to do with establishing Plymouth as a best-seller.

Al Ries and Jack Trout made positioning an ad-agency buzzword in 1972 with a series of articles in *Advertising Age*. In their book *Positioning: The Battle for Your Mind*, they say "positioning is not what you do to a product. Positioning is what you do to the mind of the prospect. That is, you position the product in the mind of the prospect."

Think back to the low-calorie beer business. Trommer's Red Label and Gablinger's positioned low-calorie beer as a drink for women or weight-conscious men. Young male beer drinkers couldn't see themselves drinking such a beer. But when Lite took pretty much the same product and used former athletes to publicize the idea that it was "less filling," the concept caught on. Beer drinkers gave it a try, liked the beer (or the positioning), and it became a huge hit.

There's no denying that repositioning has played a major role in the turnarounds of several major brands, as we shall see. The problem is that positioning works on the mind, and repositioning involves a process much like mind-reading.

Hard-Driving Cars   Volvo came to the United States in the 1950s, when cars were longer, lower, and wider. Any competition was based on looks, not performance (and certainly not on fuel economy). But, instead of basing the campaign on its looks, Volvo pegged its pitch to durability: "In Sweden, where 90 percent of the roads are not paved, Volvos last an average of twelve years."

As worries about gas-guzzling and planned obsolesence became more pronounced, Volvo appeared to be a more and more attractive alternative. It's as if Volvo had staked out a piece of turf (a position), then waited patiently to be discovered by the public. When public opinion began to value durability in a car . . . there was Volvo, ready and waiting.

To take the idea of positioning one step further, another foreign carmaker positioned itself not only as a durable car but as something of a personality. In 1959, Doyle Dane Bernbach (DDB) was assigned the Volkswagen account. The Volkswagen was a "people's car," which was commissioned by Adolf Hitler and designed by Ferdinand Porsche.

Since the design hadn't changed meaningfully in twenty years, DDB decided to make a virtue out of its sameness and poke fun at its odd looks, in spite of Claude Hopkins' warning that "spending money is a serious business and people do not buy from clowns." Instead of creating a living trademark like Betty Crocker or Buster Brown, DDB made the car itself almost human.

When a VW Beetle (nicknamed the Bug) was lowered into the water by a crane and floated for twenty-nine minutes, VW owners preened and turned Johnny Carson's gibes into something of a status symbol. If you bought a Cadillac, you'd arrived, but how many professors, students, and artists could afford one? Instead, they could avoid "bourgeois status seeking," get a VW, and learnedly discuss their mileage and the merits of rear-mounted engines.

The late Robert Kennedy campaigned in a VW in 1960, an eloquent symbol for a patrician seeking to be known as a man of the people. (White House correspondent Merriman Smith called it "keeping down with the Joneses.") When VW introduced its Transporter microbus, the ad slogan was "Do you have the right kind of wife for it?" A woman who drove one was interviewed by her local paper and said, "It made me feel cute as a button and interesting as hell."

Clearly, the VW conferred a new kind of status on its owners, and this feeling of status, this hint of specialness, is the identifying badge of a successful remarketing campaign. Motorcycle riders were considered Neanderthals before Grey Advertising got a chance to work on Honda. By featuring students, homemakers, retirees, and executives on motorcycles and suggesting, "You meet the nicest people on a Honda," Grey changed the position of motorcycles in the public's mind. Using Ries and Trout's terms, Grey found a "window" of respectability for motorcycles and used Honda to fill it.

HIRES ROOT BEER   Temperance Tantrum

Sometimes a name change can decisively reposition a product. (Remember Dr. Bunting's Sunburn Remedy and Noxzema, or Sears' Craftmaster battery, which became the DieHard?) In the case of Hires Root Beer, changing the name led to a surge in sales and also to an unfortunate clash between a devout Quaker and the forces of temperance.

Charles E. Hires had borrowed $3,000 to start an apothecary

shop in Philadelphia when he was just eighteen. Walking to his shop one day, he saw workmen excavating a cellar and realized that the "dirt" workmen were shoveling was actually fuller's earth, or potter's clay, which is used to remove stains from woolen garments. When he found out that no one wanted the "dirt," Hires had it piled in his own basement. Packaged as Hires Potter's Clay, the clay netted Hires $6,000.

He was soon prosperous enough to get married and spent his honeymoon at a New Jersey farmhouse. It was there that Hires discovered what was to become his most lasting product. The farmer's wife served an herb tea made from sixteen different wild roots and berries, including juniper, pipsissewa, sasparilla, spikenard, and hops. The same marketing instinct that led him to package the potter's clay led Hires to take the recipe back to Philadelphia and begin working on a water-soluble extract that could then be sold in grocery stores.

One of his first tasters was Dr. Russell Conwell, the president of Temple University and a close friend. Dr. Conwell loved the drink but hated the name, Hires Herb Tea. Since the beverage was made from roots and the hops made it froth, Dr. Conwell suggested the more masculine-sounding Hires Root Beer, repositioning the drink from a tea for ladies to a drink that might be served at soda fountains or taverns.

As Hires Root Beer Extract, it was sold in twenty-five-cent packages. A housewife or fountain owner could add five gallons of water, four pounds of sugar, and half a cake of yeast to make a refreshing drink that cost little more than a nickel a gallon. By the 1880s, more than 1.5 million drinks of Hires had been sold, and the nation's first branded soft drink was becoming a household word.

Then Hires learned that positioning can be a two-edged sword. In 1893, bottled Hires Root Beer went on sale nationally and quickly ran afoul of the Women's Christian Temperance Union (WCTU).

WCTU members would not accept the idea that any drink with the offensive word "beer" in it could be totally innocent. Instead of showing its disapproval silently, the WCTU took out newspaper ads saying that "fermentation of a sweet liquid at ordinary temperatures always produces alcohol." Even worse, the WCTU called for a national boycott of Hires.

The boycott was an unexpected and unwelcome stroke of bad luck, particularly since Hires had originally advertised his beverage as "the National Temperance Drink." An 1897 ad in *Ladies' Home Journal* discussed its "health-giving properties. Soothing to the nerves, vitalizing to the blood, refreshing to the brain, beneficial in every way." Scrupulous about his product's mildness, Hires refused to add caffeine to it, as Coca-Cola had done so successfully.

The Root Beer War was waged in the nation's newspapers from 1895 to 1898. Sales of Hires dropped sharply, even though Hires tried again and again to make peace with the temperance faction. When none of his attempts was successful, Hires made plans to diversify by opening a condensed milk plant in Pennsylvania.

Just when it appeared that he might have to give up manufacturing a successful product, Hires got help from an unexpected source. A chemical laboratory, attracted by the controversy, decided to submit Hires Root Beer to the standard tests for alcoholic content. After repeated trials, the lab announced that Hires had less than half the alcoholic content of homemade bread. Elated, Hires published the findings as full-page newspaper ads, and the WCTU was forced to admit its mistake. For the first, but most definitely not the last time, "white-coat advertising" in the form of an "independent clinical authority" had ridden to the remarketing rescue.

• • • • • • •

PRODUCT   ROOT BEER

Pivotal *P*: Positioning

Rather than presenting it as an herb tea, Hires positioned his drink as Root Beer, expanding his audience and giving his product a focus for marketing efforts.

Priority *P*: Publicity

When the name led to conflict with the WCTU, Hires defused the controversy by publishing an independent lab report that defended his drink.

• • • • • • •

7-UP   The Un and Only

Hires Herb Tea might have been a tough sell, but how would you have felt about trying to market Bib-Label Lithiated Lemon-Lime Soda? That was the original name of 7-Up, which became a success by stressing its "uncolaness."

Seven-Up was the second product created by C. L. Grigg, who had begun marketing Howdy Orange Drink in 1920. Howdy sold well enough until citrus growers, unable to move as much fresh produce as they'd wished, rammed legislation through in several states requiring orange-flavored drinks to contain real orange pulp and orange juice. This raised the cost of making the Howdy Company's only product and forced Grigg to diversify. He decided on a lemon-lime soda, even though there were six hundred similar brands available nationally.

Bib-Label Lithiated Lemon-Lime Soda, the brand's original name, was targeted at mothers of infants (hence the Bib-Label). The drink contained lithium, had a lemon-lime flavor, and boasted in advertising that it "tunes tiny tummies." Although the product was launched in October 1929, just two weeks before the stock market crash, Grigg was able to stick it out.

He emerged from the Depression with the decision that a name change would solve his problems and promptly bought the name 7-Up from a Minnesota candy company that made a chocolate candy bar with seven different fillings.

Even with the new name, the drink was marketed as a holdover from the patent medicine days. Long after Coke and Pepsi had forsworn making medical claims in their advertising, 7-Up was marketed as either a hangover remedy or an over-the-counter medicine for upset stomachs. A 1930s ad, for instance, reminded consumers that 7-Up antiacid lemon soda "takes the 'ouch' out of grouch."

Nevertheless, by 1940, it was fully franchised, and in 1942, the company adopted a quieter tone in keeping with wartime advertising, as J. Walter Thompson, Chicago, began working on the account. Ads stressed family themes and good clean fun. Advertised as the "fresh up" family drink, 7-Up emerged from the war as the world's third-largest-selling soft drink.

In 1959, Thompson commissioned Walt Disney Studios to create an anthropomorphic character like Elsie the Cow or Charlie Tuna for 7-Up. The animators came up with a rooster named Fresh-Up Freddie, who had the Disney touch but didn't translate into increased soda sales. As the 1960s unfolded, 7-Up dropped the family idea and switched gears; its "Wet and Wild" campaign in 1966 won a clutch of awards.

Yet, when Thompson researchers asked Chicago consumers to name five soft drinks, 7-Up wasn't mentioned by 80 percent of them—even though it was the world's third-largest-selling carbonated beverage! 7-Up had a multilayered image problem. It was considered:

- *A specialized drink.* The Seven-Up Company's executive vice president William E. Winter told a trade journal called *Grocery Manufacturer*, "From the standpoint of the consumer, we weren't even being perceived as a soft drink. . . . We were the special-occasion kind of drink." By comparison, colas were considered "normal," the kind of drink the public bought in quantity. Thompson's Bob Taylor says, "The research said that if you wanted to be a soft drink, you had to be a cola."

- *A mixer.* Seven-Up played the role of caboose in the most popular mixed drink in America at the time—Seven & Seven—Seagram's Seven Crown whiskey and 7-Up. Here, 7-Up paid the price of piggybacking, because mixers, too, are reserved for special occasions. Taylor puts the matter in perspective by asking, "Would Coca-Cola ever talk about how well it mixes with rum?"

- *A medicine.* If there is such a thing as an advertising hangover, 7-Up suffered from it. As late as the 1930s, 7-Up ads recommended buying it "when your stomach was upset or you had a little indigestion." Taylor says, "7-Up was considered a little bit like Alka-Seltzer; it was something you took to relieve an upset stomach."

In all three instances, 7-Up was perceived as belonging in a separate category, one that the public didn't associate with a soft drink.

Orville Roesch, 7-Up's director of marketing, told *Southern Advertising/Markets*, "People thought of carbonated soft drinks as brown; in fact, brown was the accepted color for all soft beverages."

Worse still, 7-Up was also taken for granted. William E. Ross, a Thompson vice president and the person Taylor credits with coining the phrase "The Uncola," told an audience of 7-Up bottlers in 1966, "People are familiar with us—they feel secure and comfortable about us. But like most things people feel secure and comfortable about—they don't think about us as often as we would like them to. And what people don't think about very often—they don't buy very often."

Part of the marketing solution, then, was to reposition 7-Up "firmly in the middle of the soft drink spectrum." The other part was to keep other "green-bottle goods"—mixers like regular and diet ginger ale, lemon-lime drinks, and quinine water—from cutting into 7-Up's mixer business; as diet drinks and drinks featuring vodka— "white goods"—became popular, Wink, Fresca, and Teem (not to mention Schweppes) became more and more popular, giving 7-Up unexpected competition.

As if these formidable obstacles weren't enough, 7-Up faced resistance from its own bottlers. Many were so-called "dual bottlers," who also distributed Coke and Pepsi as well as their sister brands, Sprite and Diet Pepsi. While they might cheer for 7-Up at sales gatherings, they were really in the Coke or Pepsi business, and 7-Up was merely a sideline for them. When Taylor and Roesch presented the Uncola concept at a bottlers' meeting in Chicago in February 1968, some dual bottlers reminded company officials of just how divided their loyalties were; many of them called the concept "too negative," because it poked fun at their biggest seller.

Fortunately, the public response was immediately positive. The first ad in the Uncola campaign talked about 7-Up as "Fresh. Clean. Crisp. Never too sweet. No aftertaste. Everything a cola's got and more besides. 7-Up . . . The Uncola. The Un and Only."

The timing was magnificent. The Uncola strategy took a uniquely antiestablishment view for the soft-drink industry. 7-Up understood that in the '60s, political, recreational, and social issues boiled down to "Them" against "Us." "They" were old, stodgy, conservative, the people the Beatles referred to in "Nowhere Man." "We," on the other hand, were hip, adventurous, iconoclastic, and fun-loving, the people you met in the Sheep Meadow in Central Park every Sunday. (One poster showed three suitably long-haired youths with the caption, "Hear no cola; see no cola; drink Uncola.") With its Uncola theme, 7-Up positioned colas as "Them" and identified itself with "Us," and was the first commercial product, outside of the entertainment industry, to take such a stance. (Remember "Laugh-In"?)

In 1968, such positioning was revolutionary for a soft drink, and it gave the brand a tremendous lift. Sales increased 14 percent in a year and had jumped 50 percent by 1973. For the first time in its corporate history, 7-Up was popular enough to sell merchandising aids—something the colas had been doing for years. 7-Up reportedly sold 60,000 Uncola lamps and 20 million upside-down Uncola soda glasses to the 16-to-24-year-old market.

The success of the campaign then prompted 7-Up to protect the Uncola name. The Coca-Cola Corporation challenged the concept for nearly four years, but on June 20, 1974, what had begun as a remarketing slogan received trademark status as well. Two years later, 7-Up celebrated the Bicentennial of "Undependence" by sending out trucks painted "The Uncola Salutes 200 Years of Un-Britain."

Then 7-Up abandoned the Uncola campaign, feeling that the '60s were dead and that a new approach was needed. Themes such as "America is turning 7-Up" and "Feelin' 7-Up" were duds. The brand repositioned itself yet again as a health craze took America by storm and young mothers of the new baby boomers (born post-1979) became concerned about the effects of caffeine on their young children. While several cola brands introduced caffeine-free versions, 7-Up was able to adopt a no-caffeine strategy—"Never Had It, Never Will."

Sales dropped drastically. Researchers were called in again, and the Gallup Organization reported that seven out of ten consumers still remembered the Uncola campaign and associated it with 7-Up. In March 1985, it was grudgingly resurrected as "The Un's The One," but without the '60s graphics or the underlying '60s feeling. The Uncola glass and actor Geoffrey Holder were there, but the magic was gone: What was decidedly daring in the '60s was deadly dull in the '80s. As marketers have learned, ads that make marketing magic in one era capture the mood of the moment but become passé in succeeding years. The backward-looking campaign was, appropriately enough, 7-Up's last gasp before its domestic operation was bought by Hicks & Haas and its foreign side was purchased by Pepsico. Even though the campaign failed when 7-Up tried to resurrect it without updating, it's a good bet that a large percentage of the public would still identify 7-Up as the Uncola.

●   ●   ●   ●   ●   ●   ●

PRODUCT   7-UP

Pivotal *P*: Positioning

Forced to attach itself to the cola category, 7-Up made an asset of its position by wooing young people, the hard-core soda drinkers.

Primary *P*: Publicity

The unique positioning stance also translated into great product publicity and supplemented soda sales with merchandise tie-ins.

●   ●   ●   ●   ●   ●   ●

MARLBORO   Sex Change

The world's best-selling cigarette—Marlboro, as in the Marlboro MAN—was originally a premium-priced, nonfiltered blend of Turkish tobaccos aimed at women.

Philip Morris introduced Marlboro in 1924 in two versions; it came with either a ruby or an ivory "beauty tip," to "keep the paper from your lips." In line with its premium image, Marlboro was made a bit longer and priced a bit higher than other cigarettes. The (sexist) idea was to play on women's vanity in an effort to get an extra few cents a pack. As an ad from 1927 noted, "Women, when they smoke at all, quickly develop discriminating taste."

Despite the ads, the tips, the length, and the price, the brand never found an audience, female or otherwise. As a "straight" (un-filtered) cigarette, Marlboro's sales never exceeded one-quarter of one percent of the market. The brand was as dead as ever when filter-tips began appearing in the early 1950s. Six of them—Winston, Kent, L & M, Viceroy, Tareyton, and Philip Morris's Parliament—managed to amass 10 percent of the entire cigarette market, despite the "sissy" image that filters had at the time.

Filters had first become popular when a New York tobacco company called Benson & Hedges began getting referrals for its filter-tipped cigarettes from Manhattan doctors, and the first warnings about the harmful effects of smoking were beginning to appear. In 1953, Philip Morris, then the smallest of the tobacco firms, hired researcher Elmo Roper to find out whether filters had a long-term future. Needing a brand to test, executives suggested that Roper use Marlboro, since it had "the least to lose."

The Roper poll confirmed that filters were here to stay, and Philip Morris decided to reestablish Marlboro as a filter-tip for two reasons: (1) registerable names are as hard to come by in the tobacco industry as they are elsewhere; and (2) with the exception of L & M, all five other filters sounded British, and so did Marlboro.

Along with the new filter and the old name, the company gave its born-again product a new kind of cigarette pack. Philip Morris had a one-year exclusive on the flip-top box, made on machines sold by Molins Manufacturing in England. The new package had been thoroughly tested with consumers and had received high marks. Smokers used to finding bits of tobacco in their shirts, skirts, pants pockets, and purses registered positive reactions in hundreds of eye-blink tests. (The tests register, by hidden camera, consumer reactions to proposed package designs.)

Although the box was seen as a tremendous breakthrough in the tobacco industry, "the first significant advance in cigarette packaging in thirty-eight years," it hadn't won new smokers over to Marlboro in May 1954, when the brand was test marketed in Dallas and Fort Worth. *Printers' Ink* wrote, "The box was getting consumers to try the smoke, but the product didn't keep them." (Packaging can only do so much.)

When sales of Marlboros remained so low as to be nearly unmeasurable in a follow-up survey, more changes were made. The tobacco mixture was enriched, and the red-and-white striped pack was redesigned, with the stripes giving way to solid red. In a significant move, the flip-top pack was tested with and without a crest in the package design. Cheskin Associates of Menlo Park, California, discovered that 71 percent of all consumers preferred the crest, feeling that it connoted a quality product and bestowed prestige on the Marlboro smoker.

Philip Morris fired Marlboro's ad agency and transferred the account to Leo Burnett in November 1954. Draper Daniels, who worked at Burnett, wrote of Marlboros, "We had to give them a reason for being. We found the reason in the middle of the Roper survey, in a sentence that said people tended to think of filter cigarettes as more feminine than masculine. . . . The problem was to make the consumer draw the conclusion that Marlboro was a filter cigarette that a he-man could smoke without being self-conscious about it."

What we're looking at was a brand with a positioning problem.

Philip Morris had reached similar conclusions. In an early meeting, Philip Morris's advertising director told Burnett, Daniels, and the other account people that Marlboro had to be known as a "cigarette designed for men that women liked." Burnett, who had created the Jolly Green Giant, agreed and told Robert Glatzer, author of *The New Advertising*, "If filters were regarded on the sissy side, and Marlboro was regarded on the sissy side, the natural thing was to look for a masculine image. I asked around for what was a masculine image, and four or five people said a cowboy."

The cowboy was an acceptable symbol of virility in its best and most American sense, but Burnett had to have other masculine figures ready for a schedule of ads ordered by the previous agency, Cecil & Presbrey, and already paid for by Philip Morris. Headlined "New from Philip Morris," the ads broke in November 1954 in Dallas and Fort Worth, and each featured a different masculine image—cowboys, sailors, aviators, and hunters. Moreover, they were not models but "real men," which added visual reality to the ads. (The cowboy in the first ad was actually a navy lieutenant commander.)

These first ads were an immediate success, which might have been expected in Texas, but worked equally well when repeated in sophisticated New York City. Marlboro expanded to twenty-five cities, box-making machines were going seven days a week, twenty-four hours a day in Richmond and Louisville, and demand still outstripped supply. One year after it was reintroduced, Marlboro was the fourth-best-selling filter cigarette in the U. S.

In 1955, Burnett added the final macho touch—a tattoo. Photographer Constantin Joffe says his wife suggested it, but Burnett claimed it came from a fragment attributed to Jack London: "Follow any man with a tattoo and you will find a romantic and adventurous past." Whatever the truth, Burnett staffers rummaged through books of elaborate tattoos before art director Lee Stanley settled on armed forces unit emblems pictured in a 1944 copy of *National Geographic.* The tattoo of an anchor, displayed prominently on a Marlboro smoker's arm in an ad, made an immediate and visceral impact on consumers of both sexes and became a part of American commercial folklore.

In *Motivation in Advertising,* marketing researcher Pierre Martineau writes that the tattoo reinforced the notion of the virility conferred by smoking Marlboro and "gave a richness to the product image, bringing it all into focus."

Sales rose from 18 million cigarettes in 1954 to over 5 billion in 1955. By 1957, Philip Morris was selling three times as many Marlboros every day as it had sold in all of 1954. Part of the change was due to the image, part of it was due to continued shrewd marketing. The brand stole a march on the competition by sponsoring NFL football in 1956, identifying Marlboro with the game just as it began to hit new heights of popularity. To influence a less macho audience, Marlboro sponsored a weekly column in college newspapers written by humorist Max Schulman; the brand was number one on every college campus that carried Marlboros before Philip Morris's national rollout.

Marlboro's rise was slowed by a 1958 *Reader's Digest* study of nicotine, which rated the effectiveness of each filter and deemed only Kent's as worthwhile. Sales didn't plummet, but they did stay flat for two years, despite another smart Burnett move—using sultry Julie

London to sing, "Where there's a man, there's a Marlboro." Kent sales more than doubled to put it second behind Winston, with Marlboro now running third.

Then in 1962, inspiration struck again. Burnett purchased the rights to Elmer Bernstein's evocative movie score for *The Magnificent Seven* and mated it with the cowboy image used in the first Marlboro ad. The result was the "Marlboro Country" theme, arguably the single most successful sustained instance of musical image-making in American advertising history.

No advertiser had ever tapped this powerful image before. The usual cowboy-themed TV commercial parodies *High Noon*: Two grim-faced cowboys walk toward each other down a deserted main street, reach into their holsters, then pull out candy bars, chewing gum, cans of motor oil, bouquets of flowers, or other purposely non-threatening products. Marlboro chose instead to play it straight.

When the Marlboro Man first rode the range in sweeping panoramic shots that would have done credit to John Ford, the strength of the image and its appropriateness to Marlboro were immediately apparent. In Marlboro Country, actors and real cowboys rode horses, rounded up cattle, or relaxed by a campfire without the forced camaraderie found in beer commercials. The commercials first aired in 1964, and Marlboro sales increased more than 10 percent a year through the mid-1970s, and have even grown 3 percent a year since 1980, while total cigarette sales were shrinking 1.5 to 2 percent a year.

Originally created for television, the Marlboro Country theme transferred effectively to print and billboards, once cigarette advertising disappeared from the air in 1961. That year Philip Morris ran a sixteen-page print insert of recipes called "Chuckwagon Cooking from Marlboro Country." A year later, the brand set an all-time record for readership scores with its "Marlboro Country Store," a six-page insert offering Western wear. In 1974, the brand offered the works of Western artist Charles Russell. Other promotions have involved traveling exhibits of antique saddles and branding irons, a Marlboro Trail Driver's Shirt, a record album called "The Music From Marlboro Country," and—since 1983—tours of modern country recording artists.

Although the cowboy has been our most enduring native myth,

no manufacturer had appropriated it for advertising purposes before Marlboro. Many have since tried to capture the magic, notably Busch beer, but Marlboro piggybacked onto the cowboy so completely that other advertisers have been largely preempted from using it.

It is also clear that the Marlboro campaign prefigured the Lite Beer campaign of the 1970s. Where Lite used recognizable athletes and humor to make it acceptable for men to drink low-calorie beer, Marlboro made an even more powerful statement by using an anonymous but archetypal cowboy to make smoking filters seem not only okay but even more manly than smoking straights.

When *Advertising Age* polled seminal figures on the leading campaigns of all time, Marlboro finished second only to Volkswagen; however, Helmut Krone, who created the Volkswagen campaign, called Marlboro the "campaign of the century." Daniel Dixon of Ogilvy & Mather commented, "When Marlboro was still a women's cigarette, advertising was dominated by words. . . . But then TV came along. . . . Imagery became as eloquent as language." The image Leo Burnett had chosen was, in Dixon's words, "strong, proud, independent, resourceful—a timeless figure in a challenging world of his own."

Marlboro has been the single largest-selling brand in the U. S. since the end of 1975 and currently controls 22 percent of the U. S. market. The leading seller worldwide since the early 1960s (due perhaps to its "Americanness"), Marlboro now sells 280 billion cigarettes a year and had revenues of $7 billion and profits of $2 billion in 1986.

• • • • • • •

PRODUCT   MARLBORO CIGARETTES

Pivotal *P*: Positioning

Making filter-tips manly enough for men called for macho advertising. The rightness of Marlboro's approach is apparent thirty-five years later as sales keep growing.

Primary *P*'s: Piggybacking, Promotion

Marlboro shunned "name" endorsers, preferring anonymous men of unquestioned masculinity. The decision to sponsor NFL football fit the position and produced fantastic ratings.

• • • • • • •

WELCH'S   Grape Expectations

Welch's, the company that compelled a generation of children to grow up whooping "Woo Woo Welch's," first became successful when its founder's son repositioned Welch's Grape Juice from a negative to a positive and was reinvigorated years later when a new CEO repositioned the entire company.

The company is the marketing arm of the National Grape Cooperative Association, Inc., whose 1,800 members grow Concord and Niagara grapes and citrus fruits in seven states—New York, Pennsylvania, Ohio, Michigan, and parts of Arkansas, Missouri, and Washington. In 1956, the coop acquired Welch's (then Welch Foods), a firm known for the taste, purity, and uniform quality of its grape products.

Welch Foods was started by Dr. Thomas Bramwell Welch, an ardent prohibitionist. Scandalized by the notion that the Methodist church he attended in Vineland, New Jersey, served wine for communion, Dr. Welch decided to make a nonalcoholic substitute.

He bartered dental services for bushels of Concord grapes. To prevent fermentation from occurring, he squeezed the grapes through cloth bags into bottles and boiled the bottles to kill any yeast particles.

But "Dr. Welch's Unfermented Wine," America's first pasteurized grape juice, was a flop. Church elders ruled it would be heretical to replace the traditional communion drink; for twenty years, only the Welch family and a few churches drank Welch's.

Dr. Welch's youngest son, Charles, also a dentist, saw the drink as something more than a replacement for wine; Charles saw the juice as a potentially profitable product—after its position was changed. Instead of being a substitute for wine at religious services, Charles saw Welch's as a healthy, wholesome drink for the whole family. Borrowing $5,000 from his father, young Dr. Welch set up a production line in a barn behind his family's home in 1892 and made it his first priority to change the product's name. Instead of Dr. Welch's Unfermented Wine, he called it simply Welch's Grape Juice, immediately repositioning the drink from what might have been a medicine to a healthy fruit juice.

Even though he abandoned the original name, Welch the younger used the same kind of health-oriented scare advertising as Charles Post. His first ads intimated that Welch's cured "typhoid fever, pneumonia . . . and all forms of chronic disease except diabetes melitus."

But where Post pounded solely on the health theme, Dr. Welch had a second advertising theme to work with—the drink's prohibitionist past. In a masterstroke of suggestiveness, he figured out a way to combine Prohibition and sex in advertising. Above an illustration of a beautiful woman, he ran the copy line, "Lips that touch Welch's are all that touch mine." (The theme has since been borrowed for anti-smoking campaigns. One said, "Lips that touch tobacco will never touch mine.")

When Prohibition passed in 1919, Welch made the only nonalcoholic grape beverage in America, and sales spurted. What was now Welch Food Company followed up with grape jelly in 1923, frozen grape juice concentrate in 1949, and Welchade in 1960. In 1972, the company reached $100 million in sales for the first time.

Welch Foods was clearly no longer a one-product company, but its very aggressiveness redounded to the company's discredit. By devoting time and attention to new brands like sparkling grape juice and red and white grape juice, the company had neglected its core purple grape products, and Welch's sales were flat from 1979 to 1983 at the same time that grape juice sales were increasing 1 to 2 percent a year, and fruit juices were becoming a multi-billion-dollar business.

A company representative says, "Those were years of huge crops. When the crops are big, the private-label guys can undercut Welch's on price. At one time, we had 44 million gallons of grape juice in storage, which is our capacity. We were awash in grape juice."

The company tried the usual steps, reviewing its advertising agency's work and creating joint promotions (piggybacking) with makers of peanut butter, milk, cereal, and cookies, with no appreciable pick-up in sales. Moreover, the new products confused Welch's corporate identity. The company's juices, spreads (jams, jellies, and preserves), frozen concentrates, and juice drinks now appeared in different aisles of the supermarket in a bewildering mix of labels, sizes, and colors. Consumers became confused and didn't immediately connect these new products with Welch's and its hard-won reputation for quality.

Worse yet, fully ninety years after it had become an active commercial enterprise, Welch's had no symbol, just a confusing jumble of packages and a logo that one package designer said "looked like the kind of thing you'd find on a motor oil."

The logo was an apt symbol for a company badly in need of some corporate repositioning. It came from Everett Baldwin, who was elected president, CEO, and named a director in the fall of 1982.

Baldwin had previously headed sales and marketing of grocery products at Pillsbury and had taken charge of operations at Land O'Lakes Foods, a cooperative of Plains states farmers very similar to Welch's in both style and substance. Both of Baldwin's former companies had well-known trademarks—the Pillsbury doughboy and Land O'Lakes's Indian maiden—which generated goodwill and recognition. The lack of such a logo told Baldwin that Welch Foods was "a sleeping, lethargic, underutilized company in terms of that asset."

Yet, instead of arriving on the scene with quick answers, Baldwin convened all his department heads, handed each a card with a definition of the word "ethos," and asked one provocative question: "What is Welch's?"

Each executive tried to capture the company's essence with a short answer, but, like an unraveling sleeve, this main question led to others: "What did consumers expect from Welch's?" and "What products could Welch's add without ruining its image?" To find out, Welch's commissioned its ad agency, Jordan, Case & McGrath, to run what is called an "ethos study." Focus-group interviews with thousands of consumers revealed that the public had good things to say about the company's "heritage" and could comfortably see it as a fruit-products firm, not just a grape company.

Baldwin then took four specific steps to get Welch's moving again. He:

1. relocated the company to Concord, Massachusetts, near Boston, where Ephraim Wales Bull had first created the Concord grape in 1853.
2. started a new products group. After only nine months of development, Welch's introduced an all-natural, frozen juice concentrate called Welch's Orchard in three flavors, all of which have been successful individually and have helped to broaden the consumer's notion of Welch's.
3. approved a switch to squeezable bottles for Welch's jams, jellies, and preserves. Consumers wanted a package that would reduce spillage, and only Heinz had used squeezables for ketchup. Welch's stole a march on fruit-products companies, and the smooth, polyethylene bottles created shelf impact and favorable reaction with consumers.
4. assigned his ad agency and packaging firm to create a coherent new scheme for all of Welch's packaging. The new products looked different from each other and different from Welch's traditional items that had shaped its identity with consumers. Baldwin told *Madison Avenue*, "To put it in practical terms, we were getting lost on the shelf."

Baldwin assigned Jordan, McGrath, Case, & Taylor to create an umbrella symbol, in his phrase, "an escutcheon," that could be used on every Welch's product. Rather than use a people symbol like the Land O'Lakes maiden, the agency came up with a garden basket overflowing with fruit and a banner with the legend "Welch's Way." This symbol was, in essence, Baldwin's "ethos" brought to life. It told the consumer that Welch's grew more than just grapes, had been around long enough to evoke nostalgia, and didn't use chemicals to flavor its foods.

Welch's sales jumped $10 million from $229 million in 1982 to $239 million in 1983, Baldwin's first year as CEO. The grape crop fell in 1984, and sales dipped to $236 million, but rebounded to $274 million in 1985, and, after another short crop in 1986 cut sales to $269 million, neared $300 million in fiscal 1987. Everett Baldwin's leading question about Welch's ethos eventually led to repositioning a sleepy grape company into an aggressive processor of fruit products.

•   •   •   •   •   •   •

PRODUCT   WELCH'S

Pivotal P: Positioning

A name change (like Hires) originally gave Welch's a new lease on life. When the family company lost its way, an outsider repositioned it as a leader in fruit products.

Priority P: Packaging

The new logo tied together the company's many products and became a symbolic rallying point for its employees and distributors.

•   •   •   •   •   •   •

Chapter Five

Opaque bags of potato chips sell better on the West coast than in the East.

Orange juice from a dark orange package tastes "sweeter" than the exact same juice from a lighter-colored container.

Even though analgesics are available in a host of forms—tablets, capsules, and caplets—some southerners still prefer to take loose BC headache powders because "they work better."

Consumers respond to packaging with a whole set of prejudices, learned reactions, and individual preferences that help make some products winners and some brand managers choose early retirement. Certain shapes, colors, sizes, and textures cause people to respond positively, while others evoke negative reactions.

Touchy Subject Even though packages are tested as assiduously as the products they contain, some misfire in the marketplace. When Welch's came out with squeezable jellies, the adults who tested them had no problems; however, youngsters couldn't create enough pressure to get the jelly out, which necessitated an expensive trip back to the drawing board.

One reason that the physical container of a product—its jar, can, carton, box, bottle, or blister pack—has so much impact on consumers is that it's the first tangible encounter a consumer has with that product. Ron Peterson, a principal in the New York design firm of Peterson & Blyth, says, "It's the sum total of your marketing effort. The package is the product."

In contrast to this tangible container, the advertising or promotional messages we receive in the home, car, plant, or office may communicate the product's name and promise exciting benefits, but they are mere abstractions as far as the consumer is concerned; packages are more "real." In his book *Packaging: The Contemporary Media*, Robert G. Neubauer points out that "In countless ways technology has cut us off from experiencing life through our senses. But the package is a reassuring exception. It is physical and encourages contact."

The Hard-Working Package   Packaging was once considered part of the production process and was regarded as so insignificant that it was overseen by purchasing people. Today, the package has become more and more prominent in marketing plans, and package designers are consulted earlier and earlier in the R & D phase of new products, repackages of existing brands, or line extensions. In some cases, a changed package enables a product manager to begin a remarketing campaign—without ever changing the product itself.

Much of packaging's new prominence can be tied to increased self-service and self-selection in retail outlets. Consumers no longer get help in choosing from an increasingly large number of different products, and as a result, packages have inherited some of the functions formerly performed by retailers themselves. Good packages include mandatory nutritional or medical information and exhibit strong "barrier properties" (keeping the contents in and any foreign substances out). They also:

- *attract consumer attention.* Convincing consumers to pick up the package in order to examine it more closely is the first step toward interesting them in buying what may well be an unfamiliar product.
- *tick off primary and secondary ways of using the product.* Ce-

real manufacturers often include cookie and snack recipes that use the product to give consumers other reasons to buy it (and use more of it).

* *provide a launching pad for premiums or related products.* While cereal manufacturers were the first to exploit the package, modern producers of all kinds are including mail-in premiums, coupons, or small product samples to give consumers other reasons to buy this or other related products.

While all these functions are valuable, catching the consumer's eye is the most important job a package can perform. Supermarkets are filled with a bewildering array of line extensions, niche products, and specialized brands. The selection in the average supermarket has grown from 5,000 to 17,000 products since the 1960s, making it absolutely imperative for manufacturers to present their goods in alluring packages.

Shelfish Behavior   In attempting to create "shelf impact," package designers use every conceivable trick of color, texture, and design to get consumers interested. This creative ability to bridge the gap between creator and consumer is often rewarded directly with increased sales; motivational studies have shown that 40 percent of purchases in supermarkets are "impulse buys"; i.e., totally unplanned until the consumer sees the package. And, according to the Point-of-Purchase Advertising Institute, fully 81 percent of the final brand-selection decisions are not made until the consumer is physically inside the store.

Given this state of affairs, an eye-catching package can easily create (or destroy) a sale. In *Packaging as a Marketing Tool*, Stanley Sacharow quotes A. C. Nielsen as saying that "the interaction between the product and the package is responsible for about 53 percent of all new product failures."

Repackaging Magic   Repackaging has become a standard way of breathing new life into products. Where it used to be done every four or five years, design changes are now made every two or three years. Structural changes either in the container or the product tend to affect both, leading to even more frequent repackaging. When liquid detergent became more popular, boxes that contained the old powdered products were phased out in favor of plastic jugs.

Repackaging has also created turnaround success stories in soft drinks, household cleaners, and toothpaste. For instance:

- Fruit Smack flavored syrup was just one of 125 mail-order products offered by Edwin E. Perkins of Hendley, Nebraska, until Perkins removed the water and sold the dehydrated syrup in paper envelopes as Kool-Aid;
- Murphy's Oil Soap in its original glass bottle was a regional brand of detergent. When it was sold in plastic bottles with snazzy labels, sales rose 31 percent (and created more profit than the costly glass).
- Most recently, Check-Up grabbed a healthy chunk of the toothpaste market by adopting a press-top pump dispenser, which made the tube look old-fashioned.

The flip-top box and the toothpaste dispenser improved the "delivery system" of cigarette and toothpaste packaging in much the same way that the pop-up box made Kleenex easier to use. More recently, easy-pouring spouts, aerosol sprays, and pumps have made motor oil, deodorants, and liquid soap easier to dispense. Some packaging stories are piggybacked to social trends; the move away from aerosols necessitated by concerns about the thinning ozone layer gave birth to a host of new, ecologically sound pump products.

Novelty Packaging   Sometimes packaging is so innovative that it qualifies as a novelty or even becomes collectible.

When the product is distasteful, the urge to merge novelty with practicality is strongest. Insecticides, in particular, lend themselves to novel packages. When Sterling Drug Company wanted to revitalize d-Con insecticide, the company packaged the liquid chemicals, not in a spray bottle, but in a felt-tip pen. And who can forget Black Flag's Roach Motel, which not only killed the varmints, but made disposing of them as convenient as possible.

When portable electronic gear—Walkmans, video games, CD players—came into vogue, battery sales surged and woke up a once-sleepy category. Since batteries were going to be purchased in quantity to make Christmas presents work in 1987, Eveready packaged part of its production run in white paper jackets with green and red trees, stars, and Santas to make the batteries look more festive (and add color to transparent flashlights and cassette players).

Aside from intentional package premiums like Jif and Welch's jelly glasses and Swee-Touch-Nee tea containers, some packages and even parts of packages become collectible. People who collect bottle caps got added value in the 1970s when the Coca-Cola Company put pictures of major leaguers on the underside of Fresca and Coke bottle caps. In a similar vein, Pepsi made a special can for the Discovery astronauts, and RC Cola commemorated the New York Mets' 1986 World Championship with a pinstriped can.

The Name's the Thing   A hundred-odd years ago, such refinements didn't exist, and neither did packaging. Although Procter & Gamble used a moon and stars design on its soap wrapper in the 1850s, there were as yet no such things as packages, only "papers." Clerks took square sheets of paper, laid them on the counter, placed the merchandise in the center, pulled the corners together, crimped them to prevent leakage, and tied them with string.

Brand names, which we always think of as "part of the package," didn't exist either. In its original, precise meaning, a brand was an initial applied with a paintbrush or a hot iron to show dockworkers where goods had come from and where they were going. A package marked

C & S
M

meant Chase and Sanborn was importing coffee from Malang in the Dutch East Indies. Later, a brand on a box or package came to mean goods that had been approved by a public inspector, giving rise to the phrase "brand names" and the public's placing trust in them. By extension, "branded goods" came to signify a certain grade of goods, much as we use the terms "prime" amd "choice" today when specifying certain cuts of meat.

Packaging as Trade Dress   The Smith Brothers, Andrew and William, had created a cough drop that had become a national bestseller in the 1860s. Unfortunately, imitators swiped their name and, in the classic manner of knock-off artists, sold inferior drops under such names as Schmitt Brothers, Smyth Brothers—even Smyth Sisters. Some consumers didn't know the difference, and the best-selling drop's reputation suffered as a result.

One early strategy to combat counterfeiting took a step toward curbing these excesses but didn't go far enough. Will and Andrew commissioned illustrations of their faces and had them emblazoned on glass jars, then instructed druggists to put their drops in the glass jars. Some did, but many bought cheap drops, passed them off as Smith Brothers, and pocketed extra profits.

Finally, the brothers decided to distribute the drops in their own packages and fill the boxes in their home town of Poughkeepsie, New York, to ensure the quality of the product. In 1872, they persuaded neighbors near their factory to fill the packages. Each evening, a wagon loaded with cough drops and a supply of boxes stopped at each of thirty houses along what became known as "Cough Drop Street." The packages not only made the drops easier to carry but also kept them fresher once an inner wrapper was added. Packaging is now considered part of a product's "trade dress" and has long been protected by copyright.

Packaging Pluses and Minuses   Consumers use what one marketer calls "hedonistic calculus"—subjective reasoning—to decide whether the pluses of the product make up for the drawbacks of the package. Scotch tape, for instance, couldn't be used efficiently for some time, because the tape stuck to itself while unrolling; then a 3M salesman came up with the idea of a saw-toothed metal edge. In the same vein, users of the original Polaroid camera put up with chemical smells and sticky hands, because the advantages of instant pictures outweighed the many inconveniences.

Structural Packaging   You'd think that the advances in structural packaging traceable to two world wars and the space program would mean the end of marketing setbacks due to physical packaging problems. No such luck. Deficiencies crop up all the time with new and established products that run the gamut from sugar to pasta to detergents.

Domino sugar used to come with a built-in metal spout; when metal prices rose, the spout was replaced by a semi-perforated "Push here" opening. One loyal but exasperated Domino customer says, "I couldn't take the chance of having bugs in my sugar, so I had to buy a canister that I could reclose."

And pasta, which may be more popular than ever, has yet to appear in a fully reclosable package. Most mass-market pasta containers are made of paperboard and are glued shut; once ripped open, they must be stored half-open and stand upright or else lie horizontally (and precariously) on shelves.

Similarly, powdered detergents come in bulky paperboard containers that are glued shut. Some are closed so tightly that one housewife participating in a focus group said, "The only time I use my screwdriver is to open the detergent box." Clearly, makers of these products could position their wares as more "user-friendly" with better packaging, but, thus far at least, consumers seem willing to tolerate structurally deficient packages.

QUAKER OATS   Unpackaged Goods

Some ideas are really quite simple and quite revolutionary all at the same time. When Quaker Oats management saw it couldn't beat the competition by going in the front door, they came around through the window with a brilliant strategy that not only made Quaker Oats a hit, but changed the history of packaging.

Back in the latter part of the nineteenth century, oats were "in." And we're not talking oat bran. Samuel Johnson defined the oat in his famous dictionary as "a grain, which in England is generally given to horses, but in Scotland supports the people."

In America it supported, in grand style, a humorless, hardworking German immigrant named Ferdinand Schumacher. Schumacher had come to America in 1850 and, starting with a small mill in back of an Akron grocery store, had almost single-handedly built a market for oats through mail order.

Back then, oats were often retailed not by grocers but by druggists, who dispensed them to invalids and infants on a doctor's prescription much as prepared baby foods were dispensed in the 1920s. Like many Americans of Scottish or German descent, Schumacher had eaten oats in the old country and clung to their familiar taste.

By renting mailing lists of subscribers to German, Scottish, and

Irish language newspapers, Schumacher was able to build a substantial market for oats. He invented a steel oat-hulling machine, enabling him to produce oats faster than anyone else. Given this important competitive edge, he gained a virtual monopoly within the United States and soon became nicknamed the "Oatmeal King."

The gruff Schumacher was more feared than admired and dealt harshly with employees, competitors, and customers alike. He refused to do business on any other basis than cash in advance, shipping prepaid 180-pound barrels of oats to customers who grumbled but grudgingly paid up, having no other sure source of supply.

He also squeezed local millers by cutting prices until they failed, and his ruthlessness put the competing Quaker mill in nearby Ravenna out of business twice. The mill had been started by Henry Seymour and William Heston, who registered the first trademark for a breakfast cereal. Seymour said he got the idea for the name while looking through an encyclopedia; Heston claimed he came up with the notion after seeing a picture of William Penn.

While we'll probably never know which version was the truth, Heston was the sole inventor of a device for cutting oats that used fine knife blades instead of millstones to grind and separate oats from their husks. This improvement reduced waste and offered an alternative to Schumacher's domination; however, Quaker Oats hadn't capitalized on it, because the pricing pressure Schumacher exerted didn't allow for much research and development. Things didn't appear likely to improve much for Quaker, when a tubercular patrician from Cleveland took over the company.

Henry Parsons Crowell had recently recovered from a congenital vulnerability to tuberculosis, which had killed both his father and grandfather. While convalescing, Crowell had a vision that God meant to save him for higher things. After he was fully cured, he showed his appreciation by giving $20,000 to Christian causes. Thirty days later, the man who inherited the Quaker Mill when Heston went bankrupt again, offered to sell Crowell the company for a few thousand dollars. Attracted by the Quaker name and convinced that God's hand was involved, he solemnly pledged himself to make the business a success.

It didn't take Crowell long to find out what he was up against. Schumacher had the oat market sewn up in Ohio, had a stranglehold on the mail-order business throughout the Northeast, and was beginning to move into grocery stores in Pennsylvania and New Jersey. Quaker Oats could only compete at the retail level and in those markets where Schumacher wasn't already fully established.

Crowell couldn't outproduce Schumacher, so he decided to outmarket him with a unique selling feature—a packaging feature.

He was personally put off by the flies that were constantly buzzing around food barrels in general stores of the day. Remembering that cleanliness was next to godliness, Crowell decided to put Quaker Oats in two-pound packages to keep it free from dirt, disease, animals, and insects. This ploy appealed to housewives, who also thought flies were a nuisance. As a further enticement, Crowell went the Smith Brothers one better by making the package not only a container, but also a selling tool: The Quaker box became the first package to provide explicit cooking directions.

Housewives picking up Quaker Oats would read:

We would call special attention to the purity, rapidity of preparation, and the fact that they [sic] did not sacrifice sweetness and flavor for the sake of rapid cooking.

Crowell took the obvious next step—adding recipes for all kinds of oatmeal dishes—and Quaker Oats later became the first nationally advertised food product in a four-color printed carton as well as the first product reproduced in miniature for sampling.

It should be noted that grocers initially had misgivings about such advances in packaging. They were used to selling food in barrels and were convinced that open pricing meant greater profits. Although it is no longer the case, packaging in the 1880s implied fixed prices with the price clearly marked on the container. Such a change threatened to put an end to the haggling at which grocers had grown so expert over the years.

Nevertheless, selling prepackaged goods offered several advantages, which had financial implications. Among other things, prepackaging:

- *reduced waste, spoilage and perishability*. Packages created physical barriers to all kinds of elements—heat, light, water, airborne gases, disease, animals, and insects—which increased return on investment.

- *speeded up packing time.* There was now no need to make individual "papers," because the packages already protected the goods. Bagging packaged goods gave clerks more time to restock shelves and make high-margin home deliveries.
- *made eye-catching displays possible.* Neat pyramids of goods created an indelible graphic impression on consumers and increased impulse buys. From the consumer's standpoint, packaging made goods easier to store at home, saved cooking time, and ended suspicion about short-weighting—being charged for twelve ounces of food and getting only ten.

Crowell's God-given talent for marketing turned Quaker Oats around and made him the first serious threat to Schumacher's domination. When Schumacher's uninsured mill burned to the ground (he was too cheap to pay the premiums), he couldn't rebuild immediately and was forced into a shotgun marriage with Crowell as part of a short-lived cereal trust.

Predictably, the two men had violent arguments about the old oatmeal barrels. Crowell said, "The barrel is open to anything; we should package and advertise our goods." Schumacher replied, "The grocers don't want packages, and the peoples [sic] don't want it neither. This advertisings [sic] is silly business! We'll save money; let our competitors advertise." At the turn of the century, in America's first large-scale proxy fight, Crowell forced Schumacher out and ran a new cereal trust himself.

Free of Schumacher, Crowell created yet another piece of marketing history by popularizing the packaged premium. C. W. Post had already included a cents-off coupon for Post Toasties in a box of Postum (see Chapter 3), but Crowell's idea made the package a mail-order marketplace. On the back of Banner Oats, another Quaker Oats brand, was the legend, "Send one boxtop of Banner Oats and twenty-five cents and start collecting this handsome set of dishes." Within two years, 2.4 million sets had been issued, and the supplier had to build twelve new kilns to keep up with the demand.

Crowell soon began giving away spoons, kitchen gadgets, and coupons redeemable for double boilers and kept the Quaker Oats name before the public on promotional billboards, blotters, calendars, and cookbooks. His promotional zeal even spread beyond the boundaries of the United States. One night, Britishers returning from Calais saw etched on the white cliffs of Dover:

QUAKER OATS

Parliament protested vigorously, giving Quaker even greater exposure in England, and the real Quakers—the Society of Friends—joined in the controversy as well. The Society instituted lawsuits against Quaker at home and abroad and petitioned Congress to bar any trademark with a religious connotation, but none of these efforts was successful.

The Quaker man's face on millions of packages became a merchandising plus, like the images of Aunt Jemima and Betty Crocker, and a real-life representation of the Quaker man made appearances at county fairs and trade shows. By the time Crowell retired to run the Moody Bible Institute, he had turned a bankrupt cereal company into a $2 billion food processing giant and played a major part in establishing packaging as an integral part of the marketing process. While it is difficult to quantify, the exposure given the Quaker man image certainly helped the Quaker Oats Company diversify into franchise extensions like granola bars and other products that bear his face.

•　•　•　•　•　•　•

PRODUCT   QUAKER OATS

Pivotal *P*: Packaging

Although grocers originally preferred open barrels, packaging meant cleaner, healthier food, easier shipping, and many selling advantages at the point-of-sale.

Primary *P*'s: Premiums, Promotion

Crowell's efforts made the cereal premium a mail-order milestone and made the Quaker man a living trademark for more than a hundred years.

•　•　•　•　•　•　•

LIFE SAVERS   Coming Unglued

Life Savers were created in 1912 as a novelty candy. The shape and flavor attracted consumers, but the packaging almost killed the brand in its infancy.

Clarence Crane had started a chocolate business in Cleveland before the turn of the century and intended to turn it over to his son, Hart. When young Crane appeared to be more interested in poetry than manufacturing Mary Garden chocolates, Crane senior began searching for a second product to give him some cash flow during the summer months. Due to a lack of adequate refrigeration, chocolate sales melted away to almost nothing in June, July, and August.

Mints were particularly popular in 1912, both for their taste and for their ability to mask unpleasant odors. The most popular ones were made in Europe and were pillow-shaped, a configuration that was fairly expensive to produce as well as costly to import. Crane decided to make less costly mints right there in Cleveland and settled on a round shape. Lacking the space or equipment to create the new product in his own factory, he subcontracted the process to a pill manufacturer. When the manufacturer's stamping machine malfunctioned and stamped out the middles by mistake, Crane kept the distinctive doughnut shape.

He named the candies Crane's Peppermint Life Savers and patented their design as "nothing enclosed by a circle."

Packed in cardboard tubes, they were shipped nationally, and Edward John Noble, a New Yorker who sold streetcar advertising, picked up a package of the new candy and was impressed with its taste, its distinctive shape, and its crafty positioning. The package read, "Crane's Peppermint Life Savers—5¢—For That Stormy Breath," and Noble was impressed that Crane was selling his candy not only as a snack but also positioning it as a way for people to deal with bad breath. Feeling he was on the track of a potentially lucrative client, Noble took a train to Cleveland with the intention of convincing Crane to advertise Life Savers nationally.

As things turned out, Crane did the convincing.

Despite the strides he'd taken with Life Savers already, and even though he knew the mints might have a future, Crane preferred the chocolate business. He said to Noble, "Look. If you think they're so great, why don't you buy them up and make them yourself?"

Noble did just that, raising $3,800 with the help of a boyhood friend named J. Roy Allen—$2,900 to buy the rights and formula and another $900 for advertising. He sold Allen on the idea that, with some advertising exposure, Life Savers could become "a $50-a-day repeat business."

A week later the partners had rented loft space in New York City and hired six young women at $5 a week to pack Life Savers. Noble was creating ads when Allen discovered that the young men had bought a product in a deficient package. The old-fashioned cardboard packaging had absorbed the peppermint flavor and had fallen apart; as a result, thousands of unprotected rolls of the candy were going stale on retailers' shelves. Allen said later, "Our dream business was indeed a dream; Life Savers were a flop."

In an effort to improve the mints' barrier properties and shelf life quickly, Noble repackaged them in tin foil (a first for hard candies), then overwrapped the foil with colorful band labels to further seal in freshness. However, when he called on Crane's old candy-store customers with the new stock, none would take new shipments of Life Savers; the most tolerant among them would merely replace the old stock with fresh mints.

Structurally deficient packaging had given Life Savers a bad reputation with retailers and had shut Noble out of the natural point-of-sale for his product. Noble had neglected some of his advertising clients, invested his savings, and was forced to find alternative distribution for a new product quickly or else go out of business.

To his credit, he explored literally every avenue for sales, going door-to-door from toy stores to barber shops to department stores. While most turned him down, Noble did sign up a few customers. He said later, "I think they felt sorry for me; I looked pretty much like a kid in those days."

One of his biggest successes came when he recalled how impressed he had been with that phrase of Crane's—"For That Stormy Breath"—and began dropping into saloons. At the time, saloons gave away free cloves (along with free lunch) to disguise the breath of their customers; however, the clove leaves grew stale quickly and were messy to chew and spit out. According to *Current Biography*, "Life Savers thus became a competitor of the standard dish of cloves at the end of the bar."

By putting Life Savers in saloons, Noble found an offbeat but nevertheless effective point-of-sale for a breath freshener; his candy saved drinkers from telltale "whiskey breath," and, in turn, drinkers saved his company from immediate extinction with a piggyback trick. The reprieve gave Noble more time to find other, less specialized distribution outlets like retail tobacconists. After approaching several tobacconists without much success, he came up with a variation on his saloon success for the huge United Cigar chain.

Noble convinced the chain's owners that smokers would use his candy as they used Sen-Sen (to cover up "cigarette breath") if he came up with a way to make it painless to buy Life Savers. He designed a lightweight cardboard shipping container that could easily be made into a miniature display case—the first of its kind. He convinced the chain's owners to "put them next to the cash register, charge five cents, and be sure to give your customers nickels in change."

As a result, Life Savers became the first nonsmoker's item to be carried in United Cigar's 1,200 stores, and, as Noble had figured, consumers began taking their change from tobacco purchases in Life Savers. Sales spurted from 940,000 tubes in 1914 to 6,725,000 two years after his Mint Products Company had almost gone bankrupt. Defective packaging had almost killed Life Savers, but the inventive display case more than made up for the initial mistake.

As more nickels rolled in, Noble was able to quit the advertising business and devote more time to building Life Savers. An early laborer in the vineyards of transit advertising, he advertised the brand nationally in streetcars. One of the cards reproduced in *Moving Images* reads:

> Mary had a little lamb
> With onions in her stew.
> Life Savers took her breath away
> So she could bill and coo!

When America entered World War I, sugar quotas cut production of Life Savers, but the mints with the hole in the middle survived. After the war ended, Noble invested in striking uniforms for young women who gave out samples on New York streets and in building lobbies. The candy began showing up in movie theaters and restaurants and in vending machines in railroad stations and even in gas stations, as the automobile became established. In 1918, Life Savers made a $280,000 profit, and in 1920 it reached the $1 million mark in profits, and underwent a name change to Life Savers, Inc. Five years later, Life Savers went public, selling 20 percent of its stock, and Allen retired with "a cool profit of $3,300,000."

Noble turned the business over gradually to other executives and, after serving briefly as Under-Secretary of Commerce, made a second mark in a new business. In 1943, he bought RCA's Blue Network (later renamed the American Broadcasting Company) for $8 million to become the first individual to own a national chain of radio stations; by year's end, he had resold chunks of it (at a profit) to several individual investors and Time, Inc.

Life Savers survived a second imposition of sugar quotas during World War II; in 1946, sales of Life Savers shot up 200 percent and have risen every year since, a fact that did not escape packaged-goods marketers. In 1956, two years before his death, the seventy-four-year-old Noble merged Life Savers with Beech-nut Products, Inc. Later bought by E. R. Squibb & Sons, Life Savers eventually became part of Nabisco Brands, Inc., in 1981.

Ironically, Life Savers, a product once barred from distribution in candy stores, is probably the single most widely distributed candy in the United States and can be purchased in more than 1 million different retail outlets. By this time, Americans have bought 340 billion of the little suckers, a figure that represents 90 percent of all the mints and fruit drops ever sold in the United States. While flavors like Horehound and Buttermint only lasted a year apiece, the original Pep-O-Mint just celebrated its seventy-eighth anniversary.

•   •   •   •   •   •   •

PRODUCT   LIFE SAVERS

Pivotal *P*: Packaging

Poor packaging caused Life Savers to be shut out of its natural point-of-sale, the candy store, but Ed Noble made them a hit in saloons and cigar stores.

Primary *P*: Positioning

Early positioning as a breath freshener made Life Savers a natural for drinkers and smokers who wanted to disguise their habits.

•   •   •   •   •   •   •

YOPLAIT   The Big Leak

Bill Bennet once said of himself, "Once I get fired up with an idea, I just put the blinders on and keep moving in one direction." But perseverance was not the Pivotal *P* in the Yoplait story. Packaging was. Bennet was just about blown out of the yogurt business by structural packaging problems.

Bennet had been a buyer and marketing specialist for Jewel Cos. Inc., the Chicago-based supermarket chain, before buying the Michigan Cottage Cheese Company in Otsego, Michigan. By the mid-1970s, the firm was generating $8 million a year in sales, but Bennet had concluded that the market for his product would never grow dramatically. Consequently, he was looking for another food item to market.

He thought he had found it the first time he tasted French yogurt. Yogurt had once been a joke food in America, a sure way for a comedian to get a cheap laugh. By the 1970s, however, yogurt had piggybacked onto the health-food revival, and Dannon, the only brand with national distribution, was growing by leaps and bounds.

Given this bedrock of support for a commodity product that wasn't being marketed with any flair, Bennet figured that yogurt-eating Americans would flock to the French version because of its creamier texture and richer taste.

Unfortunately, the two years Bennet spent on the American introduction of the French product proved to be wasted when the company was sold to a conglomerate and the deal was canceled . . . before the first bit of French culture made it to American shelves. He next tried to develop his own French-style yogurt, Mais Oui, but he discovered, while traveling in France, that SODIMA, a French company, wanted to franchise its Yoplait brand. He therefore dropped Mais Oui and became the first licensed Yoplait distributor in the U.S.

As much a missionary in his way as Henry Crowell or Ed Noble had been, Bennet spent nine months adapting the product to fit his personal vision of what Americans wanted in a yogurt that Dannon wasn't already delivering. He decided that, in addition to taste, Dannon was vulnerable on four other levels:

1. *Package*—the cup Dannon came in was a standard shape for dairy products, and the graphics were unappetizing. Generally speaking, package designers try to "tie" their packages to the leader in the category, but in this case, Yoplait came in a distinctively tapered package made of compressed waxed paper. Even though initial research showed that Americans wouldn't favor such a departure, Bennet retained the shape. He said, "I wanted it to stand out on the supermarket shelf."

2. *Size*—the size was large, compared to European containers. Yoplait was sold in four-ounce cups in Europe, while presumably weight-conscious Americans were buying Dannon in half-pound packages. Bennet increased the size of the Yoplait cup from four to six ounces, figuring he could still sell a six-ounce size more cheaply than Dannon's eight-ounce size and enable consumers to finish a cup of yogurt in one sitting without feeling guilty about the quantity.

3. *Content*—Dannon included stabilizers. So did Yoplait. Bennet, however, was convinced that the product had to be "all-natural" to fit the marketing mood of the moment. Yogurt had jumped on the organic-foods bandwagon, and Bennet decided that catering to the whims of this core group would

pay dividends in the way the product was accepted. Consequently, he removed all of Yoplait's taste enhancers and product stabilizers, which meant that he could promote it as 100 percent natural.

4. *Pedigree*—Dannon was American. Americans regard French food as the world's best, so French food confers status advantages on those who aspire to being regarded as having "gourmet" tastes. Since no manufacturer had ever tried to market French yogurt in America, Bennet felt that occasional yogurt eaters might be attracted solely by his product's pedigree and be willing to pay extra for it. To make sure that no potential consumer missed the point, Bennet had the package printed in English on one side and in French on the other.

The decisions Bennet had made combined snob appeal, rich taste, and all-natural ingredients, a combination that had already worked for another dairy-based product, Häagen-Dazs ice cream. Just as consumers had bought the butterfat-rich ice cream with the made-up fancy name, Bennet was banking on Yoplait's smooth taste and the established cachet of French food to turn yogurt—a commodity—into a "gourmet" item that could command a premium price.

Developing Yoplait took two years and cost seven figures. Bennet was prepared for neither eventuality and, in February 1976, was forced to sell 51 percent of the brand for $1.5 million. Nevertheless, the meticulous planning phase was finally over—salespeople were hired, orders were written, advertising was placed, production began, and . . . the packages leaked.

Worse yet, the leaking was not a constant problem but an intermittent one, which made it hard to pinpoint. Bennet flew the French packaging-equipment manufacturer over to America twice without coming up with a definitive answer to the problem. Meanwhile, customers complained about the new brand, which made supermarket managers uneasy and gave Yoplait a reputation in the packaged-goods field as a "leaker." This is a pejorative term in the food business (you've got your leakers and your squeakers); being classified as a leaker is like having a scarlet *A* embroidered on your cape.

Eventually, the problem was discovered to be threefold: (1) the top seal wasn't strong enough; (2) the cup material wasn't watertight; and (3) the package broke down due to the lack of stabilizers. Life Savers had fallen apart sitting on retailers' shelves, and Yoplait leaked as it sat in warehouses.

Bennet dismissed the problem as "a bad break," and refused to put the stabilizers back, contending that keeping Yoplait's ingredients all-natural was too important from a marketing viewpoint. He designed a new, tighter seal and was preparing to switch to a plastic package when his investors decided he wasn't moving fast enough and put Yoplait up for sale.

At about the same time, Steven Rothschild, then a General Mills marketing director and now responsible for marketing a good chunk of the company's food products, had been studying the yogurt business intensely. He decided that, although not many people are fond of yogurt, "People who eat it eat a hell of a lot of it." Moreover, fully one-third of the population had never tried it, and there was only one national brand to compete against.

Rothschild recommended that General Mills buy Bennet's investors out in October 1977. It took General Mills another six months to come up with a plastic cup that would hold the yogurt in place, but the wait was worth it. When it was finally introduced in Southern California, with bicycle races, hot-air balloons, and a light-hearted prime-time TV campaign, Yoplait immediately became a leading seller and even outsold Cheerios, General Mills' flagship brand, in terms of unit sales. By 1985, yogurt had become a $1 billion business, and Yoplait had 15 percent of the market as opposed to Dannon's 26 percent.

In the final analysis, Bennet batted .750 with Yoplait. He was right about its taste, its gourmet appeal, and the freshness of its tapered package, which has since inspired many imitators in the yogurt category as well as in other dairy products. However, he was dead wrong about consumers preferring an all-natural product to one that kept its physical integrity until it was used up, and the decision cost him millions, because, in all varieties, Yoplait had 1989 sales of $269.6 million.

•   •   •   •   •   •   •

PRODUCT   YOPLAIT YOGURT

Pivotal *P*: Packaging

Yoplait's founder thought the public preferred an all-natural product to great packaging. Poor packaging almost killed the brand before General Mills rode to the rescue.

Primary *P*: Piggybacking

The public tolerated Yoplait's package, because yogurt fit the national health craze. Yoplait hitchhiked onto it and became a success despite its packaging.

•   •   •   •   •   •   •

SOFTSOAP   Liquid Asset

Most packaging hits are caused when an interesting product is put into an interesting package. Softsoap made news when the product was taken out of its traditional form and therefore out of its traditional package and turned into something that was the same . . . but different.

Before it hardens, soap is a pourable liquid. Always has been, always will be. Yet soap was never used as a liquid until the 1950s, when concentrated liquid soap began to be used in factory washrooms, and Wisk and other detergent and dishwashing liquids began to appear.

It was never marketed to the general public as an alternative to wash the face and body until 1976, when liquid soap was introduced as one element of a whole shower-based cleansing system—Water Pik's Washing Machine. The device was designed to be hung up in the shower, where it would not only replace messy (and slippery) bars of soap, but would also dispense shampoo and hair conditioner, replacing three separate items and centralizing them in one neat, attractive package.

The drawbacks were: (1) the price ($24.95); (2) the installation, which involved sticking components to slippery walls; and (3) the use of a generic shampoo and hair conditioner, both of which were made up of synthetic materials. (Neither had any brand identity, and using synthetics was a mistake, considering the premium price and the target market.)

The machine didn't catch on, and Water Pik quickly withdrew it. However, Robert Taylor, a manufacturer of scented, hand-rolled soaps, saw that liquid soap, with some adjustments, could become a natural extension of his product line.

Taylor, a Stanford MBA, had left his job as a Johnson & Johnson sales manager in 1964 to start Minnetonka, Inc., of Chaska, Minnesota, in his garage. In the beginning, Taylor hired dozens of women to hand roll yellow, lemon-shaped soaps and green, apple-shaped soaps, which he sold through gift shops, eventually adding such cosmetic products as potpourri and scented shampoos. Given Minnetonka's unusual distribution system for cosmetics, Taylor and vice president Grant Wood saw possibilities in liquid soap. Taylor says, "I thought how ugly bar soap is, and how it usually messes up the bathroom."

Yet, while liquid soap was less messy than bar soap and more economical because all of it was eventually used up, merely offering a generic soap in a new package configuration wouldn't necessarily create new sales or switch previously loyal users of bar soap. Doing that would require adding value to the product, the package, or both.

The most natural way to add value was through scent, since fragrances and flavors were Minnetonka's long suit. (It was the first company to sell fruit-scented shampoos in gift stores.) Next, Taylor and Wood replaced the synthetic fats Water Pik had used with natural ones and, instead of generic soap, used an enticing blend of coconut oil, camomile, aloe, and other natural essences similar to those used in Minnetonka's "nifty gifty" soaps. Then, to give consumers a unique added benefit, they packaged what was originally marketed as the Incredible Soap Machine in a four-color floral bottle. The product originally retailed for $4.95 in 1977, and within three months, it was the single biggest-selling item in the company's limited history.

Taylor immediately saw that liquid soap could be more than just a successful specialty product. Properly handled, it could be a wedge to get Minnetonka, a company that sold mostly seasonal merchandise, into the big leagues of packaged-goods marketing. Wood says, "We were originally a one-quarter company; we used to do a lot of business at Christmastime."

Wood and Taylor decided to repackage the Incredible Soap Machine into a product that could be sold in drugstores and supermarkets, preferably alongside other Minnetonka products. Before that could happen, however, the same item that had sold well in the gift market had to be broken down and reconstructed all over again for a more broadly based audience. Several problems had to be overcome:

1. *The price.* Five dollars ($4.95) was much too high for a mass item that sold for as little as 49 cents.
2. *The pump.* The same one used for water-based detergents, it couldn't deliver the more viscous soap without clogging.
3. *The size.* The original sixteen-ounce package was too big to sit comfortably on a supermarket shelf.
4. *The shape.* Cylinders are economical for getting the maximum amount of liquid into the minimum amount of space; however, they were entirely too economical for Minnetonka's purpose.
5. *The name.* It was too long and had to be changed. "However," says Wood, "we couldn't afford to use a P & G-type name that would be familiar only after we'd spent $20 million on TV." The name had to do what L'eggs did for its pantyhose—instantly convey the essence of the product.
6. *The packaging.* Wood says, "The package had 'Incredible Soap Machine' in large letters, which is distasteful. People don't like the idea of displaying packages with big logos in guest bathrooms. They get around this with bar soap by just unwrapping the product; in our case, you couldn't unwrap the package, because, in Ron Peterson's phrase, 'the package was the product.'"

Despite these problems, success in the gift market had galvanized Minnetonka, and twelve-hour days became common in Chaska. Production engineers began to shave the price by using a less complicated pump and cutting the size to ten and a half ounces. The original target price was $1.49; they came close—$1.59. As would later happen with L'eggs (see Chapter 6), the name, the shape, and the packaging all came together at the same time, creating not only a major packaging story, but a subsequent packaging breakthrough.

Wood says, "We needed an aesthetic shape that suggested something offbeat like an oval. Then, John Matthews, one of our salespeople, came up with the idea of the wicker motif. It looked great but only required a one-color printing job, which was a big plus. It also softened the package, and Softsoap just seemed to suggest itself as a name. When we put the required legal language and the UPC coding symbol on the back, we were able to maintain a 'designer look' so people could display it in their powder rooms. By the time we finished, we had changed every element except the concept."

Part of the change involved a redirection in thinking for Minnetonka's sales staff, which had previously dealt with upscale specialty stores. They had to get an innovative product into crowded supermarkets and also get it into the right section of the market. Minnetonka spent a lot of time convincing retailers to place it in the soap sections of drugstores and supermarkets rather than alongside bubble bath and other "powder room" items. This proved to be a key point, because it made Softsoap appear more "normal" to curious consumers.

The campaign kicked off in February 1980 with $6 million worth of advertising and a blizzard of introductory cents-off coupons in newspapers. Softsoap was an immediate hit; sales exceeded $30 million nine months after it was introduced. This kind of success opened up grocery stores for Minnetonka's other products and created a mass market for liquid soap; it also brought well-heeled competitors into the liquid-soap business fast.

As a result, Minnetonka spent $15 million on advertising in 1982, and even though sales of all its products rose to $69 million, the company lost $3.8 million that year. Taylor says, "The trouble was we were creating the liquid-soap business and didn't have a basis on which to forecast except for the bar-soap business."

In 1983, Minnetonka cut back on advertising and put all its marketing efforts into coupons and price promotions on branded Minne-tonka products—for example, reduced price offers on Softsoap and Claire Burke potpourri packaged together. The strategy worked, and the company was able to regain its leadership position—a 39 percent share of a $100 million market.

Softsoap paved the way for broad acceptance of Minnetonka's products. Minnetonka had reversed its priorities from nichemanship to mass distribution and became the first company to market liquid soap in decorative dispensers along with "regular soap."

Reviewing the experience a decade later, Taylor said, "Ten percent of the success of a new consumer product is the idea. Ninety percent is the execution."

•   •   •   •   •   •   •

PRODUCT   LIQUID SOAP

Pivotal P: Packaging

Robert Taylor saw that, in the right container, liquid soap could be a popular alternative to bar soap.

Primary P's: Placement, Positioning

Rather than settle for display space with gift items, Minnetonka pushed for room in the soap section, positioning a specialty product as a mainstream alternative.

•   •   •   •   •   •   •

QUAKER STATE   Special Delivery

What the metal tube was to toothpaste, the metal can was to motor oil.

Motor oil had been sold almost exclusively in metal cans through the mid-1970s, when steel prices began rising in the U.S. Like most manufacturers being hit with packaging price increases, motor oil producers began to search for a different way to contain their product. For too many years motor oil manufacturers had been content to use a package configuration that required a separate tool as a delivery system, the familiar funnel, and was messy to boot.

Given the mystique of automobile maintenance, many consumers had been content to have service stations replace used oil and change it according to the carmaker's instructions; however, the percentage of consumers who added or changed their own oil began to rise in the late 1960s and indirectly caused a major change in motor-oil packaging. Quaker State Oil Refining Corporation saw the handwriting on the wall and began to develop distribution in mass-merchandise outlets rather than the traditional service stations. In so doing, Quaker State wound up with 23 percent of the $2 billion motor oil market, and now many American car owners change or add their own oil.

Naturally, this made motorists rather than mechanics the deciding factor in which motor oil was purchased. As consumers became direct customers, motor oil manufacturers began to put greater stock in public attitudes about their products. When an inexpensive, composite steel-and-cardboard can was perfected, Valvoline, Havoline, and Pennzoil immediately adopted it, but Quaker State, which had more than 20 percent of the $2.5 billion domestic motor oil market, initially stayed in steel.

A Quaker State marketing executive says, "In our view, composites offered zero convenience to the customer and offered more drawbacks to the distributor and retailer." Composites required the same funnel and were as messy as all-steel cans and offered the additional drawback of breaking more frequently in shipping and storage. Nevertheless, Quaker State executives hoped that what the *Pittsburgh Business Journal* estimated as a $9.5 million savings in packaging costs would make the changeover more palatable.

Things got a lot worse before they got better.

The sides of composite cans collapsed during storage; spouts inadvertently punctured the sides of cans; oil was wasted during pouring; and dirt got into open cans, making it almost impossible to use all the contents. Moreover, composites never really solved the industry's basic packaging problems and still required openers, funnels, oily rags, and other paraphernalia that mechanics accepted but consumers began resisting more and more.

During the changeover to composites, Quaker State was using

plastic cans for some specialty products like four-cycle oil for motor-cycles. Moreover, it was charging premium prices for them and getting no price resistance from consumers, even at a 20 percent premium. SAY Industries, of Leominster, Massachusetts, had developed a one-quart plastic package for motor oil in 1978, which began attracting more attention in 1980 when the shortcomings of composites became more apparent.

More than a dozen major motor-oil manufacturers experimented with plastic packages and discovered that consumers were willing to pay an extra nickel or dime for the convenience (and cleanliness) that plastic offered. Consumers were particularly impressed with the screw-on cap, which enabled them to reuse oil at their convenience. Never-theless, change came slowly. Plastic packages weren't advertised or promoted for several years.

Even though no major market research was done, Quaker State conducted focus-group research and mall intercept studies to test con-sumer reaction to plastic packaging. An internal Quaker State study predicted, "The first company to adopt plastic exclusively will reap tangible advantages in terms of increased market share; the later a manufacturer changes to plastic, the less his share will increase."

There was a definite downside in the switch to plastic—a formi-dable expenditure in new equipment. Composite can-filling machines cost $1 million apiece, but filled 340 cans per minute; American ma-chines could fill only 125 plastic packages a minute and cost $1.5 million. Eventually, however, Quaker State officials were able to find a relatively inexpensive Italian machine that filled 300 resealable bottles a minute. In the final analysis, Quaker State's size and the fact that it fills a million cans of motor oil a day made the switch to plastic affordable in the long run.

Given this long-range economy of scale and the consumer's ac-ceptance of the new package, Quaker State decided to go ahead. They even moved up the decision to switch to plastic by a whole year. In mid-1983, the company began gearing up for the change, which was announced that November by chairman Quentin E. Wood. Noting that Quaker State was known as "tight with a buck and slow to move," Wood said, "We can be quick to move . . . when the right opportunity presents itself."

The company shipped its first plastic cans of automobile motor oil in January 1984. Predictably, there was some negative reaction in the motor oil industry. One company advertised its product with the slogan, "Real men don't change motor oil with bottles."

Despite such grousing from competitors, there were measurable sales gains for Quaker State within six months. According to in-house research, the brand's market share increased from 21 percent at the end of 1983 to 23.5 percent through the third quarter of 1984. As an added bonus, plastic packages enabled Quaker State to broaden its distribution into convenience outlets like 7-Eleven stores.

Quaker State's success quickly made believers out of the other motor-oil companies, most of whom have followed the move to plastic. Manufacturers have since added improvements to plastic packages, such as more precise pouring spouts and gradations on the package to show consumers how much has been used. This feature became more valuable in 1987, when Quaker State became the first manufacturer to package its motor oil in clear, see-through plastic.

From Quaker Oats cereal in the 1880s to Quaker State motor oil in the 1980s, packaging changes have given consumers immediate, tangible advantages. Although such changes can be expensive to implement, no area of remarketing offers a "quicker fix" than improving a deficient package.

• • • • • • •

PRODUCT   QUAKER STATE MOTOR OIL

Pivotal P: Packaging

Rather than use composite cans as a stopgap measure, Quaker State made a costly commitment to plastic and reaped the rewards of increased convenience for the customer.

Primary P: Placement

When plastic oil containers became accepted, they moved into mainstream distribution outlets like supermarkets and drugstores.

• • • • • • •

Chapter Six

DON'T SELL IT IN

THE WRONG

PLACE

• • • • • •

BEFORE any product can be bought, it must reach a shelf, a bin, an aisle, a vending machine—some specific geographic location where buyer and seller can meet and transact their business.

This place, called the point-of-sale from the seller's viewpoint (and the point-of-purchase from the buyer's) has evolved as marketing has evolved, always tied closely to advances in communication and transportation.

Manufacturers have only two basic worries: How to get the product on the shelf, and, once it's there, how to get it off the shelves—and into the consumer's home and lifestyle.

Getting on the shelves is called distribution, or Placement, and it involves three things—time, place, and product—all of which are equally important for efficient distribution. If you lack one element, you blow the whole deal. For instance:

- *Time:* Kimberly-Clark's efforts to distribute Kotex were doomed until pads as a product became less taboo. After they had become accepted, however, pads became common-place in factories and vending machines.

- *Place:* Henry Ford's attempts to sell charcoal through car dealers were even less successful than the Edsel. But when Charles Kingsford bought the company and switched distribution to grocery stores, charcoal briquets caught fire.
- *Product:* Surplus military clothing used to be found in the back of camping stores, and safari clothes appeared in department stores only in combination with Africa promotions. But, put in a specialized environment and given dramatic display at Banana Republic, bush gear and aviators' jackets suddenly had the Wright Stuff.

Placement and Perception   In 1988, America's best-selling perfume was Giorgio, a brand that had been launched in a mom-and-pop store (albeit in Beverly Hills). The perfume was originally sold only in the shop and through mail order. When the perfume was offered outside Beverly Hills, only chic department and specialty stores were allowed to carry it. This tactic of limited distribution gave the product an aura of scarcity, which added to its appeal and made demand soar even higher. By reining in distribution, the makers of Giorgio established their perfume as a best-seller.

Placement and Strategy   The Giorgio distribution strategy was designed to enhance its mystique. Another entrepreneur invaded the supersaturated pizza business with a unique placement campaign. Rather than do battle with pizza parlors like Pizza Hut, or frozen pizza like Jeno's, Tom Monahan offered home delivery of Domino's within thirty minutes, or it was free. Instead of spending money on real estate and fixtures, he made one product available at a new point-of-sale—the home—and earned a big pizza the business.

Advanced Placement   Because distribution is so key to the marketing process, manufacturers are constantly finding ways to display their products in new retail outlets. Book publishers have seen the traditional bookstore become a point-of-sale for computer programs, comic books, and videotapes. In response, a publisher who specialized in books on auto maintenance found a way to hit people who didn't visit bookstores; he found a distributor of auto parts, and suddenly his books appeared in NAPA stores around the country.

One other car-related placement story: A producer of motivational audio cassettes had done well selling them in small, business-oriented magazines but wanted to attract more of a blue-collar audience. He hit paydirt by offering the cassettes to owners of car washes, who were thrilled to offer products other than beverage holders and battery cables.

Growing Customers   Under unique circumstances, companies can gain a placement foothold that will pay future dividends by creating new customers. During World War II, General Dwight D. Eisenhower asked Coca-Cola to send a vending machine to Africa to give thirsty GIs a little taste of home. Coca-Cola not only complied but sent additional machines to Europe, South America, and the Far East. When the war was over, Coca-Cola had placement capabilities around the globe, thanks to its farsighted policy.

Coca-Cola made a patriotic gesture and saw it evolve into an opportunity. Opportunistic product placement has given new life to dozens of products and helped make winners out of products as different as baby food, watches, plastic housewares, and hosiery.

GERBER BABY FOOD   Strained Relations

Convenience food was an alien notion to Americans in the early 1920s. There were no snacks in cellophane bags (there were no cellophane bags), no just-add-water cake mixes, and no mass-marketed baby food.

Grocers, convinced that mothers wouldn't buy machine-strained baby food, refused to stock it. Women with young children questioned whether food packed in tin was safe for their babies. And, despite the drudgery involved, mothers were loath to shirk the responsibility of straining food for their infants who were too young to chew.

One food packager named Clapp & Company had tried to sell strained foods in grocery stores and had failed totally. In desperation, the company sold its wares in, of all places, drugstores. Promoting the line as over-the-counter pharmaceuticals for infants with delicate stomachs temporarily solved Clapp's distribution problem; however, the drugstore sales stigmatized strained food. Now, in addition to being a slow seller, machine-made baby food was perceived as being a medicine for sick infants, rather than a source of nutrition for healthy babies.

Moreover, Clapp and other manufacturers had completely overlooked and undersold the nutritional value of prepared baby food. As it turns out, fruits and vegetables destined to be machine-strained are first steamed in huge covered vats; minerals, which dissolve in water and which are discarded in the average kitchen, are retained in factory-canning operations. The idea of providing extra nutritional value could have been one of prepared baby foods' biggest selling points, but it was completely absent from Clapp's pitch to consumers.

Appropriately, then, a woman who understood and appreciated the nutritional value of canned produce was the catalyst for prepared baby foods. Canned goods held no fears for Dorothy Gerber, the wife of Daniel F. Gerber, who ran Michigan's Fremont Canning Company with his father, Frank. In fact, Dorothy Gerber was uniquely equipped to see just how much drudgery was involved with straining fruits and vegetables several times daily, a repetitive job she knew could be done by a machine.

One summer Sunday in 1927, she spent the afternoon straining peas for her infant daughter before getting dressed to go out for the evening. Frustrated with chopping and straining vegetables for the third time that day, she asked her husband why the job couldn't be done at his food-processing plant. "To press the point," she said, "I dumped a whole container of peas into a strainer and bowl, placed them in Dan's lap, and asked him how he'd like to do that three times a day, seven days a week."

Dan Gerber later commented, "The following twenty minutes shouldn't happen to any man . . . I pushed and squashed valiantly, and the peas were everywhere but in the strainer." When his wife arrived, all dressed for the evening, she asked, "You can puree tomatoes at the plant, why not vegetables for Sally?"

Several days later, Sally and the children of other employees tasted the first production batch and gave it thumbs up. When similar tests in their home town got rave reviews, the Gerbers contacted nutritionists, domestic science teachers, and pediatricians for their reactions; each group was enthusiastic and lent the products some credibility with endorsement letters. (And, while they dared not say so publicly, food and health professionals secretly welcomed machines that would do the job of straining food with greater uniformity and efficiency than some mothers managed.)

When Gerber's staff gave samples to thousands of mothers and did follow-up interviews, they made a series of discoveries. The bad news was that, yes, many women did psychologically equate the arduous task of straining peas with loving their babies. They consequently felt anxious about giving up this key responsibility and were unmoved by the increased convenience of prestrained foods. But there was good news too. Dan Gerber had planned on drugstore distribution for his line; however, when 90 percent of the mothers said they would prefer to buy strained foods in the grocery store, he changed his plans, particularly when doctors who were interviewed agreed with the mothers.

The single most surprising result of consumer research was the fact that mothers didn't flinch about paying high prices for prepared baby foods. Due to high start-up packing costs, Fremont originally had to charge fifteen cents for four-and-a-half-ounce cans of strained peas, prunes, carrots, and spinach to make a profit; in contrast, an eighteen-ounce can of regular peas cost only ten cents. What made the difference for mothers—the key selling point—was increased nutrition; they were willing to pay a premium for more consistently nutritious food to feed their children.

Given this enthusastic response from consumers, Gerber was faced with a seeming paradox. For two generations, the Gerbers had enjoyed excellent relations with the various middlemen of the food business—food brokers; however, in this instance, Gerber knew that the brokers and distributors had a blind spot about strained baby foods. How could Fremont Canning enter the marketplace with an unproven product and, at the same time, protect the good relations he and his father had spent years building?

Gerber decided to go directly to the consumer who had to sit there straining the peas, "three times a day, seven days a week." Gerber said, "Our friends in the trade argued very strongly against the idea of starting national advertising without a bit of distribution. But without advertising we felt that we could not get the goods on dealer's shelves."

The Gerbers committed $40,000 to an advertising campaign; each ad carried a coupon offering consumers six cans of Gerber's Strained Vegetables for a dollar with the return of a coupon. Mothers were asked to fill in the coupon with their names and addresses—and the names of their local grocers—and return them to Fremont Canning. Naturally, if consumers responded, Gerber would present the coupons as evidence that there was a sizable market for prepared baby foods just waiting to be tapped.

Since $40,000 was a major expenditure for his company, Dan Gerber decided to get the biggest bang for his buck by running as many small ads as possible, and Frank Gerber suggested using an illustration to attract attention. A number of life-sized oil paintings were submitted and admired but were eventually rejected. At the last minute, commercial artist Dorothy Hope Smith submitted an unfinished charcoal sketch of a baby girl named Ann Turner, and it was chosen to symbolize Gerber baby foods.

That October, after ads featuring the adorable infant had already been produced for the *Journal of the American Medical Association, Good Housekeeping,* and *Children* (then the name of *Parents' Magazine*), Fremont Canning began approaching food brokers, who quickly divided themselves into two groups: those with young children, who immediately bought; and those without youngsters, who merely asked for further information and, after several sales calls, placed only small orders.

Gerber was worried until Fremont began to be flooded with mail—at the rate of 20,000 units a month. There were coupons and dollar bills plus letters from mothers with questions about child care, requests from 600 pediatricians for samples of the product, and thousands of requests for reprints of the ad itself. Of course, not all mothers bought those magazines, and not all who did responded. Accordingly, Gerber told his sales staff to count the number of diapers they spotted drying on laundry lines; by spot-checking, salespeople could roughly estimate the number of babies along their sales routes.

Armed with positive consumer response backed by dollars and

informal "projections," the company was gradually able to convince retailers that there was indeed a grocery market for strained baby foods. As Gerber had suspected, when strained baby food was sold in grocery stores, it was immediately repositioned in the consumer's mind as food that all babies could enjoy. Within six months, Gerber's Strained Vegetables were in most major market areas, and Fremont grossed $345,000 its first year in the baby food business.

By creating physical evidence of consumer demand for strained foods in the form of coupons, the company was able to refute the idea that such foods were unsalable and ended up creating a major category of convenience foods. Even though Gerber attracted sixty-eight competitors by the 1930s, the company sells 70 percent of the baby food in America and grosses $600 million annually.

•   •   •   •   •   •   •

PRODUCT   STRAINED BABY FOOD

Pivotal P: Placement

Gerber's coupon strategy forced grocers to stock strained baby food despite its poor sales history. Mothers not only bought it but were willing to pay a premium for it.

Priority P: Piggybacking

Doctors reinforced the nutritional value of canned baby food, helping some mothers overcome the guilt they felt about not straining food for their babies themselves.

•   •   •   •   •   •   •

TIMEX WATCHES   Time Bombs

Consumers get used to buying certain products in certain places. Changing these established distribution patterns can be difficult, but it is often the only road to survival for a product. In one case, a weapons maker faced extinction and made a comeback by taking watches out of the jeweler's case and putting them next to the corn plasters.

The Waterbury Watch Company of Middlebury, Connecticut, had converted to wartime production of fuses in 1942 and, during the war, had become the largest producer of timing fuses in America.

In its last full year of wartime production, Waterbury registered sales of $70 million; however, the orders stopped in 1945, and by 1948, annual sales had fallen to a paltry $300,000. The company desperately needed a new product, and president Joakim Lehmkuhl decided to make watches, "because it seemed the only thing to do."

Before the war, Waterbury had marketed the Ingersoll pocket watch, which sold for a dollar and was much favored by railroad conductors. Lehmkuhl, who had been born in Norway and educated at Harvard and M.I.T., had returned to Norway to run a small shipbuilding firm in the 1930s. Also the publisher of an anti-Nazi newspaper, Lehmkuhl fled Norway just before the start of World War II and eventually settled in Connecticut.

He and a group of businessmen had bought Waterbury Watch with the sole aim of converting it to defense production. Now, with no military market to supply, Lehmkuhl decided his only realistic choice was to capitalize on the precision-tool techniques the firm had used in making fuse timers and combine them with automation to turn out low-cost watches.

The resulting design was infinitely simpler than a Swiss watch, because metal bearings replaced the jewels used to maintain balance in the movement (in fact, the prototype was based on the mechanism that was used in Mickey Mouse watches). Moreover, since it had withstood the punishment to which children subject watches, Lehmkuhl reasoned, the watch should easily stand up to adult wear and tear.

Lehmkuhl originally thought that people might remember the Waterbury name fondly. Instead it proved to be a millstone. He said, "When the public saw a Waterbury watch, all they remembered was a dollar pocket watch. You couldn't get a $1 watch after the war." Lehmkuhl changed the company name to U.S. Time Corporation and dropped the tarnished Ingersoll name for Timex, which sounded "precise and modern." After some retooling, U.S. Time produced a sample run of watches and sent its salesmen out to show them to jewelers, the established distribution system for watches.

Lehmkuhl had expected that Timex's ease of operation and low cost ($6.95) would be attractive to jewelers; however, he badly underestimated the marketing reorientation jewelers would have had to undergo to sell Timex. For years, jewelers had regularly realized $50 profit on $100 watches (100 percent) and $400 profit on $600 watches (200 percent).

It was difficult if not impossible for them to have any interest in a $7 watch that gave them a $2.10 profit (30 percent margin). While cost was the overriding factor in the jewelers' original rejection of Timex, there was a second negative element in Lehmkuhl's marketing plan— Timex's disposability. U.S. Time salespeople preached that it was just as cheap to buy a new Timex as it was to repair an old watch. This argument totally alienated jewelers. Jewelers looked on repair work not only as a small but additional profit center but also as a valuable way of giving service to build loyalty with their (generally) well-to-do customers.

When Timex salesmen threw watches against the walls to impress dealers with their durability, the dealers could only imagine how appalled their upscale customers would be at such cheap theatrics. A jewelry store then was a refuge of elegance, a sacrosanct environment of velvet plush and gleaming gold. In such a place, the Timex sales force was as welcome as a bull in a china shop.

Rejected by jewelers, U.S. Time salesmen tried china shops and just about every other kind of retail establishment. The place where Timex took off was the corner drugstore. Nestled among the prosaic cold remedies and toothbrushes, the Timex had pizzazz. Where jewelers had looked down on the watch as a downscale "mass item," druggists were thrilled to sell what to them constituted "class merchandise." Fully 80 percent of Timex's early sales came in drugstores.

This matching of product and distribution network was poetic justice. The Timex had been designed as a practical, low-maintenance item. Robert Mohr, Timex's vice president in charge of sales, told *Advertising Age*, "We promote the watch as something for everyday use that people don't have to worry about because the cost is low."

Buoyed by initial sales, Lehmkuhl tried a series of print ads built around the Timex's indestructibility. One ad showed Ben Hogan with a Timex attached to a golf club, another pictured Mickey Mantle with the watch circling a Louisville Slugger. The ads tried to make the point that the watch could take tremendous punishment and still keep time, but some consumers remained unconvinced. Such photographs could be faked, and still pictures were a poor substitute for salesmen smacking watches against the wall. Print wasn't a dynamic enough advertising medium to bring this sales point to life.

Then, in 1954, Timex took the same concept and presented it in a more dramatic way. The company created an award-winning, point-of-purchase display that used levers to dunk a Timex into a container of water, then dropped it on an anvil where it was struck with a hammer; when the retailer fished out the watch and showed a potential buyer that it still worked, consumers got the message loud and clear.

Such a rock-'em, sock-'em sales aid would have been woefully out of place in a jewelry store, but it attracted a lot of attention in drugstores, which were, at this point, keeping Timex in business. Once the basic concept of a low-cost, low-maintenance watch proved to be salable, Timex produced a waterproof watch meant to retail for $12.95. Although some druggists were wary of the higher price, the waterproof Timex also was soon on display at drugstores, stationery outlets, tobacconists, even hardware stores.

The watch-against-the-wall routine, which had failed in person and as a print ad, surfaced again when U.S. Time Corporation had generated enough revenues for a television campaign. Beginning in 1956, newsman John Cameron Swayze, the host of NBC-TV's *Camel News Caravan*, emceed a series of famous TV "torture tests" by throwing a Timex into a paint mixer. In the words of the commercial, "It took a licking and kept on ticking."

What made the commercials work was the fact that they were done live. No camera trickery was possible, and the public could see for itself whether or not the watch still worked. Taking a chance that a Timex wouldn't work—live on national television—was the twentieth century equivalent of the Sherwin-Williams money-back guarantee. It told the public volumes about the manufacturer's belief in the product, because no sane manufacturer would take such chances if there were any possibility of failure.

When Timex sponsored a program like a Bob Hope special or an NBC "White Paper," viewers knew they would be entertained while being pitched, adding an element of fun and anticipation to the commercial. The attitude was, "What will those crazy people at Timex think of next?" The public even began dreaming up its own torture tests, and Timex got 1,000 suggestions a month. (One was from an Air Force pilot who volunteered to crash an airplane to prove that Timex had the right stuff.)

Even when the live demonstrations didn't work exactly right, Timex sold watches. In one live commercial, a watch that was attached to the spinning propeller of a motorboat flew off. Newsman Swayze straightfacedly assured viewers, "It worked perfectly during rehearsals." The audience howled, and the watches kept right on selling. By the time the series stopped airing, Timexes had been attached to surfboards, a marksman's arm, a racehorse's leg, and the wrist of a high diver plunging off the La Perla cliffs 135 feet above Acapulco.

By 1960, Timex was grossing $70 million again and was selling 7 million watches a year in the United States—one out of every three watches sold, according to market researcher Alfred Politz. Nor was this an isolated case. Timex was selling a third of all the watches in Great Britain and had factories producing watches in England, Scotland, Germany, and Besançon, France, just twenty-seven miles from the Swiss border. In 1962, Timex began selling a twenty-one-jewel Timex, which sold for $21.95 and, by offering jewelers a 44 percent markup, was finally able to add some jewelers to its roster of 100,000 retail accounts.

Other manufacturers were impressed with Lehmkuhl's engineering skills. Now Timex Corporation, the company supplied parts for Polaroid cameras, and the military-industrial complex, which had made Waterbury Watch prosper in the 1940s, became a big customer of Timex's in the 1970s. The company maintains "the cleanest room in the world" in Irvington-on-Hudson, New York, for work on gyroscopes and timing devices, which are used by both the U.S. Navy and the U.S. Air Force.

As Timex moved into higher-priced watches, the torture tests were retired for more "image-oriented" advertising; however, the tests remained firmly rooted in the public consciousness. Timex revived the theme during the 1986 Super Bowl with a commercial that cost a cool $1 million to film. The spot featured two divers discovering buried treasure—a 1½-ton, 60-by-20-foot fiberglass and plywood model of Timex's Atlantis 100. It was, of course, still ticking.

•   •   •   •   •   •   •

PRODUCT   TIMEX WATCHES

Pivotal P: Placement

Designed as a low-cost, low-maintenance item, Timex was cut off from the established point-of-sale, jewelry stores, but received tremendous acceptance in drugstores.

Priority P's: Promotion, Publicity

Timex stressed the punishment it could endure in a series of television commercials that generated favorable publicity nationally for many years.

•   •   •   •   •   •   •

TUPPERWARE   Party Line

The peacetime economy that nearly made military suppliers like Waterbury Watch extinct was a boom period for makers of housewares and furnishings as reunited couples bought houses for the first time or moved into larger second homes. Amid this rash of expansion, the inventor of a unique plastic container came close to financial disaster. In the end, however, an enterprising woman convinced him that, when it comes to selling housewares, there's no place like home.

Earl Tupper was the very model of the postwar wonder boy.

A self-proclaimed "ham inventor and Yankee trader," Tupper had taken a paraffinlike substance he called Poly-T (we know it as polyethylene) and made it into an unbreakable, shape-retaining plastic. It was temperature-resistant, could be molded into all sorts of containers without cracking or splitting, and Tupper improved it even further by inventing a seal that made the container waterproof and airtight.

By 1948, his process was used to make nesting cups for thermos bottles, snack bowls sold with Canada Dry beverages, and 300,000 inexpensive cigarette cases for Camels. Over and above its applicability to packaging, Tupper created lines of double-walled ice cube containers, poker chips, and bowls with close-fitting caps. (A Massachusetts insane asylum particularly liked these; they were so much quieter than aluminum containers.) To top it off, New York's Museum of Modern Art put two Tupper bowls on permanent display, and the Massachusetts farmboy told *Time* that he expected annual sales of $5 million.

It might have worked out just that way had Tupper not become obsessed with selling plastic housewares. He believed the airtight seal was a natural for preserving leftovers, but the public disagreed. Consumers were much more used to using glass and tin to preserve food and had trouble working the plastic seal. Many containers that had been sold were returned because they "didn't work like the man showed me." Retailers didn't want to take the time to be Tupper's (unpaid) demonstrators, and the bowls and containers began gathering dust on the shelves of houseware stores. By 1951, Tupper had abandoned selling plastic wares at retail; but then he met Mrs. Brownie Humphrey Wise.

A veteran of the "home party" system of selling, Wise had hawked Stanley Home Products, working her way up to a distributorship. Since Stanley didn't offer a complete line of housewares, she had often used Tupperware to fill out her line. Given the time to demonstrate the tricky seals in a low-pressure atmosphere, Wise was able to make housewives understand the practical application of Tupperware in their homes.

She arranged a meeting with Tupper and pointed out that the home-party format kept a potential buyer in and around Tupperware for an average of two hours, plenty of time to dispel its newness and unfamiliarity. Moreover, the relaxed atmosphere lowered sales resistance, and the "party" made housewives more likely to spend. In April 1951, Tupperware Home Parties, Inc., was formed. According to *Business Week*, "the company cleared out of all retail outlets, [and] settled on the home party as its only point of sales."

When the program became established, Tupperware dealers (95

percent of whom were housewives) received 35 percent of the gross sales from each party (which averaged $56). Once dealers put together groups of four fellow dealers, they became unit managers and got a small override on the other dealers' sales. As distributors, they got an even larger discount but also had to warehouse the goods.

From miniscule sales in 1950, the home-party idea produced $25 million worth of business in 1954, and Tupper sold the company to Rexall Drug Company in 1958 for more than $9 million. When Tupper died in 1983, there were an average of 75,000 Tupperware parties a day around the world, and they are just as popular today.

•   •   •   •   •   •   •

PRODUCT   TUPPERWARE

Pivotal *P*: Placement

Retail clerks didn't want to waste time showing off Tupperware's features. Put in the home and demonstrated by friends to other friends, the product quickly became established.

Priority *P*: Promotion

The party atmosphere transformed the mundane purchasing of such goods as melon ballers into an "event." The party made buying "fun," a social occasion, and it lowered sales resistance.

•   •   •   •   •   •   •

L'EGGS   Stocking Feat

Home—and home parties—were increasingly left behind as more and more women entered the work force. Seeking to be as comfortable as possible in the workaday world, women began replacing girdles, stockings, and garter belts with pantyhose in the mid-1960s, even though they were expensive and unreliable as to fit and durability. A manufacturer solved the problem by merchandising what had been a specialty fashion item as if it were a commodity.

Pantyhose were very expensive initially ($8 a pair) and could be found only in specialty and department stores. As they spread to drugstores and supermarkets, toward the end of the decade, prices dropped but the product remained unreliable. With as many as six hundred private brands competing for consumer attention, there was no market leader, no bellwether to make pantyhose, rather than stockings, the standard for working women.

The Hanes Corporation, of Winston-Salem, North Carolina, was selling a product about the same as 599 others until the production department developed a stretchable, nonsagging pantyhose. They were more expensive to produce than even Hanes's department store brand, but they fit nearly 90 percent of all women, a possible mass market.

Hanes executives were split on which direction to take with the new pantyhose. Some executives wanted to take the high road, raise the price, cater to women with high disposable incomes, and capitalize on high profit margins.

Robert Elberson, president of the company's hosiery division, had a different idea. He had noticed Lady Brevoni, a West German brand, on supermarket shelves in ready-to-display cartons. Even though Lady Brevoni sold for seventy-nine cents, its manufacturer was still offering the retailer a 40 percent profit margin. Elberson decided to go the mass market route rather than rely on high margins to make the new product profitable.

Making the leap to a commodity product in what had previously been a specialty category required an executive with packaged goods experience. David E. Harrold, formerly with General Foods, was given the assignment of bringing Hanes pantyhose to drugstores and supermarkets and immediately shook up the conservative hosiery industry by hiring not one, but two marketing research firms and paying them $400,000, an unheard-of figure.

What emerged from the studies was rampant distrust of bargain brands of pantyhose. Women complained that the same brand would sag one week and bind the next. Additionally, those that bought pantyhose despite the problems generally bought them in department and specialty stores; only 12 percent of pantyhose were sold in supermarkets.

Harrold had a tough assignment. He and his colleagues had to create a national market for a product that wasn't regarded as a quality item, accepted as a necessity by its target audience, or established in the mass-merchandising market. On top of everything else, the product had to appear familiar yet be different from hundreds of other brands and be presented in the smallest, most eye-catching amount of space.

Dancer-Fitzgerald-Sample was assigned by Harrold to advertise the new Hanes brand and gave the packaging assignment to Lublain, Smith, Carnse, and Ferriter. After crushing a sample pair of pantyhose in his hand, Roger Ferriter decided on an egg-shaped package because it "is the most beautiful package in nature. It was familiar and conducive to the shelves of the supermarket." He combined the egg, the leg, and an apostrophe to give L'eggs a distinctive name, a dash of French flavoring, and a symbolic shape to the shapeless pantyhose.

Then a Hanes engineer designed a free-standing display rack as innovative in its way as Ferriter's package. The rack made L'eggs stand out at the point-of-sale, and, since it was only two feet high, it was ideal for high-traffic areas. The unit held twenty-four dozen pairs of pantyhose in many colors, styles, and sizes and had space for coupons and promotional literature.

The finishing touch was the introduction of 450 Hanes "route girls." Originally clad in red, white, and blue hot pants, these women restocked shelves, arranged brochures, collected sales data (to make the company more responsive to buying trends), and reported any discounting of Hanes's fair-trade pricing policy.

Add this all up and look at it from the retailers' point of view. They had no responsibility for stocking the attractive unit, earned a 42 percent profit margin (seven times the average return on a per-square-foot basis), and didn't pay for the goods, which were delivered on consignment, until they were already sold. The route girls caused a lot of positive in-store comment and, as an added bonus, L'eggs was introduced with $10 million worth of TV advertising with the slogan, "Our L'eggs fit your legs."

L'eggs debuted in Milwaukee, Kansas City, Sacramento, and Portland, Maine, in May 1970, and was introduced into major cities six months later, in October. It was regularly identified as "my regular brand" six months after introduction by 25 percent of all women. With limited distribution, Hanes rang up sales of $9 million in 1970, $54 million in 1971, and $112 million in 1972. By March 1973, 30 percent of all the hosiery sold in drugstores and supermarkets was L'eggs.

•   •   •   •   •   •   •

PRODUCT   PANTYHOSE

Pivotal *P*: Placement

Rather than charge premium prices for pantyhose in department stores, Hanes chose mass distribution and made its profits on volume rather than margins.

Priority *P*'s: Packaging, Promotion

L'eggs's package gave it instant familiarity. The display rack made the product more noticeable, and route girls created favorable word-of-mouth publicity for L'eggs.

•   •   •   •   •   •   •

Chapter Seven

DON'T **PRICE** IT

WRONG

• • • • • • •

DON McLean, the composer of "American Pie," wrote another song called "The More You Pay, the More It's Worth."

Well, it just ain't so, Don. In 1979, Peter C. Reisz, a professor at the University of Iowa, tried to relate the prices of 679 brands of packaged foods with their ratings by Consumers Union over a period of fifteen years. He concluded that "The correlation between quality and price for packaged food products is near zero."

That would be bad news for marketers except for the fact that old habits die hard. Consumers are accustomed to paying higher prices for certain products and would resist changing the long-held notion that "If it costs more, it's got to be better."

Of course, this is nonsense. While prices can be created using Lotus 1-2-3 and other spreadsheets, pricing remains an art, not a science. Consider the case of two liquor products with declining sales. Fleischmann's gin wasn't selling well at $4.50 for a 750-milliliter bottle. The price was raised fifty cents with no change and sales rose; when a new package was used and the price was raised another fifty cents, sales rose even faster.

You can even see sales decline and make more money with shrewd pricing. Heublein, which makes Smirnoff vodka, also makes Popov, which was selling slowly. The average price of $4.10 a fifth was raised by 8 percent with no change in the product itself. Sales declined 1 percent, but because of the higher price, profits increased 30 percent.

Pricing Makes Products Primo   The winner of an NBC soap opera contest wrote the show's promotion director a six-page personal letter, which included the information that "My favorite foods is gormay."

What transforms popcorn into gourmet popcorn or makes Stouffer's Lean Cuisine gourmet frozen food? The answer is—Price.

Ice cream used to be Breyers and Dolly Madison. Now it's Häagen-Dazs, which sounds Swedish but started in the Bronx, Frusen Glädjé (another made-up name), and DoveBars. Michael Stefanos, son of DoveBar founder Leo Stefanos, says, "The moment my dad said, 'Son, I've invented the DoveBar,' I knew I wasn't going to grow up to be a veterinarian."

DoveBar sounds expensive, and its name is one reason that superpremium ice cream products have relegated Breyers and Dolly Madison to the back of the ice cream case. While it can be (and is) argued that superpremiums taste better, the buyers of flavors like Cherry Garcia and Heath Bar Crunch are clearly buying image, just as Volkswagen buyers bought it in the 1950s. When you serve DoveBars, you make a statement that can't be made dishing out Breyers.

Tiered Pricing   Pricing is a tricky business. Consumers assume that prices are set in stone, when prices are perhaps the most fluid part of the marketing equation. A leading hotelier once said, "Anyone who pays rack rate (list price) for a hotel room hasn't asked for a better one."

The airlines industry even assigns different prices to different segments in advance of delivering its service. Writing in *Business Horizons*, professor Thomas Nagle says, "Many airlines . . . could not survive if they treated all segments of the transportation market alike. Were every traveler required to purchase first-class service at a first-class price, airlines would soon go broke for lack of passengers."

Instead, computers create models for each flight which take into account weekend, weekday, and holiday travel patterns, weather and climate, time of day, and local festivals and fairs. Arriving at an estimate of how crowded the flight will be (the "load factor"), the computer decides how many tickets will be available for advance purchase and how many will be offered at other discounts. The long lead time needed for travel plans gives the airlines plenty of notice to figure prices most efficiently.

Price and Positioning The public may desire a certain characteristic in a product but be unwilling to pay for it. One good example is "sportiness" in a car. Analyze the nebulous concept of "sportiness," and you discover that it entails rounded, sculptured bodies, which involve more precise molds and are therefore more costly to manufacture than rectangular shapes.

Nevertheless, through extensive study, Ford discovered that a market segment existed that valued "sportiness" but didn't want to pay for a "sports car," which was viewed as expensive. The only way to make a product to fit this market segment was to use its eventual selling price as a target before it went into production, then check costs every step of the way to reach the goal of producing a low-priced, "sporty" car. The result of this "buyer-oriented" pricing policy was the Mustang, one of the most successful new product introductions in Ford history.

Pricing often involves finding "niches" that will pay more for your product and "segmenting the market," as the cigarette business has done with filters, premium length, and reduced nicotine. Margarine was just margarine until Imperial trumpeted itself as "the high-priced spread," segmenting the market and positioning itself as "worth the extra pennies."

One of the constant battles in marketing is monitoring the tension between products viewed as "commodities" and others viewed as "specialty items" which command higher prices. Soap was a commodity until Softsoap came along. On the other hand, decaffeinated coffees were a specialty item until anticaffeine advertising increased sales to the point where it became a commodity. (The explosion of generic brands in the late 1970s signaled that a whole slew of "specialty items" had, in fact, become commodities.) New products (and new segments) are hampered by high production costs until enough consumers decide, "I've just got to have one of those."

SINGER SEWING MACHINES   Buying Time

One entrepreneur found the right way to market with a unique price-cutting move. Instead of lowering the price, he strettttched it a little.

Hailed by Mahatma Gandhi as the world's most useful invention, the sewing machine went largely unsold for sixty-six years after it was first patented. For one thing, it didn't work all the time. For another, it cost too much. Finally, it couldn't be marketed to its target audience because of social pressures (a perception problem if ever there was one). But it was on the subject of price that the Singer Sewing Machine Company made its breakthrough and changed the world of buying and selling as well.

Elias Howe patented the first American version of the machine, although it lacked several essential features. Precisely because it didn't work very well, Howe's version attracted more attention from other inventors.

One of them was Isaac Merritt Singer, who, along with lawyer Edward Clark, formed the oddest couple in American business history. Singer, a flamboyant inventor, was loutish, nearly illiterate, and completely amoral. Formerly an actor and manager of a theatrical troupe, he cadged money from partners whenever possible, hectored them for living off his genius, and once said, "I don't care a damn for the invention. The dimes are what I'm after." Equally cavalier with the weaker sex, he fathered twenty-four children by five different women, only two of whom he married.

The methodical Clark, in contrast, was a junior partner in the New York City law firm of Jordan, Clark and Company and the scion of an old and wealthy family from Cooperstown, New York. Originally a Sunday school teacher, he studied law and quickly rose to eminence in Cooperstown, then Albany, and ultimately New York City. In addition to these impressive credentials, he had also made an advantageous marriage; senior partner Ambrose Jordan was Clark's father-in-law and was later named attorney general of New York state.

Singer and Clark came from divergent backgrounds, had different ethical standards, and brought separate skills to their partnership. Singer contributed mechanical excellence and played the role of Acclaimed Inventor with consummate skill, serving as a model for Thomas Edison. Clark's contributions were not, as you might expect, oriented toward legal skills like negotiation or litigation. Instead, as events would prove, the man was a marketing genius who had no training in this field yet performed brilliantly when circumstances dictated.

They had first met when Singer invented a machine for carving wood-block type, and Clark had traded his legal services for 37 percent of the invention. It looked like a good deal when bookseller George Zieber paid $3,000 for the rights and set up a machine shop in Boston for Singer. Unfortunately, the building was destroyed in a fire that killed sixty-three people; the invention died completely when mechanical typesetting was introduced.

Nevertheless, Clark had been impressed with Singer's mechanical aptitude, and when Singer approached him about working on the sewing machine, Clark made one of history's best barter deals: He traded his services for one-third of what was then I. M. Singer & Company. (Clark later became an equal partner when Singer forced Zieber to sell his interest.) Singer was anxious to get Clark involved in the sewing machine business at once, because Elias Howe had seen Singer's son William demonstrating a machine in the window of a New York clothing store, and Singer feared legal reprisals.

Clark patented Singer's invention on August 12, 1851, and made ready to go to war when Howe sued for $25,000. From 1851 to 1856, American newspapers and courts were the battleground of "the sewing machine war," as Howe, Singer, and several other manufacturers sued and countersued each other. Despite Clark's attempts to prove that the Chinese had invented the sewing machine two thousand years earlier, Howe won a $15,000 judgment against the I. M. Singer Company in New York state.

Despite this victory, it wasn't clear that Howe would make a lot of money. Sewing machine patents had become entangled because no single complete machine had ever been invented by a single person. Every inventor had added a new wrinkle, and by 1867 nearly 900 improvements had been patented. Howe, Singer, and two other firms—Wheeler & Wilson and Grover & Baker—each controlled valuable patents, although Howe had the lion's share. These partnerships were paying Howe royalties on each machine, but the basic patent issues remained unsolved.

Orlando Potter, president of Grover & Baker, broke the deadlock with the ingenious idea that the four holders of principal patents should pool them instead of wasting time and money in court. The pool, formally called the Sewing Machine Combination, agreed to split a fifteen-dollar licensing fee for every machine produced, while Howe was to receive an additional five dollars for every machine sold in the U.S. and a one-dollar override on every machine exported.

The patent fight had been fierce, but now it was over and the business at hand was not inventing or producing sewing machines but selling them. Since there were as many as 30,000 professional seamstresses at the time, the market potential was there.

In *A Capitalist Romance: Singer and the Sewing Machine*, author Ruth Brandon says, "Looked at in the abstract, in terms purely of ideas and markets, the sewing machine could not fail." She points out that men's shirts, which took fourteen hours and twenty-six minutes to stitch by hand, could be completed in an hour and sixteen minutes with a sewing machine.

But potential alone never sold anything, and the sewing machine had three problems to overcome from a marketing standpoint. Such devices were:

- *Unreliable*—The 10,000 machines that had been sold by 1856 were all handmade, which made parts almost impossible to replace. Consequently, sales were restricted to big-city tailor shops and clothing stores, which could call in repairmen quickly if needed.
- *Complicated*—As a practical matter, women were not hired then to do jobs that required them to use machines. Accordingly, the target market for the sewing machine was restricted from using it by history and social pressures.
- *Expensive*—Even if most women had believed they could op-

erate the machines, sewing machines were enormously expensive, costing $125 in pre–Civil War dollars at a time when the average annual family income was only $500, four times the cost of the machine. The contraption was a meaningless luxury.

Given this perception, the price issue was the one that occupied most of Clark's time, and his ad hoc adaptation of a Cyrus McCormick idea eventually became marketing dogma. McCormick, the inventor of the reaper, had faced a similar problem—selling an expensive, unfamiliar machine. He had allowed farmers to split the payment for his reapers into two parts, one before and one after the annual harvest. Even so, few farmers could afford two large cash payments, just as few consumers could afford to make two payments of $62.50 for a sewing machine.

Then Clark hit upon the idea of cutting the two large payments into many small ones with his "hire/pay plan," what we know today as the installment plan. Consumers put five dollars down and paid the rest off at three to five dollars a month, including interest. Although local furniture manufacturers had offered such time-payment plans, I. M. Singer & Company became the first merchant with national distribution to offer installment-plan buying.

Clark's ads read:

> Why not rent a sewing machine to the housewife and apply the rental fee to the purchase price of the machine? Her husband cannot accuse her of running him into debt since he is merely hiring or renting the machine and under no obligation to buy.

The message used language that women of today would find degrading, and Clark's ploy of "renting" the machine was a flimsy disguise for a sale. Moreover, the whole concept of installment buying remains a disputed moral and economic question more than a century later, particularly in the United States, the world's largest debtor nation. Nevertheless, lawyer Clark had found a clever way to sidestep the issue of high prices and had gotten the sewing machine into the American home where women could get accustomed to using it.

The idea immediately bore results as this table of sales figures shows:

1853	810
1854	879
1855	883
1856	2,564

Clark knew that women were the group he had to convince about the sewing machine, both for immediate sales and for long-range planning. He tempted those with local clout—wives of teachers, clergymen, and newspaper publishers—by offering them 50 percent discounts, then merchandised these sales to "influentials" by linking the sewing machine to building character in children. A company booklet read, "The great importance of the sewing machine is its influence upon the home . . . in the increase of time and opportunity for that early training of children, for lack of which so many pitiful wrecks are strewn along the shores of life."

In addition to lowering prices and gathering endorsements, Clark came up with another brainstorm to make sewing machines less daunting to women. He hired seamstresses, taught them how to use the machine, and placed them in the front windows of his retail stores as demonstrators. Female passersby could see for themselves that there really wasn't much to working a sewing machine. Demonstration changes perception.

When I. M. Singer & Company subsequently franchised sewing machine agencies, the agent had to agree to hire a female demonstrator and show her sewing in the window for a set number of hours a day.

By 1856, it had become abundantly clear that Clark's Sunday school teacher exterior hid the persona of a born salesman. Even though the partnership had just gotten on its feet, Clark was impatient with growth and saw yet another way to boost sales more quickly by further reducing prices. Beginning in 1857, I. M. Singer & Company offered the first "trade-in allowance," couching the innovation in a believable argument. Clark's thesis was that the public wouldn't buy new Singers while they still had their old Wheeler & Wilson and Grover & Baker machines. In masterful copy, Clark "confided" to the public that, "These worthless Machines now stand directly in the way of the sale of good ones. Their existence causes great pecuniary loss to us." Accordingly, it was to his firm's advantage to get rid of these machines, and the fifty-dollar trade-in was an inducement to retire all non-Singer machines, even those that were "inferior or wholly worthless."

This tactic, another prong in the price war, gave Singer an aura of leadership in the field, and sales in 1857 exceeded those of the two previous years combined.

A bit later, I. M. Singer & Company also became the first American-based multinational corporation. While Singer sewing machines were selling in America better than they had been originally, Wheeler & Wilson outsold them nearly two to one. Clark established offices in Paris, Glasgow, and Rio de Janeiro, and by 1861, more Singers were sold in Europe than in the United States.

The outbreak of the Civil War in April 1861 eventually made Singer number one in America because shipments of raw materials were interrupted, delaying production for all manufacturers. But more important, a wartime series of taxes added levies every time the product was resold, making the price higher from manufacturer to wholesaler to retailer. Foreign sales faced no such taxation, and Singer's revenues from worldwide sales essentially funded production expansion that lowered manufacturing costs. By 1870, Singers sold for sixty-four dollars at retail, and Singer became America's lowest-priced and most popular sewing machine.

Singer's reaction to this success was to play the Great Inventor at every turn, which proved to be his undoing. One day, he was driving with one of his many women in a canary-yellow carriage of his own Brobdingnagian design. (It held thirty-five passengers and also had room for a nursery and a small orchestra.) He was spotted by an enraged Mary Ann Sponsler, the unwed mother of eight of his children, who hauled him into court. The resultant publicity revealed that, unbeknownst to his conservative partner, Singer had been supporting no less than four separate families in New York for at least nine years.

Clark, already chafing under the idea that he had made the sewing machine a household staple while Isaac Singer got the credit, used the opportunity to sever his ties with Singer. After a number of bitter exchanges, Clark and Singer parted ways, each with 2,075 shares of stock, and I. M. Singer & Company became the Singer Manufacturing Company in July 1863. By 1958, every share was worth $36,000 after stock splits and had paid an additional $131,340 in dividends.

Since both men were convinced that their contributions alone had made the business work, they felt that, upon their retirement, any office boy could run the Singer Manufacturing Company. Inslee Hopper, the office boy at the time of the break-up, remembers Singer saying, "Clark won't let me be president—and I swear I won't let him. Our president ought to be a married man—the office requires some dignity. You are pretty young, but we think if you are married we could try to get along with you as president." The dazzled Hopper said he knew a girl and told a historian, "That evening I hurried round and told her my dilemma. She was nice about it, and five weeks later we were married and I was drawing $25,000 a year salary." It was the fastest rise from office boy to president in American corporate history.

That ended the founders' involvement with sewing machines, but not their mark upon history. Singer's son Paris married Isadora Duncan and helped finance the building of Palm Beach, Florida. According to author Ruth Brandon, Isaac Singer's last legal widow, Isabella, was the model for the Statue of Liberty. Clark's heirs have beautified Cooperstown, New York, and endowed both the National Baseball Hall of Fame and the Metropolitan Museum of Art.

Despite their obvious personality differences, the flamboyant genius and the lawyer-marketer had combined their efforts to make the sewing machine affordable, reliable, and a success with consumers around the world.

When social conditions changed, and more women began working, the Singer Company began diversifying into other durable goods like refrigerators. Sewing machine sales peaked at 3 million in 1978 and, in 1979, the company began directing more and more of its efforts to aerospace; on July 5, 1986, the sewing machine division was spun off as SSMC (Singer Sewing Machine Corporation) to become what a press release calls "the oldest new company in the world."

•   •   •   •   •   •   •

PRODUCT   SEWING MACHINE

Pivotal P: Price

Edward Clark reduced the cash outlay for the sewing machine by letting consumers buy now, pay later, then added the trade-in allowance to make purchasing even easier.

Primary P's: Perception, Promotion

Women weren't confident about working sewing machines until Singer put female demonstrators in store windows, which changed this perception.

•   •   •   •   •   •   •

BARBASOL   Close Shave

Everybody loves a comeback story, particularly one involving an old favorite. Barbasol Shave Cream, an oldie but goodie, has come from oblivion all the way back to the top and now leads the $182 million aerosol-foam segment of the shaving-cream category, the first time since the 1940s that Barbasol has led even a submarket.

Other marketers may wax poetic about the bonds between older products and consumers, but Rom (short for Romulus) Cartwright of Pfizer, Inc., told *Fortune*, "If you're going to revive an old brand, you've got to have a reason other than nostalgia." The reason that Pfizer remarketed Barbasol turns out to be lackluster marketing by the competition.

Once a category of image brands like Noxzema ("Take it off, take it alllll off"), shave cream became more and more a commodity as health and beauty aids began showing up on supermarket shelves. Consumers don't attach much status or imagery to products jammed between mops and trash bags.

This change was good news for Barbasol, a product that once reminded radio listeners that it was: "No brush, no lather, no rub-in/Wet your razor and begin." And it was good news for the guys at Pfizer who were smart enough to grab opportunity by the *P*'s.

When foam aerosols like Rise first appeared in the 1950s, tubed shaving creams like Barbasol became old hat. When the company tried its own me-too aerosol, it bombed. (One executive says, "It dried up immediately and felt like you were shaving with sandpaper.") From that point until 1985, Barbasol was a ghost product, there on the shelves but largely unadvertised and given a minimum of marketing attention.

Then Pfizer decided to change its tactics. Bob Unger, Barbasol's vice president of marketing, says the company decided on a four-point strategy, which included:

1. *Changing the price.* Barbasol raised its price originally, which changed consumer perception of the brand. Says Unger, "Psychologically, Barbasol was now a regularly priced shave cream which, occasionally, you could get at a lower price." Then, Pfizer concentrated on price promotions while competitors were using coupons, refunds, and sweepstakes. Unger says, "Every man eighteen to sixty needs shaving cream. By running specials, retailers may catch them when they want to stock up."

2. *Advertising on television.* The pricing strategy carried over to Barbasol's TV commercial, which shows a rich man and a butler in a lavish bathroom. The idea is that His Nibs can afford to buy any shave cream, but he saves money on Barbasol and then spends it on luxuries. The commercial has run for five years and has cost Pfizer only $3 million in TV time.

3. *Introducing new "flavors."* Until 1984, every brand of foam aerosol came in regular and menthol. Then, Edge introduced lemon-lime and it started to take off. Unger says, "We jumped on it, had immediate success, and got into other line extensions which proved even more successful." Pfizer introduced Barbasol Skin Conditioner Shave Cream in 1985 and Sensitive Skin, which became the company's second biggest

seller, in 1986. Together, these line extensions make up a
third of Barbasol's business.

4. *Riding the wave.* Unger frankly admits that Barbasol down-
   priced its product just when shaving cream ceased to be an
   image product. "The market had started to shift toward
   'value brands' anyway; now Barbasol, Palmolive, and store
   brands account for 40 percent of sales."

The remarketing effort began in February 1985. Unit sales of
aerosol shave cream fell by 2 percent that year, but Barbasol's rose 12
percent. Within a year, it had passed Noxzema to place third, and it
took over first place in 1987.

• • • • • • •

PRODUCT   BARBASOL

Pivotal P: Price

Barbasol, a ghost brand, gained significant market share by becoming a low-
priced brand just at the time shave cream ceased to be an image product.

Primary P: Promotion

Rather than apologize for its stance, Barbasol made a plus out of downpricing
with a commercial showing a rich man who used Barbasol to save his pennies.

• • • • • • •

CULLIGAN   Deep Water

Everybody falls in love with an idea now and then, sometimes with
disastrous results. Emmet J. Culligan fell in love with the idea of softening water, and it took him fourteen years to turn his million-dollar
idea into a million-dollar business. He succeeded by pricing his product as if it were a service.

At age twenty-one, Culligan inherited $38,000 from his father
and invested it in Iowa and Minnesota real estate. The land had been
worth $200,000 at one time but lost nearly all its value during the

1921 farm depression, when corn sold for eleven cents a bushel and cost twelve to plant. During liquidation, he accepted $18 for a $600 car.

He returned to St. Paul to live with his mother and shortly thereafter ran into a friend working for a water-softening company. The friend showed him how magnesium and calcium were filtered out, thus "softening" the water, and got Culligan a job as the firm's Iowa sales manager. After a week, Culligan told a superior, "You charge too much for your product. Nobody can afford to pay $400 for a water softener." He was fired.

Culligan had learned just enough to become interested in water softening just when his sister Anne was studying chemistry at the University of Minnesota. One of her professors showed him how to make zeolite, the active ingredient in water softening. (It is made by combining and then drying sodium silicate and sodium aluminate.)

After experimenting on his mother's stove, Culligan moved to Phoenix and began selling zeolite there. Just when he was becoming successful, he was sued for patent infringement and was forced to finance a seven-year court fight. He "won," but wound up owing $41,000 in legal fees.

In debt at the height of the Depression (1935), Culligan still searched for a way to lower the cost of water softening and eventually created a 9-by-42-inch tank filled with zeolite. (When the zeolite was used up, the company replaced the entire tank.) Instead of selling the equipment, he decided to sell a water-softening service. He reasoned that the consumer didn't know or care about the equipment, what was important was the service, which could be provided at a far, far lower price than the equipment.

Unable to afford a scouting trip to the Southwest, Culligan looked for land in the Chicago area and discovered several miles of paved, vacant land on either side of the Milwaukee Railroad tracks in Northbrook, Illinois. The streets had been paved in hopes of attracting industry, but the plan died during the Depression.

Using $50 in savings and a $500 bank loan, Culligan rented space in Jock McLachlan's blacksmith shop. When McLachlan, a member of the town council, heard of Culligan's idea to manufacture zeolite, he approached his fellow council members, and the town *gave* Culligan the land, figuring correctly that a successful water-softening firm would markedly raise employment in Northbrook.

Culligan offered his service through municipal water departments, which had to make house calls to read meters anyway. The problem was that meter readers didn't like carrying the 165-pound tanks up and down cellar stairs. Eventually, Culligan sold franchises, and by 1941, he had 151. When postwar inflation raised the costs of labor, cars, and gasoline, Culligan developed a smaller, automatic water softener that could be recharged right at home. Even with finance charges, consumers could lease the machine economically and maintain it for a small monthly fee.

By the mid-1950s, Culligan was advertising on radio. In 1958, commercials written by Dallas Williams and voiced by his wife, Jean, made America reverberate to the cry of "Hey, Culligan Man!"

Jean Williams's voice not only got the audience's attention but also let housewives know that it was all right for women to be interested in such a dull, technical matter. *Business Week* commented, "If you have a product with a sales message that's hard to get across to customers, try selling them the salesman rather than the product."

The salesman talked about benefits—less money spent on soap, shinier hair, cleaner bodies—and didn't dwell on the details. Sales doubled from $11.2 million in 1958 to $22.5 million in 1963. By 1986, the company was generating over $100 million annually as part of Beatrice Foods.

•   •   •   •   •   •   •

PRODUCT   WATER SOFTENER

Pivotal *P*: Price

Rather than sell a high-priced machine, Emmet Culligan decided to lease water-softening equipment, which cut the price of getting the service.

Priority *P*: Promotion

Jean Williams's voice got women interested in the subject of softening water and made them more aware of its health and beauty benefits.

•   •   •   •   •   •   •

PEPSI-COLA   The Price Is Right

None of the success stories recounted in this book is as dramatic as the remarketing of Pepsi-Cola, which began before Franklin D. Roosevelt took office and continues to this day.

Pepsi-Cola's history is a textbook example of all the *P*'s in action, and you'll have no trouble spotting them as you study the company's ups and downs. Despite this plenitude of *P*'s, Pepsi would not exist today had it not been for a price gimmick.

In 1931, Pepsi was suffering from its third bankruptcy, while Coca-Cola was the world's best-selling, best-known, best-packaged, and best-advertised product. By 1986, after changes in the formula, packaging innovations, promotional wizardry, and dramatic repositioning, Pepsi had become:

- a corporation with annual sales of $9.3 billion versus Coca-Cola Corporation's $8.4 billion;
- the world's largest operator of restaurants;
- the leader in U.S. cola sales in supermarkets.

Caleb Bradham, a pharmacist in New Bern, North Carolina, made the first Pepsi-Cola in 1893 by mixing the cola nut with pepsin, sugar, vanilla, oils, and spices. When "Brad's Drink" became popular in surrounding communities, he changed the name and incorporated as the Pepsi-Cola Company on December 30, 1902.

Within a year of the drink's invention, Bradham was producing 8,000 gallons of syrup, and five years later sales hit 100,000 gallons. Then Pepsi got whipsawed in the commodity crunch of 1920; sugar, which Bradham had bought at twenty-two and a half cents a pound in May, was worth just three and a half cents a pound in December, and he lost $150,000. (Coca-Cola convinced its bottlers to pay the difference between the regular price and the inflated price of sugar it had been forced to pay.) Bradham took the loss alone and had no choice but to declare bankruptcy on March 2, 1923. Wall Street financier Roy C. Megargel bought Bradham out, went bankrupt himself in 1925, and, with the company's "network" of bottlers down to two, filed his second petition of bankruptcy on May 18, 1931.

The very next day, a shrewd entrepreneur named Charles Guth decided to buy Pepsi. He wanted the company, not because he believed in the product and thought he could turn it around for fun and profit, but simply for spite.

Guth had gained control of the Loft's Candy Store chain in 1930 and had observed that Loft's was selling lots of Coca-Cola at its 115 soda fountains. In 1930, in fact, Loft's had bought 31,000 gallons of Coca-Cola syrup and had served 3.9 million Cokes. Guth was, as we shall see, always one to look for an edge, and he felt that the syrup volume he was generating entitled him to the wholesale price. Coca-Cola turned him down in a series of increasingly bitter meetings. Enraged, Guth discovered Pepsi-Cola's abject financial condition and agreed to loan Megargel $10,500 to buy its assets at the bankruptcy sale. Loft's replaced Coke with Pepsi at all its outlets, and although the Coca-Cola Corporation sued, contending that Loft's customers expected to be served Coke, the suit was quickly dismissed.

Guth bought Megargel out, and Pepsi-Cola chemist Tom Elmezzi changed the drink's formula, dropping the pepsin that originally gave the drink its name. Despite the changes, Pepsi's presence in the marketplace didn't improve: From 1931 to 1933, Pepsi sold only $100,000 worth of syrup, nearly all of it to Loft's. Sales were so poor that a contrite Charles Guth even offered to sell out to Coca-Cola; his offer was firmly declined.

Since he couldn't sell the company, Guth searched for a way to differentiate Pepsi from Coke and the dozens of other colas on the market. He couldn't attack Coke on the basis of advertising; his distribution was awful; and he couldn't begin to outpromote Coke—so he decided to compete on price. Since Coke came in six-and-a-half-ounce bottles, Guth began bottling Pepsi in twelve-ounce beer bottles. Even though soda drinkers could now get an extra five and a half ounces of Pepsi for the same dime as they spent for a Coke, there was little reaction.

When his first attempt to shake things up didn't work, Guth made the decision most responsible for turning Pepsi around. Starting in September 1933, he began to sell twelve ounces of Pepsi for just a nickel. Now, Pepsi drinkers were getting nearly twice as much soda for half as much money as Coke drinkers. Money-conscious consumers (and who wasn't in the Depression?) began buying Pepsi in unprecedented numbers.

In 1934, Pepsi showed its first substantial profit in fifteen years; a year later, the company was growing so rapidly that Guth left Loft's and took 91 percent of Pepsi's stock with him. As it turned out, however, he had purchased Pepsi, not with his own money, but with funds misappropriated from Loft's.

Enter entrepreneur Walter Mack, who had cofounded Phoenix Securities Company to create new companies out of the ashes of older ones. After a long legal battle, Mack ousted Guth, then was forced to turn his attention to another legal tangle. The Coca-Cola Corporation, which claimed to have won such cases against other manufacturers using the word "cola," sued Pepsi-Cola for trademark infringement in New York state.

Pepsi's chances appeared even slimmer when a newspaper ran a story about how Coke had recently forced Cleo Cola of Orange, New Jersey, out of business.

The next morning, Mack got a call from Mrs. Herman Smith, wife of Cleo Cola's president. She told Mack that Coke would put him out of business, "just like they did my husband. . . . My husband thought he was right too, but they still put him out of business. And I still have a photograph of the check they gave him."

Stunned by the news that Coca-Cola had paid Herman Smith, Mack said, "I could hardly believe what I was hearing. My mind was racing." He quickly made arrangements to borrow the photograph (which showed both the front and back of the check) and says in his biography, No Time Lost, "What Coca-Cola had done, in effect, was to buy the decision, and they had perpetrated a fraud in court by not disclosing it." He also speculates that Coke "may have bought a lot of their decisions."

The next day, Dave Podell, Pepsi's lawyer, submitted the photograph of the check as an exhibit in the infringement case and asked Coke's lawyers why the company had paid Smith $35,000. Aghast, Coke lawyers quickly requested a three-day adjournment. Early the next morning, Coke's Robert Woodruff called Mack, met him for lunch in the Waldorf Towers, and suggested settling the suit. Mack wrote an agreement out on plain Waldorf stationery, and Woodruff signed it, putting an end to Coca-Cola trademark-infringement suits against Pepsi in the U.S.

Mack then built a streamlined bottler organization with a packaging gimmick. Despite the two-cent deposit they could earn, beer-makers in the 1930s never recycled their twelve-ounce bottles, because of the expense involved in shipping them back to the breweries. Mack bought every used beer bottle he could lay his hands on and let his new bottlers have them for a quarter of a cent a bottle; then the bottlers added a paper Pepsi label and brought them back to local stores to collect a clear profit of a cent and three quarters a bottle, which was more than chicken feed in those days. A few thousand bottles later, the entrepreneurial bottlers had instant working capital.

Not all of Mack's ideas were so brilliant. In one instance, he spent a lot of executive time and effort trying to buy the rights to Popeye, intending to make Pepsi rather than spinach the sailor's "signature" food.

But he hit the jackpot with a jingle that cost all of $2,500. Alan Bradley Kent and Austen Herbert Croom updated "D'Ye Ken John Peel," an old English hunting song, and turned it into one of the most famous jingles in advertising history:

> Pepsi-Cola hits the spot
> Twelve full ounces, that's a lot
> Twice as much for a nickel, too
> Pepsi-Cola is the drink for you.

The jingle almost never made it onto the air: Mack wanted to dispense with the spoken word and just run the music for thirty seconds, but in those days broadcast time was customarily sold to advertisers in five-minute minimums. Even Mack's college classmate at Harvard, Alan Marsh of CBS, refused to sell him time in blocks of anything under five minutes. Undeterred, Mack soon found radio stations in New Jersey that were more than willing to air the jingle alone; two weeks later, Pepsi sales were up phenomenally wherever the jingles were heard, and Mack kept buying spots by the hundreds. CBS was forced to break precedent for Pepsi, the other networks followed, and the thirty-second radio spot became a staple of radio and television.

Two years after its debut, the jingle had been broadcast an astounding 296,426 times in a number of versions. It was given a Latin beat for Hispanic audiences, a twang for country music fans, and Mack even got it played on New York's leading classical station, WQXR. (It was rendered sedately on a solo celeste.)

While most people can't remember a time when Pepsi-Cola was not Coca-Cola's biggest competitor, Royal Crown Cola, 7-Up, and Dr. Pepper were still ahead of Pepsi in the late 1930s. Then another catchy advertising phrase, "More bounce to the ounce," gave Pepsi an image boost, and it became second only to Coca-Cola in soft drink sales. Coke sales slumped, Pepsi sales soared, and for the first time Coca-Cola acknowledged the competition in a most symbolic way. Woodruff offered Mack the presidency of White Motor Company at $250,000 a year, five times what he was making at Pepsi-Cola. Mack declined, but might have changed his mind if asked a few months later.

When America entered the war, Coca-Cola rolled up its sleeves, and Woodruff offered to sell servicemen a nickel Coke anywhere in the world as "a patriotic gesture." Coca-Cola constituted 95 percent of all the soft drinks dispensed at overseas PX's. In 1945, it was estimated that U.S. servicemen had drunk 5 billion bottles of Coke during the war, and *PM*, the defunct liberal daily newspaper, commented, "What do they think this war is—the cause that refreshes?"

Worse still for Pepsi, sugar prices rose sharply in a second fit of postwar inflation, and it was no longer possible—or profitable—for Pepsi to sell twelve ounces of soda for a nickel. The price was raised to six, then seven cents a bottle, and the incredibly successful jingle had to be changed, because consumers were no longer getting "Twice as much for a nickel too."

Increased production costs forced Pepsi-Cola to raise its prices, when its reputation had been made as "the poor man's drink." Mack consciously tried to change Pepsi-Cola's image, using New Yorker-type cartoons, adopting a fancier swirl bottle, sponsoring exhibitions of modern art, and funding Pepsi-Cola scholarships, but it was a case of too little, too late. In the 1940s, Pepsi-Cola's market share dropped from 22.7 percent to 15.7 percent, while Coca-Cola's rose from 77.3 percent to 84.3 percent. Walter Mack had made Pepsi-Cola a contender, but changing circumstances blunted the effects of his greatest contributions to Pepsi-Cola's advertising.

Pepsi-Cola needed new leadership, and, of all places, it came from Coca-Cola headquarters in the person of vice president Alfred N. Steele. A flamboyant sales executive who, according to one employee, "could talk the horns off a brass bull," Steele had peaked at Coca-Cola and realized that his way of doing business would never fit the conservative pattern so pronounced at Atlanta headquarters. He joined Pepsi-Cola in 1949 and brought with him fifteen key management people and an intimate knowledge of Coca-Cola.

Having worked the other side of the fence, Steele knew that Pepsi had two problems: an image problem, resulting from the pricing decisions of the 1930s, and a distribution problem. Coca-Cola remained unbeatable at soda fountains and in mom-and-pop grocery stores, but both were located mainly in downtown areas, and the flight to the suburbs was already a fact of life. Steele saw this demographic shift as a golden (placement) opportunity to establish Pepsi-Cola with the suburban middle class. To encourage them to switch allegiance, to "move up," Steele began establishing an image of quality for Pepsi-Cola. For the first several years, he pushed "quality statements" in Pepsi advertising and pictured white-coat lab scientists guaranteeing Pepsi's "purity." Then, a second flight of ads suggested, "Be Sociable, Have a Pepsi." Suddenly, the "poor man's drink" was appearing in ads cheek by jowl with women in ball gowns and French poodles.

Whether these ads moved the public was moot, but it is a fact that Pepsi-Cola bottlers loved them, because raising Pepsi's image was packaged with small rises in Pepsi's price. While Walter Mack's jingles had built recognition, they had also squeezed Pepsi's bottlers, who had to fight hard to get the price raised to six and then seven cents a bottle.

Over and above raising Pepsi's image with consumers and mending fences with bottlers, Steele turned Pepsi around by:

- Investing $38 million in new plants and equipment.
- Instituting a "Guaranteed Profit Concept," which allowed retailers to return unsold product for full credit.
- Standardizing Pepsi's taste. By establishing mobile sampling
  laboratories, Steele ensured that consumers could enjoy the
  same Pepsi anywhere in the country.
- Reducing its sugar content. Part of standardizing Pepsi's taste
  lay in lowering its sugar content, a change that was very
  much in tune with the growing national interest in dieting.

To Steele must also go the credit for planting the seeds of what
became "the Pepsi Generation." Pepsi-Cola's ads in 1958 positioned it
as "the light refreshment," which had ramifications both with weight
watchers and with young people. By pointedly using young, slim models and music with rock-and-roll flavoring, Steele began the process of
repositioning Coke as "heavy" and "old-fashioned." By 1959, Pepsi's
profits had increased a thousandfold since 1951, and it commanded an
astounding 31.6 percent of the soda market.

Steele died of a heart attack, but his successors built on the "light
refreshment" idea to reposition Coca-Cola as "out of step, out of
touch, and out of date." The ad campaign began in 1961 as a jingle,
sung by Joannie Summers, "Now it's Pepsi for those who think
young." The jingle was catchy, and younger consumers slowly began
to change their attitudes about Pepsi. In 1963, Pepsi-Cola built on this
success by introducing "You're in the Pepsi Generation," created by
Pepsi ad guru Alan Pottasch.

Pottasch essentially piggybacked onto a whole generation and
preempted the youth issue for Pepsi. The adept and timely slogan
made Pepsi drinkers feel young the same way VW owners felt hip and
Marlboro smokers felt manly. "The Pepsi Generation" entered the
language, became shorthand for the early '60s (the prewar '60s) and
was eventually the focus of a *Time* cover story.

Pepsi's boss then was Donald Kendall, the man who convinced
Richard Nixon to install a taping system at the White House and
arranged to have Nikita Khrushchev drink Pepsi at a Moscow trade
show. Kendall brought Pepsi-Cola into the food business via a merger

with Frito-Lay in 1965. As PepsiCo, the new company became number one in snack food sales, and executives in Purchase, New York, began to adapt to the strange new feeling of leadership.

Riding a wave of increased sales and tons of publicity, Kendall bought more major food chains to increase mandatory soda-fountain sales of Pepsi-Cola. PepsiCo purchased Pizza Hut in 1977 for $300 million and Taco Bell a year later for $148 million worth of stock. In 1979, PepsiCo topped the Coca-Cola Company in total corporate sales by $140 million, and in 1981, for the first time, Pepsi-Cola edged Coca-Cola in supermarket sales.

While PepsiCo has still not taken over the cola market, the bank-ruptcies, the horse-and-buggy distribution, and the legal battles are things of the past. Over a fifty-year period, Pepsi-Cola's string of aggressive leaders—Guth, Mack, Steele, Kendall, and, lately, Roger Enrico—contributed to its overall success with key contributions in every area of remarketing. From stumblebum to megalith, the remarketing of Pepsi-Cola is complete . . . at least for now.

• • • • • • •

PRODUCT   PEPSI-COLA

Pivotal P: Price

Guth's decision to sell twelve ounces of Pepsi for a nickel was the bold stroke it needed to compete, even though it later caused image problems.

Priority P's: Placement, Positioning

Steele moved Pepsi into supermarket leadership, the "Pepsi Generation" gave the company an edge with young people, and Kendall added fast-food distribution outlets.

• • • • • • •

Chapter Eight

IF you ever zapped a Martian with your Buck Rogers Ray Gun, bought Red Heart Dog Food for the baseball cards offered on the can (even though you didn't have a dog), or collected Welch's jelly glasses, premiums worked their magic on you.

Premiums have always been popular, because they offer an inexpensive way for manufacturers to reward loyal consumers. They also:

- *Encourage trial.* If Gillette attaches a new type of razor to its Rise shave cream and doesn't charge for it, consumers get to try it for free and the company saves on sampling costs by only reaching people who shave.
- *Increase usage of the product.* The recipe booklets distributed by Jell-O (see Chapter 2) offered a great way to encourage consumers to use more of it.
- *Raise prices.* Consumers may be willing to pay a higher price for a product that includes a premium with perceived value. Spending to save is a long-accepted shopping strategy.
- *Help segment the market.* Manufacturers can use premiums

159

that appeal to different groups—rock-and-roll fans, Hispanic families, car buffs, children. In the 1970s, small children weren't frequenting midwestern McDonald's franchises as often as other age groups. Kansas City advertising executive Bob Bernstein came up with the idea of packaging fries and a burger in a small box that contained prizes and also had colorful games and puzzles on the outside (a container premium). The idea gave Mom and Dad a moment's peace while the kids played with the prizes and did the puzzles. Happy Meals are now responsible for 40 percent of McDonald's profits.

Premium as Package   Soapmaker Benjamin Talbert Babbitt introduced the premium in 1865. Where most manufacturers sold just bare chunks of soap, Babbitt wrapped his in printed paper to make them more attractive. Since consumers thought they were paying separately for the fancy wrapper, he printed the word "Coupon" on it and redeemed ten of them for a "beautiful lithograph picture"—a great way to sell more soap.

Author-publisher Elbert Hubbard gave away a brass reading lamp with every case of his books. The canny Hubbard said, "The premium method of merchandising will live as long as trade itself, because it moves with the tides of the human heart." (Translation: "Everybody likes to get something for nothing.")

Packaged premiums had been introduced by Henry Crowell in 1901 (see Chapter 5) and were well established by the 1930s. Nevertheless, radio dramatically increased their popularity. When General Mills gave away a Jack Armstrong torpedo flashlight in 1939, it sold 13 million packages of Wheaties in two weeks.

Premiums also helped lower resistance to unfamiliar products like strained baby foods. Gerber offered beautiful stuffed dolls for a dime and a package label and created a premium in the 1930s that's still available—a baby spoon engraved with the child's name and birthdate for six labels and a quarter. The price is now six labels and a dollar, but consumers order more than 100,000 a year.

Extra Points   You can also score points with the public when your product is a ticket. The ballpark giveaway was born when St.

Louis Browns owner Bill Veeck found a sporting goods store about to go out of business. The inveterate promoter bought 5,000 Little League bats for just pennies, gave them away at Sportsmans Park, and fans buzzed for days about the giveaway.

At the time, the owners of baseball's fifteen other teams huffed that Veeck was "damaging baseball's reputation." Now, such promotions are commonplace. In the early 1970s, basketball's Utah Stars held a Diamond Night to attract more women. Every female coming into the arena reached into a barrel and pulled out 1 of 5,000 stones. Two actually were diamonds, but, since it was difficult to tell the real from the fake, interested parties could have them appraised. As you may have guessed, the promotion was sponsored by a local jewelers' association.

Premiums with a Purpose   Quaker Oats was bedeviled in the 1970s, like all cereal companies, with complaints about "empty calories" in children's cereals. Jack Lewis, who heads a marketing consulting firm in Westport, Connecticut, was given the assignment to promote Quaker's Cap'n Crunch brand with a premium that had to be:

1. squeaky clean and overwhelmingly positive;
2. divorced from a contest or sweepstakes that might be viewed as "commercial" or "gimmicky"; and
3. a tangible builder of goodwill as well as a successful sales device.

Lewis decided to give away a classic toy and settled on a fire truck. When he sought to tie his campaign to American fire departments, he discovered that fire chiefs had their own public relations problem. Adults no longer rubber-stamped pay raises for fire departments, and, in an age of astronauts, firefighters commanded little attention from children. Moreover, kids were turning in false alarms in increasing numbers.

Lewis contacted the International Firechiefs' Association and created a program that would give youngsters honorary membership in the IFA and a free tour of any firehouse in the United States. The membership card was printed on the back of the Cap'n Crunch box

with a proof-of-purchase seal; any child sending three of the seals to a
P.O. box got a free toy fire truck.

The campaign mollified Mom, built goodwill for a public institution, and delighted children, not to mention Quaker Oats. Max La-
mont, then working on sales promotion and package design for Cap'n
Crunch's and now a senior vice president at Quaker, called it "the
most successful promotion ever run for the brand."

To Be Continued   Some premium programs, called continuity
programs, are structured to keep consumers buying a specific product for a very long period of time. (Henry Crowell's sets of dishes
[see Chapter 5] is an example.) Raleigh cigarettes, Brown & Williamson's first brand, has been offering premiums since the 1930s and is
the longest-running continuity premium program in American merchandising history. Loyal Raleigh smokers save coupons religiously
for ceramic log lighters (1,550 coupons), fruit dryers (3,300 coupons), and computers that tell fishermen which lure to use (6,100
coupons). Coupons can be combined with cash on 550 of the 760
items offered; for instance, a metal detector is available for either
6,100 coupons, 1,525 coupons and $33, or 100 coupons and
$47.50.

While three hundred other brands slug it out for market share by
latching on to the most visible trend, the hottest celebrity, or the
lowest tar, Brown & Williamson hasn't changed its marketing approach since the early 1930s. At this juncture, the makers of the leading brands of the day—Old Gold, Lucky Strike, Camel, and Chester-
field—raised the price of a pack of twenty cigarettes from ten to
fifteen cents. Consumer reaction was swift, and per-capita tobacco
consumption declined for the first time since the 1870s.

Instead of lowering the price of Raleighs, however, Brown &
Williamson chose a different strategy; they added value to the brand in
the form of premiums. While users of other brands saw their invest-
ments go up in smoke, Raleigh smokers could proudly point to a
household item their loyalty had helped to purchase.

As of June 1987, more than 54 billion B & W coupons have been
issued, and better than 82 percent have been redeemed. Every year,
the company ships merchandise with a retail value of $15 to $20

million and sends its *Welcome Home* magazine to 514,000 catalog requesters and coupon redeemers.

According to *The Maxwell Report*, a tobacco industry newsletter, Brown & Williamson's two coupon brands (Raleigh and mentholated Belair) collectively enjoy a 1.4 percent share of the $33 billion cigarette market, worth about $462 million.

WRIGLEY GUM   Premium Product

In 1878, Washington Atlee Burpee started a Philadelphia mail-order business to sell purebred fowl and livestock and offered grain seed as an afterthought. When he got more orders for seed than for stock, Burpee changed businesses to become the nation's largest seed supplier. Similarly, Edwin W. Cox gave up selling aluminum pots to promote his S.O.S. soap pads, and when customers admired his shiny floors, Samuel C. Johnson stopped pushing parquet to market Johnson's Wax. None of these premium-to-product stories matches the saga of how the baking-powder salesman who failed finally got rich selling chewing gum.

William Wrigley, Jr., would live to be called "the greatest salesman since John H. Patterson" (see Chapter 1) and the greatest showman since P. T. Barnum. At age nine or ten, however, all he was was the town bad boy in Philadelphia. He was thrown out of school every two or three weeks in the 1870s and regularly ran away from home until his soapmaker father laid down the law. Twelve-year-old Willie got the toughest job in his soap factory—stirring the thick vats of soap with a paddle for ten hours a day at $1.50 a week.

Willie yearned for a promotion to salesman, and after what amounted to a year of hard labor, he became the boy salesman and made friends, influenced people, and charmed his father's customers for sixteen years.

Despite his efforts, Wrigley's Soap was never a best-seller, because it sold for only a nickel. Retailers were more interested in higher-priced soaps, which returned higher unit profits. To break through this barrier of dealer indifference, Wrigley persuaded his father to raise the price to a dime and then gave dealers cheap umbrellas to keep or to sell with every box of soap. Even though all 65,000 of them dripped red dye at the first hint of rain, Wrigley suffered only a minor setback; despite the problems, soap sales rose, proving the basic soundness of his strategy.

From this simple and admittedly flawed beginning, Wrigley developed the something-for-nothing concept like no one before or since. He gave away weighing scales, cuspidors, and cash registers, slot machines, hatchets, mandolins, gramophones, baby carriages, and accident insurance. He even introduced early versions of the fountain pen and the home movie camera as premiums.

All this merchandising activity made it easier for Wrigley to switch products himself. He added a brand of baking powder as a giveaway, then copromoted it with a cookbook. The cookbook took off, and, in 1892, when he was selling 50,000 cans of baking powder a week, he got out of the family soap business.

A year earlier, he'd started a gum company to give away spruce and paraffin gum with his baking powder. When demand for the gum outstripped demand for the powder, Wrigley was into a new business again, this time for good. He marketed Vassar gum to women (talk about piggybacking) and introduced Juicy Fruit and Wrigley's Spearmint in 1893. (Of course, dealers who placed large orders got free coffee grinders, cheese cutters, lamps, and ladders.)

Premiums had gotten him into the gum business, and after several false starts, advertising heavily when other gums were pulling back made him a success. Two $100,000 campaigns had failed, leaving Wrigley penniless. Yet, in the midst of the Panic of 1907 and a subsequent depression, he borrowed $250,000 more and was able to buy $1.5 million worth of advertising at bargain-basement rates. Spending this amount of money when the average annual ad budget was $25,000 caused the nation's newspapers to notice the former soap salesman and his reputation as a marketing genius began to grow.

As usual, Wrigley took care to find a way to involve dealers in his campaign. He distributed thousands of coupons to them which could be redeemed for free boxes of Spearmint. Within a year, sales jumped from $170,000 to $1 million. By 1910, Wrigley's Spearmint was America's leading brand of gum.

Later in his career, Wrigley put posters extolling his gum in 62,000 subways, mailed four sticks of gum to all 1.5 million telephone owners in America, and enrolled 100,000 boys in a fictitious Indian tribe in connection with a radio show called "The Lone Wolf." At the time of his death in 1931 (two years after the stock market crash), he owned a big league baseball team (the Chicago Cubs), owned America's most beautiful resort (Catalina Island), was a director of forty corporations, and left an estate of $20 million. He attributed his success to lack of fear. "I've been broke three times since I started business, and it didn't cause me a minute's loss of sleep."

• • • • • • •

PRODUCT   WRIGLEY GUM

Pivotal *P*: Premiums

William Wrigley used premiums to woo dealers instead of consumers. The tactic led him from soap to baking powder to ultimate success as a manufacturer of chewing gum.

• • • • • • •

KRAFT CHEESE SPREADS   Gift Box

Delivering in-pack premiums (the kind kids find in cereal boxes) can present problems. Many require labor-intensive insertion or specialized packaging. One classic way around these problems is to make the container itself a reusable premium. It can become a sewing box (Swee-Touch-Nee tea canisters), a geranium planter (Breakstone's cream cheese box), or a scooter (Borden's milk container).

No container premium success story is more dramatic than that of "Swankyswigs," the glass containers in which Kraft sold processed cheese spreads for more than twenty years, beginning in 1933.

The spreads were marketed in 1931 in paper containers called "Kleen Kups." The four-ounce containers were rendered in opaque pastels—Wedgwood blue for Cream Relish, light green for Roquefort

Spread. Although the colors were specifically chosen for mass display in grocery stores, consumers didn't find them attractive and, of course, they couldn't be reused.

In re-evaluating the promotion and the packaging, John H. Platt, Kraft's marketing vice president, proposed a reusable, decorative container, like the wooden box. Of all the possible packaging materials, Platt liked glass, despite the problems it presents as a packaging material. It's breakable, heavy to ship, and containers with narrow openings can be difficult to sterilize. On the other hand, glass feels cool to the touch and is also transparent, a fact that pleases consumers, particularly where dairy items are concerned.

Once the decision had been made, the Hazel-Atlas Glass Company was hired to develop a glass container that had a thin enough rim for drinking, used a top-sealing cap rather than a more expensive screw-type closure, and could be painted by hand at high speeds. Since the art of hand-decorating glasses at production speed was primitive, the simplest type of decoration—a one-quarter-inch red horizontal band with a black hairline was selected. Eventually, 280 women, working around the clock, hand-painted the tumblers.

After months of planning, Platt provided the unusual name for the containers. Paul Butler, a former Kraft employee and the nation's foremost Swankyswig collector, says, "The company wanted a container strong enough to withstand damage from knives used to spread the cheese and handling by children, yet attractive enough for the finest 'party' company. The name 'Swankyswig' seemed to fit."

The program started in October 1933 and was an immediate runaway success. Housewives appreciated the smooth, thin rim that made Swankyswigs the first reusable food containers truly suitable as drinking glasses. In the first year of Swankyswig's existence, sales rose a phenomenal 601 percent, and retailers established ordering patterns in advance to be able to meet demand and satisfy their customers. A survey showed that 94.3 percent of the women who had purchased Kraft spreads had saved the glasses, and four out of five said they collected Swankyswigs in sets of six or eight.

In addition to originating what amounted to a continuity-container premium, Kraft also created a market for glassware premiums. When

Swankyswigs began turning up by the thousands in the institutional market—schools, clubs, churches—leading glass manufacturers gave new thought to the possibility of promoting premium sales.

As an added bonus, the transparent glasses, which eventually sprouted tulips, sailboats, and checkerboard patterns, sold themselves. Kraft was able to use the jar tops, previously used for cheese spread copy, to market its other products, giving it a source of free advertising. The company also used Swankyswigs in piggyback promotions with its other products.

When it became clear that housewives were sold on Swankyswigs, Kraft and J. Walter Thompson, its advertising agency, began pretesting other designs. Whenever one pattern showed signs of losing its sales punch, it was replaced and remaining stocks were cleared out through high-volume retail outlets.

The only pattern that failed to sell well was the 1939 Carnival Ware, which had several drawbacks. Unlike the transparent originals, the Carnival glasses frankly imitated Fiesta Ware, then at the height of its popularity. Housewives surveyed said they disliked the fact that Carnival Ware was opaque and "looked like pottery." Others said the colors chosen "didn't match their dishes," while retailers complained that it was hard to read the labels against an opaque background. (Carnival Ware is now collectible.)

Despite this misstep, new Swankyswigs were created until America entered World War II and glass was needed for defense use. The glasses were reintroduced in 1947, but by the early 1950s, it was evident that hand painting Swankyswigs was no longer feasible economically. In addition, the idea wasn't proprietary, and jam and jelly manufacturers tailored glassware specifically to children by featuring the stars of kids' TV shows on their glass containers.

Nevertheless, Swankyswigs proved, beyond the shadow of a doubt, that design changes in the container itself—independent of any modifications in the product—could create significant sales increases. By this time, Swankyswigs are established as a collectible with some pieces bringing $25 or more, and Kraft still receives more calls and questions about the containers than any other subject in its eighty-five-year history.

•   •   •   •   •   •   •

PRODUCT   KRAFT CHEESE SPREADS

Pivotal *P*: Premiums

Cheese spreads, which failed to sell well in paper containers, became hits when packaged in reusable glasses with hand-painted designs.

Primary *P*'s: Promotion, Piggybacking

Kraft advertised its other brands on the tops of Swankyswigs and pushed its other dairy products in two-products-for-one promotions with the cheese spreads.

•   •   •   •   •   •   •

PUFFED RICE   Land Grant

As we have already seen with Wheaties (see Chapter 1), radio brought cereal premiums to new heights of popularity by mentioning the premium items in radio scripts. Young buyers got milk pitchers with Shirley Temple's likeness, diagrams showing Tom Mix's twenty-two knife wounds, and Jack Armstrong's Torpedo Flashlights.

By the mid-1950s, however, radio had given way to television, which changed the effectiveness of premiums. Where radio seemed to spur consumers to action, the passivity induced by television seemed to work against mail-in offers. Only one in-pack premium from the early days of television proved popular, one that several people literally risked their lives to create.

For years, Quaker Oats had sponsored "Sergeant Preston of the Yukon" on radio and continued to sponsor it when it came to television. By 1955, the company had created a wide range of in-pack premiums for its Puffed Rice and Puffed Wheat brands, including a skinning knife, a compass, and a fire-lighting prism ring. Nevertheless, sales were still slumping.

Quaker asked its ad agency to figure out yet another way to use the cereal box as a promotional vehicle for an in-pack premium to generate new excitement for the brand. The day before the agency was set to make its presentation, account executive Bruce Baker dimly remembered a sweepstakes that had involved giving away small pieces of Oklahoma real estate. He convinced his bosses and Quaker's merchandising department to give away land in the Yukon by enclosing miniature deeds in Puffed Rice and Puffed Wheat boxes.

Baker and company lawyers flew to Dawson, Alaska, selected a 19.11-acre plot of ice on the Yukon River from the air, and bought it for $10,000. Baker wanted to go home, but the Quaker lawyer insisted on investigating the land close up by boat.

As it turned out, the boat developed a leak in the middle of the half-frozen river, and the passengers were forced to jump overboard. They gamely paddled back to shore, only to find they'd missed their dogsled connection back to the airstrip. As darkness fell, the Quaker contingent was forced to walk six miles in subzero weather to meet the aircraft and go home.

As luck would have it, the promotion was nearly worth all the aggravation. After buying the land, Quaker Oats passed title to the Big Inch Land Company, Inc. Big Inch subdivided the land into 21,000,000 inch-square parcels, each properly designated by individual letter and number to differentiate it from its neighbor. Deeds were duly inserted in boxes of Puffed Wheat and Puffed Rice at no charge and were snapped up immediately. A follow-up promotion, offering an ounce of bona fide Yukon soil, sold 20,000,000 more packages of Puffed Rice, meaning the premium was responsible for sales, in all, of 41,000,000 boxes of cereal.

The only drawback involved a collector who had amassed 10,800 deeds and wanted to consolidate his holdings of approximately seventy-five square feet into one parcel; after some discussion with company officials, he was dissuaded and profited eventually by selling the mass of deeds as a collectible.

● ● ● ● ● ● ●

PRODUCT   PUFFED RICE

Pivotal *P*: Premiums

Quaker Oats used an inventive packaged premium to revive Puffed Rice in the 1950s and did equally well a bit later with a piggybacked tie-in premium.

● ● ● ● ● ● ●

CRACKER JACK   Prize Package

There was Scorcher—"It goes fast."
    There was Yellow Kid—"Say it's out er sight."
    There was Honey Corn—"Largest box in the world."
    There was Unoit—"Crisp Molasses Popcorn with Nuts."
    There was Goldenrod—"Nutritious Nuts and Blood-enriching Sweets."
    There was Honey Boy and Western Scout and Little Buster, Jolly Time and Razzle Dazzle, Happikrax and Kor-nut, Osmun's Dandy Snack and Shenkberg's Nutty Corn and Five Jacks and Maple Jack and Sammy Jack, and then there was Cracker Jack.
    Of all the confections involving popcorn, peanuts, and a sweetener (molasses, caramel, sugar, or maple sugar) in the 1900s, none was more interesting than Cracker Jack, produced by the firm of F. W. Rueckheim & Brother. German-born Frederick Rueckheim and his brother Louis had made popcorn in Chicago since Mrs. O'Leary's cow set the city ablaze in 1871. It sold so well that they moved to larger quarters six times in seven years. The business was a success by 1893, when Chicago played host to the Columbia Exposition and 21 million Americans. Many of them sampled Aunt Jemima pancakes and a nameless popcorn-peanut-and-molasses confection the Rueckheims had created as a novelty.
    The novelty caught on, and by 1896, the Rueckheims had figured out how to keep the candy from sticking together and how to distribute it outside Chicago (in wooden tubs). That same year, an anony-

mous salesman tasted it and, using a slang expression of the day, said, "That's a cracker jack!" Cracker Jack took the form we know today in 1899 when E. G. Eckstein, a packaging expert, created the first waxed carton, which protected the product's flavor and crispness. Sales jumped from 68,000 cases to 170,000 cases in four years and continued to grow in 1908, when songwriter Jack Norworth immortalized the candy in his song, "Take Me Out to the Ballgame."

While all these improvements generated sales, Cracker Jack remained just one of several hundred "caramel candies," the generic name for these confections. At the time, distribution was limited and production was cheap. The basic strategy of candy manufacturers was to get an idea, introduce it to wholesalers, and see if the taste, name, or package caught on. Because marketing was so inexpensive, brands came and went quickly; a full 78 percent of the 60,000 candy bars and confections created in the United States got their start before World War I.

This already fierce competition intensified when movie houses began springing up. Now, brands could be slapped together and "tested" in nickelodeons without approaching candy wholesalers. In 1912, when "movie bars" began to make their presence felt, the volume of Cracker Jack fell to 58,000 cases. Initially, the Rueckheims played the candy-bar game and marketed Hunky Dory chocolate bars, Pastime peanut brittle, Taffy à la mode, and dozens of other brands. When none found an audience, the brothers decided to concentrate on Cracker Jack.

In thinking of ways to make Cracker Jack stand out from its competitors, the Rueckheims considered a whole range of promotional options. One possibility was a system of coupons, like the ones Richard Sears and Alvah Roebuck had introduced; when collected in large enough numbers, these on-pack coupons became redeemable for Sears merchandise. Another was a premium program like the kind Henry Crowell used in 1901 with Banner Oats (send in the boxtop and some small change, build a set of dishes).

The brothers had used premiums in the mid-1890s and tried them again in a way that wouldn't hurt the Cracker Jack name if it flopped. Prizes were introduced in Chums, another Rueckheim product, and the legend "Novelty Package" was emblazoned on the package front. The response, however, was almost nil, for reasons that were unclear.

Since in-pack premiums hadn't worked with Chums, Cracker Jack began a coupon premium program in 1910, offering household items like clothes and sporting goods, and a few toys like bouncing balls and cloth animals. The majority of the premiums were meant to appeal to adults, and for a while sales picked up, then fell again. According to legend, Louis Rueckheim then suggested putting small toys directly into the boxes to appeal directly to children, because children were more likely to make repeat purchases than were their parents. The combination of Cracker Jack's name value and the packaged premium directed toward children made the difference. In 1912, spinning tops, metal whistles, pins, puzzles, and yo-yos began appearing in Cracker Jack boxes, and sales rose immediately. Small toys that offered instant gratification were a far bigger hit with children than coupons that might bring toys in some faraway future.

By 1914, Cracker Jack was enclosing baseball cards in boxes, and the set became a national craze. The company printed 15 million cards, making it, at the time, the single most popular premium in America. (A complete set is now worth $50,000.) A year later, the coupon program, which had proven costly to administer, was discontinued entirely, as sales hit an all-time company high of 257,000 cases.

Predictably, other candy manufacturers tried to duplicate the success Cracker Jack had achieved by making premiums part of the product. McNamara Brothers of Austin, Texas, came up with The Monkey Popcorn Prize Box; Plows of St. Louis introduced King Prize Popcorn; and McDonald's, a Salt Lake City manufacturer, introduced Polly Prize Box. None caught on, owing to the lead the Rueckheims had developed in finding toys. They asked for and got many toys on an exclusive basis, and their many imitators soon fell by the wayside. The last piece of the Cracker Jack marketing puzzle fell into place in 1918, when Frederick Rueckheim decided to add a sailor-boy logo as a patriotic gesture. (The boy was modeled after his grandson Robert, and when he died of pneumonia shortly thereafter, the logo was emblazoned on his tombstone.)

Despite this personal loss, Cracker Jack became a national phenomenon in the 1920s, and million-box years became commonplace. When sales nosedived during the Depression, the company hopped onto the radio bandwagon by sponsoring a rash of national and local mystery-oriented radio shows and introducing special "Question Mark" or "Mystery" packages keyed to the plots of the shows. These contained "presidential coins," which enabled children who joined to receive a variety of special toys as prizes; within two years, 230,000 children had joined. When interest in the coins flagged, movie-star cards featuring Jean Harlow and Clark Gable appeared, and later intricate porcelain toys, wire puzzles—even a complete set of trains—kept kids collecting.

On the eve of World War II, the superpatriotic founders decided to end production of toys in Japan, Hong Kong, and Taiwan, and all Cracker Jack toys have been contracted to U.S. companies ever since. During the war, metal figures of soldiers, sailors, and pilots and cards identifying every U.S. battleship and airplane were used as prizes. When the candy's target market—five-to-twelve-year-olds—became interested in space and television, the prizes used were plastic rockets and toys featuring popular TV characters like Davy Crockett.

Every year, Cracker Jack creates fifteen new series of toys, each with twenty to twenty-five novelties, and distributes 25 million prizes. By this time, more than 16 billion copies of more than 20,000 different prizes have been distributed, and each has been inserted by hand. To make sure that no consumer is ever disappointed, three electronic eyes on every packing machine monitor each box; if the box doesn't contain a toy, the eye will detect that the box is underweight and will reject it. (In one case, the electric eye goofed, and the something-for-nothing concept was so ingrained that a little girl sued Cracker Jack. The case was settled out of court.)

Research has proven—unalterably—that the little prizes are the number-one reason people buy Cracker Jack. The prizes have become an acknowledged category of collectible, and a bank vault in Columbus, Ohio, protects 10,000 of the most difficult to find. Oddly enough, the single rarest item is the 116-page catalog issued in 1912 that showed items that could be redeemed for coupons but was itself replaced by the free prize. Bought by Borden in 1964, Cracker Jack still pops eighteen to twenty tons of popcorn every day and is, according to the Brand Rating Index, one of the five most recognized product names in America.

•   •   •   •   •   •   •

Cracker Jack

Pivotal *P*: Premiums

Putting a toy in each box of Cracker Jack made it stand out from its competition and offered children instant gratification.

Primary *P*: Positioning

Cracker Jack became "the candy with the prize" and was able to stay current by leaving the product unchanged but constantly updating the premiums it offered.

•   •   •   •   •   •   •

Chapter Nine

WE live in the twilight of advertising.

More and more, the primary ways product managers sell their products employ one or more kinds of promotion—sampling, product demonstration, premiums (see Chapter 8), coupons, games, and sweepstakes.

From the 1920s through the early 1980s, advertising was king, but no longer. Now, nearly two-thirds of all money spent on marketing goes toward promotional efforts, and only one-third is allocated to advertising.

Donnelley Marketing's tenth annual survey of promotional practices in 1986 showed that 39.3 percent of all expenditures goes to trade promotion and 25.5 percent goes toward consumer promotion; only 35.2 percent goes toward media advertising. Russ Bowman, a columnist for *Marketing & Media Decisions*, estimates that the $165 billion spent on promotion in calendar year 1986 is growing 12 percent annually, as opposed to the $58 billion spent on advertising, which is growing at less than 10 percent annually.

Eric Douglas, president of Riverside Marketing of Westport,

Connecticut, sees what's happening to packaged goods as an instant replay of what happened in the fast-food business in the 1970s: "It's a condensation of what happened in fast food. Fast food was so successful, so right for the times, that it was almost impossible to make a marketing mistake."

In the late 1950s and early 1960s, when Douglas was marketing director at Jeno's, "It cost $25,000 to open the doors, and most people made back their investments in the first month of operations." Calling this the bricks-and-mortar phase of fast food, he says the next step was the entry of advertising into a business that had needed very little marketing help.

Advertising was the route used by several fast-food empires, most notably Wendy's, which was able to compete with the entrenched McDonald's and Burger King by relying on what Douglas calls "key-attribute marketing." A study asked the public which attributes were the most important for a fast-food chain. Cleanliness ranked first, followed by the wish to have hot food actually served hot. The idea that fast food should be juicy (not dried out) placed eleventh on the list.

Says Douglas, "Wendy's took two attributes, hot and juicy, and based their entire marketing campaign around that theme line. The hot-and-juicy commercials practically wrote themselves, and the company prospered. Later they changed to other advertising concepts. "Where's the beef?" was popular for about a minute, but there was no central theme line, and sales began to slump and have never fully recovered. Advertising isn't enough any more. For at least ten years, fast food has been a battleground for market share, and that market is becoming increasingly segmented."

Linking Douglas's history of fast-food marketing to today's business climate makes it clear that advertising alone is no longer adequate to manage the marketing function. Selling one product is an easy job for advertising ("I'd walk a mile for a Camel"), but selling multiple products or their different facets in a segmented marketplace is not something that advertising does well.

That's where promotion comes in. There are three basic reasons to run promotions:

- *Trial*: Convince people to try the product.
- *Continuity*: Get them to buy it more often.
- *Loading*: Induce more spending on the product by selling more of it (getting the consumer to load up) or by adding allied items to the purchase.

"After World War II, we had a love affair with advertising," explains Chris Sutherland, president of the Promotion Marketing Association of America. "We loved to be wooed the way advertising did it. Now we're imaged out and it's easier to see the limits of advertising. Advertising is based on image; promotion is based on performance."

Push and Pull   There are two main branches of marketing thought—pushing and pulling—and the abstract ideas behind them are embodied in all marketing plans as either promotion, advertising, or a combination of both. The "push" school relies on influencing dealers and getting them to stock the product heavily. The argument is that you're better off selling the dealers, because they can give you the distribution you need, plus in-store merchandising support. Of course, it'll cost you, but then again there's no free lunch.

Pushing—in essence, trade promotion—is potentially very expensive, because it cuts margins to the bone. It can include inducements like higher-than-normal markups (say an extra 10 percent), free goods (buy ten, get two free), consignment billing (you don't pay for it until you sell it), easy credit terms (120 days), and payment for prime display space (the end of a supermarket aisle). This type of payment, also known as "shelf money" and "slotting allowances," has taken over more and more of the budget as products proliferate.

In addition to these direct costs, pushing also involves promotional incentives to help the dealer sell the new item. Traditional techniques include point-of-purchase displays, national publicity, in-store promotional appearances, cooperative local advertising, heavy couponing, and training and incentives for the salespeople or the dealer.

The other branch, the "pull" school, relies on creating demand directly with the consumer and spends heavily on advertising. Their philosophy is to forget the dealer. You've got to convince consumers to buy, so you're better off aiming all your efforts at them in the first place. Spend your time and money cultivating the customer.

Pull strategies are generally three-step affairs: (1) advertising directly to the consumer; (2) sampling the product generously, or, if it's a toy or a machine, demonstrating it in high-traffic areas; and (3) praying that advertising and sampling translate into demand so that the retailers stock your product. It may sound like a backward approach, but it has worked repeatedly.

Adopting a pull strategy means advertising an untried and unfamiliar product nationally. It is surely not for the faint-hearted, but when it is successful with either new categories or dormant ones, the results can be spectacular and can break down dealer resistance at a stroke. There's also a bonus in that this approach makes the consumer feel more a part of the decision-making process, which reinforces brand loyalty. When Gerber Foods was forced by circumstances to take such an approach (see Chapter 6), buyers felt it was somehow "their" brand and supported it vigorously when competition began to appear.

Pushing and pulling offer different advantages, but they are mutually exclusive in the beginning, because new product budgets rarely allow manufacturers to do both simultaneously. Claude Hopkins, the advertising copywriter who resurrected brands like Palmolive soap and Puffed Rice in the 1920s, wrote in *My Life in Advertising*, "One can rarely afford to sell to both dealers and consumers. If you sell the consumer the dealer will supply the demand." Hopkins learned his trade selling patent medicines by direct mail, which probably colored his judgment.

Most manufacturers try push strategies first with new products, because it requires less effort to give them national distribution—even though it cuts profits. If (or when) retailers turn thumbs down on new products, because they're "too risky" or "unproven," the pull strategy is usually invoked for a remarketing effort.

Couponing   Couponing, the leading promotional category in the mid-1980s, is an aspect of another *P*, price. A cents-off promotion is one of the best ways to get consumers to try a new product or to revitalize a sluggish one. Especially in commodity products, where consumers have a small inner voice that tells them, "There's only one way to make aspirin," purchasers are more willing to give one-time trial to a product that is virtually the same as the previously chosen brand. In fact, a high percentage of shoppers have no brand loyalty whatsoever and alternate through several based only on price.

Couponing in America is a proven way of saving money. There is an ethic among a large percentage of shoppers that couponing is smart business; that it "pays" to shop smart . . . to use coupons. Coupons are therefore distributed at point-of-purchase; inside or as part of the package and in newspaper (or magazine) inserts or advertising pages. A large percentage of the food section of any metropolitan newspaper is a mass of advertisements with coupons.

Only a small percentage (6 percent) of coupons printed are ever redeemed, so the couponing process is actually two-fold: It serves as advertising and reaches a wide market (when inserted in various media) and then serves as a price break for those who choose to go the distance and actually buy the product. A coupon is a tangible reward for both the consumer, who has just saved money, and for the marketer, who has just sold a product through a traceable and very real means of doing business.

Games and Sweepstakes   Games and/or sweepstakes are usually used not to introduce new products but to stir up sales or to add sparkle to a category that hasn't seen much glitter lately. Promoting a humdrum cleanser is a difficult task, but a Procter & Gamble brand manager gave sixty-year-old Spic and Span cleaner a shot in the arm with a game that used an in-pack premium; he hid five hundred synthetic cubic zirconia diamonds, each worth $600, in boxes and bottles of the product. Sales for the first quarter of 1985 were up $8 million over a similar period in 1984.

Such a campaign was out of character for staid Procter & Gamble, which generally identifies a product need, buys or develops a technology to produce it economically, tests every element, and then decides to go ahead, staying in long after other firms would have given up. Nevertheless, this time the game revived a product in a crowded category when every other form of promotion had failed.

Demonstration as Promotion   A percentage of new products make perfect sense to those who invent and/or market them and seem obvious to all but the simplest of minds, yet they bomb in the marketplace. Why? Because the product cannot get the attention or engage the consumer's imagination in the same way it attracts the people who work with it daily.

There's only one way to reach those who will not see: Show them. Demonstration—the grown-up version of show-and-tell—is the indispensable visual aid most of us need on occasion to "get it," to understand what a product is, how it works, how it can benefit us.

Demonstrations, most specifically at the point-of-purchase, are particularly effective in introducing breakthrough products or technologically advanced products. Although Raytheon made its microwave ovens successful primarily by changing the concept of what they were selling, the second-most-important aspect in the repositioning of that product was the actual cooking of popcorn right there in the store (see Chapter 3).

Sampling as Promotion   When you've developed the right product, targeted the largest market, and crafted a compelling sales pitch, and still your product isn't moving, there's one strategy left to you. And it's not suicide.

If you can't sell it; GIVE it away.

Think about it. How can your potential audience know how your food tastes or how your machine performs unless you tell them or show them, let them try it for themselves? You can make the opportunity even more appealing by removing the pressure of spending money for something new and untried.

Giving the product away is called sampling. Sampling—getting the product free the first time—in addition to all its other charms, probably lowers consumer expectations and reduces their normal resistance to new products. It's based on the entirely reasonable notion that if consumers like a new product they've been given for free, they may very well buy it on their own and, as a bonus, tout its virtues to their friends. Word of mouth is still one of the most compelling forms of advertising.

Sampling has been around from the early beginnings of American business. It used to involve going door-to-door and physically handing something to someone. While this form of sampling still exists, most sampling is done in more sophisticated ways.

One step up from the house call is public one-on-one sampling. The most familiar example features hired actors and actresses passing out packs of a new brand of cigarette on a big-city street corner, but that's just the tip of the sampling iceberg. Add to that:

- *Direct sampling*, especially of prepared foods, is a daily event in supermarkets around the country. When frozen foods went gourmet, microwaves began sprouting in supermarkets, offering consumers little, bite-sized portions of tortellini, crepes, dim sum, and other slightly unfamiliar goodies.
- *Mailed sampling*, directed to "Occupant" or "Householder," even "Boxholder," is favored by detergent, hand lotion, and shampoo manufacturers. Procter & Gamble is a leader in this field and sends out samples by the millions every month.
- *In-pack sampling*, in which you get a little something more than you bargained for, is practiced especially by cereal manufacturers, who include samples of candy or cookies in their packages. The samples are either of brands produced by the same company or of brands from a manufacturer who is paying for the privilege of reaching the cereal company's young customers.

Sampling has become so sophisticated that it's now done demographically by computers. Packages of infant-related products are given away at Lamaze classes, hospitals, birthing homes, and adoption agencies. In 1989 through sample distributors, Johnson & Johnson distributed 1.5 million packs of baby shampoo, corn-starch, lotion, and swabs.

One distributor, Long Island-based Giftpax, caters to the baby market and also distributes grooming aids and personal-care products to junior high schools, high schools, and colleges; packets of household items to newly married couples at county courthouses, wedding chapels, and bridal shops; and products for senior citizens to nursing homes, retirement communities, and recreation centers.

Promotional samples are also distributed to media people—columnists, reporters, and broadcasters—in hopes that they will then recommend the product to others in print or over the air. Had it not been for this kind of promotional sampling, the food processor might never have succeeded.

Amateur chef Carl G. Sontheimer attended the Paris housewares show in 1971 and was fascinated with a French machine that could grind, chop, mince, pulverize, mix, and blend with stunning speed. He secured U.S. distribution rights for the Robot-Coupe, improved its slicing and shredding discs, and rechristened it the Cuisinart.

It was introduced at the Chicago housewares show in January 1973 and bombed; department-store and kitchen-shop buyers failed to see the Cuisinart as anything more than a souped-up blender with a fancy price tag.

Then Sontheimer came up with a way to turn things around. He sent "demonstrator models" of his processors to America's food gurus—Julia Child, James Beard, and Craig Claiborne—with instructions on how to grate, slice, and julienne, processes no blender of the day could duplicate. Their enthusiastic reactions in print caused food buffs to become, in effect, his "sales force," motivating dealers to stock the machine and creating acceptance for the food processor in general and Cuisinart in particular.

Demonstrations like this are to machines what sampling is to packaged-goods products. Manufacturers can't afford to give away expensive items like food processors, home appliances, video recorders, and computers, except as prizes in sweepstakes. But they can offer a "free home demonstration" by the manufacturer's rep or let the consumer use it "for ten days in your own home."

Product demonstration and sampling, then, give manufacturers a chance to show off the benefits of new products with no cash outlay on the part of the consumer. Moreover, they don't need the cooperation of retailers to make the connection with consumers on new products, which is just as well, because retailers don't really like new products. As they are only too quick to remind salespeople, "We're not in business to help you create demand for your new item."

Retailers function beautifully as middlemen when a product has already proven its appeal in the marketplace and they can buy it and resell it quickly at a profit. The more they sell, the more shelf space the product gets. Simple. But, when a manufacturer needs them most—to stock a new product—where are they? Nowhere. The maker of a new product is lucky to get an order for a third of a case.

VASELINE   Soothing Samples

You're sitting at home in the 1860s. A stranger drives up in a buggy and tells you that some new stuff he's hawking will heal all kinds of bug bites, soothe chapped lips, and bind up minor cuts. "What's the downside?" you ask. (You're no dummy.) "Well," he says, "it's gooey, it's taken out of the ground by huge machines, no doctor will recommend it, and no druggist will stock it."

That just about describes the situation that Robert Chesebrough faced in the 1860s. A Brooklyn chemist, Chesebrough had, at age twenty-one, begun refining cannel coal to make a living. A variety of bituminous coal that burns with a bright flame, cannel oil was ultimately made into kerosene for use in reading lamps.

Chesebrough made a modest living, but it was threatened in August 1857, when Edwin Drake struck oil in Titusville, Pennsylvania, the first oil strike in the United States. It soon became clear that kerosene could be made more cheaply from petroleum than from cannel oil. With his livelihood threatened, Chesebrough took the train to Titusville and began asking questions about every part of the drilling operation. As he questioned oil workers, they would often mention "rod-wax," a colorless paraffinlike residue that formed around the pump rods.

The drillers had mixed feelings about rod-wax. They cursed it when it gummed up the works and stopped the machinery; one driller called it "the single biggest nuisance in the oilfields." But, just as often it seemed, the crew blessed rod-wax after using it to soothe wounds caused when they cut or burned themselves.

Chesebrough knew that oil had been used as a healing balm by the Egyptian pharaohs and convinced himself that rod-wax had mysterious healing powers. He took some back to Brooklyn, did hundreds of experiments with it, and finally extracted a concentrated residue of it in the form of a translucent jelly. To test it, he deliberately cut and scratched himself and repeatedly burned his hands with acid. The jelly healed every wound. He gave jars to construction workers, ditchdiggers, and bricklayers; they verified that he wasn't a special case—it salved their wounds, too.

In 1870 he decided to name his invention Vaseline, after the German word *wasser* (water) and the Greek *elaion* (olive oil), and raised money to set up a plant. As a marketing strategem, he sent hundreds of free samples to physicians, apothecaries, and scientific societies and then planned to use their enthusiastic reactions (the old piggybacking-on-the-physician trick) as a wedge to create drugstore distribution. He waited for their reorders in vain; his refined rod-wax was simply too new and unproven to elicit testimonials from cautious folk like doctors and drugstore owners.

It was clear to Chesebrough that, lacking quick commercial distribution for his product, he would have to create demand among consumers himself. Driven by the zeal of the entrepreneur, he embarked on what *Reader's Digest* called "probably the first giveaway campaign."

Dressed in his Sunday best, the determined Chesebrough hitched up his horse and buggy and headed for upstate New York. He gave a jar of Vaseline to every single person he met en route and dropped one off at every farmhouse. When he first told these unsophisticated people that the jelly came from oil underneath the ground, some were afraid to try it, thinking that it might explode; however, such fears disappeared once Chesebrough showed them how useful the jelly could be for soothing cuts and burns.

When they inevitably ran out of this first sample jar, consumers would ask local druggists to reorder Vaseline. Thus, Chesebrough's second sampling effort, the one directed at consumers, was a total success. He sent a dozen other horse-and-buggy hawkers into New Jersey and Connecticut and was soon selling a jar a minute. Six years later, *The Lancet*, Great Britain's prestigious medical journal, noted Vaseline's value to medicine, and when the Equitable Life Assurance Building in New York caught fire in 1912, hundreds of pounds of the jelly were used to treat burn victims.

Once Vaseline became established as a salve for cuts and burns, consumers began to suggest other uses for it (as they had for Kleenex, see page 18). Chesebrough's rod-wax has been used to protect long-distance swimmers from chills, simulate tears for movie actors, and, in a pinch, even work as trout bait.

When an employee cringed at the news that people in India were using Vaseline to butter their bread, Chesebrough reassured the young man, "I eat a spoonful every morning as a general panacea." In truth, after he was stricken with pleurisy in his fifties and nothing else seemed to work, he prevailed on his nurse to rub him with Vaseline from head to toe; he lived to be 96.

By directing his marketing efforts toward the end user when he'd been turned down by retailers, Chesebrough was able to "pull" orders out of them by using the endorsements of satisfied users. Vaseline became the cornerstone of a $3 billion consumer goods company recently acquired by Unilever.

•   •   •   •   •   •   •

PRODUCT   VASELINE

Pivotal P: Promotion (direct sampling)

When doctors refused to endorse Vaseline, Robert Chesebrough started the first large-scale sampling effort and created consumer demand with his pull campaign.

Primary P: Perception

The medical community's eventual endorsement stilled fears about Vaseline and allowed the public to discover new uses for it, as people had done earlier with Kleenex.

•   •   •   •   •   •   •

VICKS VAPORUB   Mentholated Mail Order

Thanks, in part, to Vaseline, petroleum's healing properties were established by the 1880s. Nevertheless, Vicks, another petroleum-based home remedy, sold poorly until it too was sampled. When it became clear that Chesebrough's horse-and-buggy style had become outdated, more efficient sampling methods, combined with couponing, did the trick for Vicks.

In the 1880s, the common cold was even more common than it is today. Where we now have specialized remedies—antihistamines, fever reducers, and different kinds of cough medicine—colds back then were treated with two different panaceas: (1) poultices—flour and mustard plasters—and (2) vapor lamps. Poultices were used to relieve congestion by giving off fumes that helped open nasal passages, but they were unreliable and often caused painful blisters. Vapor lamps conveyed fumes of medication to the sufferer's air passages, but they were also awkward, expensive, and too complicated for general use.

Lunsford Richardson, a druggist in Selma, North Carolina, had grown "sick and tired" of hearing his customers complain about colds and congestion, but he didn't do much about it until his older son, Smith, turned out to be a "croupy" baby. When colds became a more personal concern, Richardson decided to combine the limited virtues of plasters and vapor lamps and simultaneously try to eliminate their negative aspects.

He used a petroleum base like Chesebrough's, added camphor, nutmeg, and eucalyptus oil, and made a lucky guess by including menthol, a substance then new to America, which proved to be effective in opening nasal passages. Melted by the heat of the patient's own body, Richardson's Croup and Pneumonia Salve soothed and opened air passages. According to *Everybody's Business*, the Richardsons originally pushed their product with the slogan "Rub it on, sniff it in, it's good for you, it's made by Presbyterians."

In 1898 Richardson started a medical wholesale business in Greensboro but soon sold the business and, at age fifty-one, invested his life savings in the Vick Family Remedies Company, which offered twenty-one separate home cures. His son Smith joined the company in 1907, organized a small sales force, and called on every drug and general store in North Carolina. It quickly became evident that only Vick's Croup and Pneumonia Cure Salve (named for Dr. Joshua Vick) had any real appeal. The other twenty products were dropped, and Lunsford Richardson renamed his remaining product Vick's VapoRub.

The shorter name didn't do much to increase sales, because Richardson had a one-product company. Pharmacists then and now aren't interested in a new company with just one product and an unproven one at that; they preferred to spend their time with salespeople from major companies whose sample cases bulged with dozens of familiar items.

Shut off from the drugstore-distribution mainstream just as Chesebrough had been, the Richardsons decided they needed a more dynamic way to demonstrate the product and a more direct way to stimulate demand.

One of Richardson's salesmen created a unique product demonstration that became known as the "spoon test." When a tin spoonful of Vicks was warmed by a lit match, the pungent odor never failed to make an impact on the startled store owner. This was a demonstration with a punch that made even skeptical retailers agree that Vicks just might work.

What turned things around for Vicks VapoRub in the South was sampling and word of mouth. Any merchant buying twelve dozen jars of Vicks got twenty-four jars free to give to selected women customers. When the Richardsons invaded the North, they placed coupon ads in newspapers, offering free samples of Vicks to the public. A few days later, salesmen would visit druggists and would offer them a case of twelve dozen jars with the proviso that the druggist give seventy-two jars away to good customers. Richardson then reimbursed the druggist at the full retail price of twenty-five cents a jar.

After salesmen signed up the stores, Vicks ran a second set of newspaper ads listing the names of the stores that would stock Vicks, increasing store traffic and providing impulse sales of other products as well.

There was no comparable way to sample in the West without adding sales reps, until 1917, when the U.S. Post Office began allowing mail to be delivered without naming a specific individual at a given address or box number. Given their success with sampling, the Richardsons naturally became the first marketers to do mail-order sampling on a national basis. They sent eight freight-car loads of Vicks samples to western states and asked local post offices to supply the box number or address of each local resident. Over a seven-week period, most of America's 31 million western "Occupants" received samples in their mailboxes.

Just as their eastern counterparts had done, westerners requested drugstores to stock Vicks, and, at the end of World War I, nearly every American household had gotten a free sample of Vicks, and every druggist knew the product by name. Sales increased from $75,000 in 1912 to $613,000 in 1917.

When the Spanish influenza epidemic struck in 1918 and 1919, sales of Vicks more than doubled again. The Richardsons' pioneer work in sampling—tying sampling to newspaper coupons and then expanding the process through direct mail—created demand and distribution that built a one-product, horse-and-buggy company into $1 billion Richardson-Vicks, bought by Procter & Gamble in November 1985. Vicks went on to become a model example of piggybacking by introducing several franchise-extension product categories centered around cold care—nasal sprays, cough drops, cough medicine, and the Vicks inhaler.

• • • • • • •

PRODUCT   VICKS VAPORUB

Pivotal *P*: Promotion (couponing/mail sampling)

The Richardsons finally got Vicks off the ground with an innovative couponing strategy, then extended their promotion with the first large mail-sampling campaign.

• • • • • • •

HOOVER VACUUMS   Clean Sweep

Around the turn of the century, housewives were resigned to sweeping their homes daily with a broom—even though they knew this method didn't pick up all the dust. Periodically beating the carpet in the backyard loosened some of the dirt, but never really did the job of cleaning efficiently. Although the vacuum cleaner had been invented, housewives didn't know what they had been missing until Boss Hoover gave them a free home demonstration.

In 1901, the year Queen Victoria died, an Englishman named

H. C. Booth had demonstrated the usefulness of suction for cleaning by enthusiastically sucking the dust from the upholstery of a London restaurant with his mouth. Not to be outdone, Americans came up with two other contenders, an electrical gadget that sucked dirt into a wet sponge, as well as the precursor of the industrial vacuum, which depended on a complicated network of ducts to do the job.

Neither caught on, but in 1907, an aging would-be inventor named Murray Spangler was motivated to improve on these earlier, unsuccessful efforts. Reduced to cleaning the floors at a Canton, Ohio, department store, Spangler found the store's bulky carpet sweeper too heavy to move around; it also stirred up dust, aggravating his chronic cough, and he decided he could make a better cleaning machine himself.

Gathering spare material in an assemblage that would have made Rube Goldberg weak with envy, Spangler took a motor from an electric fan, tied a pillowcase around it, mounted the contraption on a soap box he'd sealed tight with adhesive tape, stapled on a broom handle, added wheels, and created what he called the "electric suction sweeper."

It may have looked like hell but it worked, and Spangler thought there could be commercial possibilities in such a device. He tried to raise financial backing to no avail and finally he gave a machine to his cousin Susan. After she'd tried it and liked it, she showed it to her husband, saddlemaker William "Boss" Hoover. Faced with a declining market for his product in light of the horseless carriage, Hoover bought all the rights to the horseless suction sweeper—even though only 10 percent of the United States was wired for electricity at the time.

When he began marketing his new product, Boss Hoover was firmly convinced that the key to selling vacuum cleaners was to "develop a strong national network of hardware-store owners who would act as Hoover dealers." His first idea was to convince local electric companies to be his dealers, offering them $20 profit per machine and another reason for consumers to want to go electric. Predictably, however, the local power companies moved too slowly for Hoover, who then created an imaginative variation of the Richardsons' coupon strategy with Vicks.

His campaign proceeded in three logical, interconnected steps:

1. Attract attention with national advertising. Faced with creating interest in an unfamiliar product that, at sixty dollars, was also expensive by the day's standards, Hoover relied on coupon ads in national magazines to give authority and urgency to his sales pitch. The consumer ads, prepared by Lord & Thomas, offered interested readers a ten-day free home trial of the machine.

2. Direct interested consumers to a local retailer. Hoover answered every consumer inquiry and assured the writer that the trial machine would be delivered by a local store in her area. Hoover would look up local retailers in Dun's directory and Bradstreet's directory (they hadn't merged yet) and write the dealers advising them that Mrs. Prospect's trial suction sweeper was being sent to them—prepaid.

3. Make the product easy to sell. Given this procession of events, the dealer's sole investment was the time needed to deliver the machine. If the customer bought the sweeper, the merchant took the $60, sent $40 on to Hoover, and pocketed the difference without doing a lick of selling. If the machine were returned for any reason, the dealer got to keep it as a free sample to interest other potential customers.

The plan was an inventive way to build a dealer network for a pioneering product, and it should have worked like a charm, but it didn't.

The first ad ran in a December 1908 issue of the *Saturday Evening Post* and produced a flood of inquiries. Letters went to dealers, and many of them duly delivered the machines; unfortunately, they couldn't (or wouldn't) demonstrate them—which killed many prospective sales.

Hoover shook his head. He'd given the dealer many of the classic "push" incentives—no cash outlay, a qualified sales lead, and a free demonstrator—all to no avail. His strategy had failed to foresee that dealers had neither the time nor the inclination to spend their precious selling time demonstrating his machine. Moreover, store owners didn't even want to train their clerks to demonstrate this relatively complex new device; it was a lot easier for them to concentrate on moving pots and pans, which were already proven sellers. Hoover sales crept up from 2,140 cleaners in 1910 to just 4,659 during the 1913 economic boom.

Largely as the result of publicity generated by winning gold medals at industrial expositions in Tokyo, London, and the Panama-Pacific International Exposition in San Francisco, Hoover sales increased to 7,415 in 1914, 11,756 in 1915, 24,251 in 1916, and 48,878 in 1917, when President Woodrow Wilson put the first Hoover in the White House and 24.3 percent of the United States was wired for electricity.

Just when things appeared rosy for the Hoover Company, the War Industries Board declared vacuum cleaners nonessential to the war effort. The Manufacturers' Association of Vacuum Cleaners appealed to the board that "cutting off this industry plants a germ of discontent in the people at home, which will pass on to the soldiers in the camps abroad." In other words, stop making vacuum cleaners and we'll lose the war. After some debate, Hoover was allowed to make two models, but had to cut production to 75 percent of the 1917 level.

In the fall of 1918, Hoover hired a new sales trainer, named E. C. "Sub" Marine, who had a new selling strategy. Marine had sold popcorn machines to drugstores as a boy, convincing managers that proceeds from the machines would more than pay for their rental. He sold Hoover on the same idea, which became known as "the Resale Plan." Under this novel arrangement, a Marine-trained Hoover salesman would demonstrate the machine in the dealer's store, but be paid by Hoover. Dealers would have their commission cut from $33^{1}/_{3}$ percent to 15 percent; however, they would save the time demonstrating the machine or training their clerks to demonstrate it.

The Resale Plan directly addressed the problem of demonstrating the machine and cut the retailer's responsibility to merely providing space. To balance this negative factor, the demonstrations increased store traffic and generated charge accounts for the stores, because most machines were sold on time. Dealers began selling machines and ordering more, with about a third of the country (34.8 percent) wired for electricity.

In the postwar boom, orders shot up to 273,176 units in 1920, but collapsed in the postwar depression later that same year. Dealers began sending machines back as fast as they had ordered them, and by the end of the year, when money became scarce, 100,000 had been returned unsold.

Marine went back to the drawing board, and in 1921 he came up with a new approach—direct canvassing. Where previously Hoover salesmen would go to a home only if invited, Marine decided desperate measures were called for to clean out the warehouse. As things worked out, door-to-door selling not only sold the returned machines, it also solved a persistent problem the Hoover company had had with the Resale Plan.

Women who saw the machine demonstrated at the hardware store were often impressed with it but didn't want to make the decision to buy a large piece of machinery on their own. They would say things like, "I'm anxious to see what it will do for my own carpets, but—I'd like to talk it over with Elmer first. I'll bring him in over the weekend." Most Elmers never quite made it in to the store.

After losing numerous sales this way, Marine pondered the subtleties of the two-person purchasing decision and eventually came up with a flanking maneuver. Beginning that spring, demonstrators would put the machine through its paces in the store and elicit excited reactions. Then, even before the housewife could mention Elmer, the Hoover salesman would say something like, "Well, I'm glad that you're excited about our machine, and I know you'd like your husband to see what it can do too. What would be a convenient time for me to come to your home to demonstrate it for you both?"

This speech postponed the buying decision, in violation of the accepted rules of selling. But it did change the venue for demonstrating a new and unfamiliar product from a possibly crowded public store into a private, familiar setting—the home. Moreover, the relaxed husband and wife could both try out the machine before giving the sales rep a yes or a no. Faced with the machine and the actual cleaning situation, even Elmer could see that, yes, this suction sweeper was one handy little item and, no, he didn't want his wife doing a dirty job when there was a reasonably inexpensive alternative.

By the summer of 1922, nearly half the United States was wired for electricity, and 748 Hoover sales reps were out canvassing and making at least the required fifteen demonstrations each week. That works out to 549,780 product demonstrations in a forty-nine-week year. It's no wonder that direct selling led to domestic sales of 172,000 vacuum cleaners, a record year for Hoover.

The home demonstrations had a success rate of 31 percent, and, better yet, produced no returns. People who bought Hoovers in their homes stayed sold.

"The Hoover man" became a familiar neighborhood sight throughout the 1930s, which turned out to be the peak years for door-to-door selling. When consumers began fleeing to thinly populated suburban areas, the Hoover Company discovered that direct canvassing was no longer cost-efficient and discontinued the practice. Nevertheless, the Hoover Company expanded into a $700 million company before being bought by Chicago Pacific Corporation in 1985.

•   •   •   •   •   •   •

PRODUCT   HOOVER VACUUM CLEANER

Pivotal P: Promotion (coupon/demonstration)

Boss Hoover qualified sales leads with coupons until he saw that demonstration was vital. He succeeded by dropping retail distribution for home canvassing and demonstration.

Primary P's: Placement, Perception, Price

Just as Earl Tupper's plastics had to be demonstrated at home, seeing the Hoover clean the living room rug changed the perception that it was expensive.

•   •   •   •   •   •   •

POST-IT NOTES   Padded Sell

If any corporation can claim to be the spiritual home of remarketing, it is the 3M Corporation of St. Paul, Minnesota. In its eighty-eight year history, 3M keeps getting stuck with "lemons" and winds up selling tons of lemonade. So it was with Post-it Notes, a product which, despite its simplicity, no one knew how to use.

The company, which used to be called Minnesota Mining & Manufacturing, was even founded on a faulty premise—its principals thought they had discovered a lode of corundum, a mineral used in grinding wheels and other high-grade abrasives. Although their find turned out to be only anorthosite, a relatively worthless mineral, 3M's management made enough sandpaper out of it to start a thriving industrial company. In later years, the company tried to make a masking tape for carmakers who wanted to give their automobiles two-toned finishes. It failed, but the tape, mated with cellophane, became Scotch tape—the world's largest-selling adhesive.

Against this background, in 1973, some 3M staffers showed Geoffrey Nicholson a curious new adhesive that had flunked all of 3M's standard tests. Since Nicholson was one of the company's technical directors, the idea of a totally imperfect adhesive caught his fancy. Although he tried to imagine a use for it, he never did find one himself. But someone else in the office did.

While singing in the choir at St. Paul's North Presbyterian Church one Sunday morning in June 1974, Art Fry kept trying to mark the place in his hymnal with a piece of paper, but the makeshift bookmark kept falling to the floor. After several frustrating attempts, he analyzed the problem and decided he needed a marker that would stick to the page for as long as he wanted but could then be lifted off easily without tearing the hymnal. Fry needed a new kind of adhesive, one that could be, to coin a phrase, "permanently temporary." Then he remembered Geoffrey Nicholson's adhesive that had always failed.

The following Monday morning, Fry got a lab sample of the goo, dabbed some on a piece of paper, and immediately had a crude, "permanently temporary" note. He remembers, "I realized very quickly that this was a systems approach to note taking. It had the means of attaching it and the means of removing it built right into it."

Fry later made a formal presentation to Bob Malinda, the product manager for 3M's commercial tape division, and got a go-ahead to continue his research on company time. Getting a workable product proved to be a headache, and some marketing people saw only limited uses for the pads. Nevertheless, Fry insists, "I saw it as something that could eventually grow into something as useful as Scotch tape." Malinda supported him and, according to 3M custom, allowed him to "bootleg" funds from other projects for unofficial research.

Despite Malinda's support, Fry was unlucky in one respect. His concept of the product ran counter to 3M experience in one significant detail. For more than seventy years, the company had been successfully making adhesive products in rolls; accordingly, all its machinery was designed to make rolls of this or that material—adhesive paper, cellophane, or nonwoven material. Fry envisioned his product marketed in the form of a tear-off pad, which would require dramatically different production techniques.

Selling a product in pad form proved to be a liability as Fry began asking several 3M business development units for further funding. He recalls, "No one said 'No' to me, but then, no one said 'Yes' either." Fry decided to go ahead and build a production prototype anyway—in his basement.

After many months, he was able to crank out several pads and invited Malinda, Nicholson, and key figures from several business development units to his house to see the machine. Everyone was impressed and immediately wanted to move Fry's machine back to the factory, only to find it was too big to clear the stairwell. That weekend a 3M construction crew broke down the wall just long enough to remove the machine and then rebuilt it.

When production did begin on intracompany samples of the pads, Fry passed out what were then called Press'n'Peel notes to 3M staffers, recorded the names of those to whom he gave samples, and noted how long it took them to ask for a refill. Nicholson took a similar tack and passed his samples to top 3M executives. He says, "My secretary started getting so many requests that my office started resembling a supply depot."

Intracompany reaction prompted 3M's marketing people to go ahead; the notes were formally test marketed in 1977 in Denver, Tulsa, Tampa, and Richmond, Virginia. Before the test 3M visited retailers in the test cities with Press'n'Peel notes in 8 1/2-by-11 and all the standard sizes. The company placed advertising inserts in local and regional editions of trade magazines for office managers and secretaries and sent their subscribers descriptive brochures and product samples.

Results were so-so in Denver and Tulsa, but downright poor in Tampa and Richmond; then-marketing director Jack Wilkins said, "Nobody really knew what it was good for."

Press'n'Peel was a cool disaster.

Nicholson and Joe Ramey, the division's new general manager, went to Richmond to find out why things had gone so badly. Ramey told *Corporate Report*, "My reaction when I went out into those markets was that we probably had a dead duck on our hands, and it just wasn't going to make it."

Ramey and Nicholson went into office buildings and made cold calls in Richmond and the other test cities and immediately discovered the missing element. Just supplying the pads wasn't enough; as simple as they were, they had to be demonstrated to be effective. Marketing had originally distributed few samples and had made no allowance for demonstrations, which meant that every bank and business office had to get personal instruction from Ramey or Nicholson. It was worth it; they wrote orders at nearly every stop along the way.

Ramey says in retrospect, "Our communications package was put together very badly, and the consumers didn't really understand the product. To get people motivated to buy this product, we had to get a sample into their hands."

After checking with salespeople, they discovered that in Tampa, as in Richmond, there was a lack of dealer enthusiasm, little promotion, and—most important—no demonstration of how the notes worked or what they were designed to do.

At this point, the pads were pulled out of the test markets, and marketing people designed new merchandising materials for a 1978 campaign, since dubbed "the Boise Blitz." Still sold under the Press'n'Peel name, the notes were advertised with eight two-color insertions in the *Boise Statesman*, promoted with window, counter, and ceiling displays, and offered at a special promotional price. The final touch was the mass hiring of temporaries from the Manpower agency who offered samples and demonstrated the pads by going from office to office in Boise's business section.

While Fry had always maintained, "If you put a pad in someone's hand, they'll know what to do with it," the Boise Blitz proved otherwise. The simple show-and-tell slogan "Press it on, peel it off" made no impression until people could see for themselves just how the little notes worked and how useful they could be. Lynn Wilson, the new marketing coordinator, says, "Once people see it, put it down, and pull it off, the light comes on real fast."

Post-it notes, renamed in 1980, went into national distribution that year and immediately caught on. By 1984, they were the most successful new product in 3M's history and one of the top five products in the office-supply industry—of all time—along with Scotch tape, liquid paper, copy paper, and file folders.

Six years after they first became available nationwide, sales of "the little yellow pads" exceeded $100 million annually. 3M now also offers printed notes for premiums and specialty advertising, imprinted trays to hold the notes, notes in cube form and dispenser packs, and dozens of other Post-it products.

•　•　•　•　•　•　•

PRODUCT   POST-IT NOTES

Pivotal P: Promotion (demonstration/sampling)

Post-it notes were originally mismarketed because no one thought the product had to be demonstrated. When they were widely sampled and demonstrated, Post-its became a huge hit.

•　•　•　•　•　•　•

Chapter Ten

ONE warm spring afternoon in 1884, Pete Browning, champion slugger of the National League's Louisville Eclipses, strode to the plate, his favorite bat in hand.

The pitcher wound up, Browning swung, and the bat splintered in half. Disgusted, Browning returned to the clumsily made bunch of short poles that passed for bats, took one, and struck out.

John "Bud" Hillerich understood Browning's plight completely, because he was an apprentice in his father's woodturning shop. After the game, he offered to make Browning a bat and, while the slugger waited, used a lathe to turn a piece of white ash into a carefully honed bat that was just the way Browning wanted it.

The next day, Browning got three hits, each of them a screaming line drive, and the *Louisville Courier-Journal* wrote a story about Browning, Hillerich, and the bat. Soon, every Louisville player was clamoring outside Hillerich's shop; the legend of the Louisville Slugger was born.

If you think things like this can't happen today, think again. Bob Greene, a columnist for the *Chicago Tribune*, wrote a rave about Canfield's Diet Chocolate Fudge Soda, a regionally distributed carbonated drink. The next day, the company was deluged with calls from New Hampshire, Florida, and Goteborg, Sweden, each one from a distributor who wanted to stock it.

These are "product publicity stories," one small branch of a large, misunderstood craft called public relations. When you want to tell your boyfriend, girlfriend, wife, or husband something, you communicate it with body language, eye movements, or the special vocabulary every couple uses to convey information.

That's private relations.

You can't communicate a message the same way to 260,000,000 Americans. That requires public relations.

The PR Game   Public relations is a form of indirect communications that covers radio, television, newspapers, magazines, theater, books, movies, billboards, brochures, and even advertising messages inserted in fortune cookies. No matter where you receive the information (home or office), its form (written words or moving images), or its subject (a product, a rock star, a country), you're forming an opinion based on abstracts (words, pictures) without using the product, meeting the rock star, or visiting the country directly. The message is being directed at a series of publics (people who shave, Van Halen fans, American Express cardholders) without direct personal contact, in other words, without private relations.

Tell someone you're in public relations, and they may immediately assume that you:

- drink a lot;
- lobby Congress;
- plan parties;
- arrange press conferences;
- know a lot of famous people;
- hobnob with investment analysts;
- spy for a foreign government.

Public relations people have done all these things and many more. But, in the world of marketing, they are generally hired to get their clients what is redundantly called "free publicity."

By definition, publicity is free as opposed to advertising, which is paid. With advertising, you craft the message with words and images you choose, pay for the space (in print) or the time (on TV or radio), and pray that people get the message and act on it. While there are obvious exceptions (Marlboro, Volkswagen, 7-Up) the public often places little faith in advertising because the message has been bought and paid for. Studies show that only 12 percent of advertising is even noticed, much less believed or acted on.

With publicity, you present the idea to the media, hope they decide to devote coverage to your client, and are totally at their mercy about what is said and in what way. On the other hand, since the (supposedly objective) media, rather than the client, is determining what is said, the public gives it greater credence. It is rare that one story will create demand as with Canfield's and the Louisville Slugger; however, it is not unusual to establish a personality with a wave of stories (Madonna and Donald Trump would be examples).

Word-of-Mouth   Sometimes, the most believable publicity doesn't come from the manufacturer but from a total outsider. Food salesman Joel Cheek created a coffee in the 1890s and persuaded the Maxwell House hotel in Nashville to serve it. When management agreed, he dubbed it Maxwell House coffee.

Shortly after the turn of the century, President Theodore Roosevelt was the guest of honor at the Hermitage, Andrew Jackson's Nashville home. Maxwell House was served, and when the hostess asked if he wanted a second cup, Roosevelt replied, "Delighted! It's good to the last drop!" Newspapers picked up the comment, and Maxwell House quickly became a regional, and later a national, favorite.

Honorable Mentions   Sometimes a chance mention can bring a product tremendous publicity with no planning at all. Think of how Cracker Jack benefited by being included in the lyrics of the song, "Take Me Out to the Ball Game." In another example, Shirley Temple sang about "Animal Crackers in my soup" in a movie, and a brand that had been around for thirty-three years took off (seemingly) overnight.

In a related example, a candy maker named a log-shaped bar Baby Ruth—not to honor Babe Ruth—but to honor Ruth Cleveland, the fully grown daughter of former president Grover Cleveland, who as a child had been the nation's pet. The Curtiss Candy Company promoted the bar by parachuting samples from biplanes. Six years after its introduction, Curtiss was selling five million Baby Ruths a day.

Promoting Publicity   Sometimes, advertising or promotion leads to publicity by establishing a Living Trademark. Mr. Peanut and the Quaker man were advertised so extensively that the characters could be used to generate local publicity at store openings and the like. (NBC weatherman Willard Scott got his start playing Ronald McDonald in Washington.)

Similarly, contests and sweepstakes can generate publicity and focus attention on a given product. Dr. William Scholl began marketing foot-related products in 1904, and was doing pretty well by 1916, when he sponsored a Cinderella foot contest. Women all over the country walked into shoe stores to leave their footprints on a "Pedograph" to see if their pedal extremities had the right balance and weight distribution. As you might expect, the contest generated tremendous publicity and helped make Americans conscious of the importance of wearing good shoes.

AUNT JEMIMA   Pancake Makeup

In 1889, two men who knew practically nothing about cooking huddled over a kerosene stove in St. Joseph, Missouri. The novice cooks experimented with a ready-made pancake batter, the first ready-mix food product of any kind. Like many great ideas, it didn't fly immediately and might have never made it, except for a brilliant publicity campaign that helped turn a long-time loser into a big-time winner.

Chris Rutt, an editorial writer for the *St. Joseph Gazette*, and Charles Underwood, a friend in the milling business, had bought the Pearl Milling Company and were trying to create a new product that would use a lot of flour, like pancakes. The problem with pancakes back then was that they were tricky to make the same way every time because of variations in the recipe. To lessen this margin for error, the partners focused on creating self-rising flour, which would cut down on the inconsistency of pancake making. After weeks of experimenting, they mixed wheat flour, corn flour, phosphate of lime, soda, salt, and milk together, tasted it, and decided the results were excellent.

At first, their concoction was sold in plain paper sacks with no trade name, but Rutt got an idea for a name after watching two vaudeville comedians in blackface. When Rutt saw Baker and Farrell perform their hit cakewalk number, "Aunt Jemima," he found the name for his product and also appropriated Baker's costume—the apron and red bandanna headcover northerners usually associated with a southern "mammy."

The name was no panacea, and sales remained slow. Convinced that trade-show promotion was the answer to their problem, they took a booth at the New Era Exposition in St. Joseph. The public still wasn't interested in ready-made pancake mix and distrusted any food that boasted more of its convenience than its flavor. The company folded soon thereafter, and Ritt returned to the newspaper. Underwood persevered, forming the Aunt Jemima Manufacturing Company with his brother Bert as the money manager. Their only accomplishment was registering the Aunt Jemima trademark. This company also failed.

After two bankruptcies, Underwood decided he would trade a possible windfall for a steady paycheck and went to work for the R. T. Davis Milling Company, selling Davis the Aunt Jemima brand in return for a job. Davis, who had fifty years of milling experience, improved the flavor and texture of the product by adding rice flour and corn sugar and simplified cooking it by adding some of the powdered milk popularized earlier by Gail Borden. Now all the housewife had to do was add water to the first packaged ready-mix food.

Despite this innovation, the brand still didn't catch on. Four years after Aunt Jemima had first appeared on the market, consumers remained suspicious of ready-mixed foods. In particular, ready-mixed pancakes were looked on as an impossibility, because preparing them seemed complicated and dependent on real cooking skills.

The brand was about to be retired for good when Davis decided to capitalize fully on the Aunt Jemima name and literally bring her to life. In so doing, he decided to piggyback onto a pair of accepted truisms, one of which would rightly be regarded as racist today:

1. "You just can't beat southern hospitality."
2. "Black women are the best cooks in the world."

By inventing a "real" Aunt Jemima, Davis saw that he could take commercial advantage of both of these myths. By associating them directly with a real person who represented his product, he could create a living trademark for his brand and capitalize on the goodwill that already existed for southern manners and black female cooks.

He told food brokers what he was looking for, and Charles Jackson, a Chicago wholesaler, found Nancy Green, a famed black cook from Montgomery County, Kentucky, with an attractive manner and an easy-going personality. Davis signed her to a lifetime contract and, in modern parlance, "bet the company" on one all-out publicity stunt built around her that probably cost $10,000 (perhaps $1.5 million in contemporary terms).

On May 1, 1893, President Grover Cleveland himself cut the ribbon opening Chicago's Columbia Exposition to commemorate the four-hundredth anniversary of the discovery of America. Millions visited the fair and, inevitably, their attention was attracted by a circular building 12 feet across, 24 feet long and 16 feet in diameter—"the world's largest flour barrel." When they walked inside, they found themselves in the parlor of that noted southern cook, none other than Aunt Jemima herself, and sampled free pancakes.

Yes. Sampling does enter into the story, and the brand couldn't have survived nearly a hundred years if the pancakes didn't taste good. But Davis wanted to leave people with more than just the taste of pancakes in their mouth. Nancy Green brought the fantasy of the southern mammy to life with her songs and stories of the Deep South before the Civil War. Her talent, warmth, and friendliness inevitably rubbed off on "her" pancakes, and her endorsement generated goodwill and eased consumers' minds about ready-mixed foods. Cooks who might have felt humiliated to be using a ready-made product couldn't feel the same way once they had met the "real" Aunt Jemima.

When she left the booth, crowds followed her, asking for cooking tips and autographs. When she was in the booth, it became so crowded that Davis had to hire special policemen to control the mob. By the time the fair ended, an estimated 1.2 million people had tasted Aunt Jemima's pancakes, and Exposition officials crowned her Pancake Queen. On a more commercial note, Nancy Green's hospitality had generated what Davis later claimed were 50,000 orders for Aunt Jemima pancake mix from all over the world.

After the Exposition, Davis published a souvenir booklet entitled *The Life of Aunt Jemima, the Most Famous Colored Woman in the World,* and his salesmen fanned out across the country to arrange in-store appearances for Aunt Jemima. Nancy Green would give cooking demonstrations and make friends. The demonstrations taught an entire generation of housewives cooking shortcuts and paved the way for convenience foods and the ready-mix revolution. Not one to overlook a promotional opportunity, Davis eventually created one of the most famous boxtop premium offers in merchandising history. For one trademark off the carton and twenty-five cents, consumers got an Aunt Jemima rag doll. The promotion proved so successful that Arthur Marquette says in *Brands, Trademarks and Good Will,* his history of Quaker Oats, that, "Literally almost every city child owned one." Eventually, a whole family of Aunt Jemima dolls—Uncle Mose and the twins, Diana and Wade—was spun off. It was followed by 4 million sets of Aunt Jemima and Uncle Mose salt-and-pepper shakers, 150,000 copies of a cookie jar shaped like Aunt Jemima, and a plastic syrup pitcher that sold 1 million copies as well.

Just when it appeared as if Nancy Green could keep Aunt Jemima alive forever, Davis died, and without his promotional flair, the company went into bankruptcy again in 1900. It was reorganized in 1903 by former general manager Robert Clark, who pushed the southern hospitality theme as hard as he could: "Years ago, Aunt Jemima refused to tell a soul how she mixed her batter. In those days, only her old master and his guests could enjoy her pancakes." The appeal of the pre-War South once again worked its magic and brought the brand back to profitability.

Aunt Jemima's legend was powerful enough to survive yet another crisis. When rationing during World War I forced the company to find a substitute for wheat flour, sales dropped abruptly. James Webb Young, then of J. Walter Thompson, rode to the rescue with a series of dramatic ads featuring episodes from Aunt Jemima's "life" and using Nancy Green's features. Each ad carried a four-color illustration by N. C. Wyeth, the father of Andrew Wyeth, and told of incidents like the night Aunt Jemima revived the flagging spirits of passengers who had jumped off a burning Mississippi riverboat.

The series worked brilliantly, but Nancy Green's death in a 1923 car accident put an end to the first Aunt Jemima. Quaker Oats acquired Aunt Jemima Mills in 1926 for $4.2 million.

When the brand went downhill during the Depression, Quaker officials decided to bring back Aunt Jemima. Once more, ads were run in the Chicago papers to find a new Aunt Jemima. Fittingly enough, the new Aunt Jemima, 350-pound Anna Robinson, debuted at another big trade show, the Chicago Century of Progress Exposition in 1933—forty years after Nancy Green had "created" the character. Anna Robinson filled Aunt Jemima's shoes so well that the familiar trademark on the package had to be redone by artist Haddon Sundblom to reflect Anna's facial features.

If there were any lingering doubts about the staying power of the Aunt Jemima fantasy, they were resolved when Disneyland opened in 1955. With Aylene Lewis serving as the third and last Aunt Jemima, the Aunt Jemima Kitchen proved to be such an attraction that it had to be torn down and expanded. Although there is at present no human Aunt Jemima, her name was used for a chain of franchised restaurants in the 1960s, and her pancake mix remains the world's best-selling ready-made.

In an example of piggybacking poetic justice, a name itself stolen from a vaudeville song nearly a hundred years ago graces no fewer than thirty franchise extensions, including various flavors of French toast, waffles, cornbread, and syrup. When Aunt Jemima Toaster Browns, hash brown potatoes prepared in a toaster, were introduced, the music played underneath product shots in the TV commercial was "Nothin' Could Be Finer Than to Be in Carolina."

• • • • • • •

PRODUCT AUNT JEMIMA PANCAKES

Pivotal *P*: Publicity

By using a black woman to embody myths about southern hospitality and home cooking, R. T. Davis created a living trademark, a rich symbol, not just a pancake mix.

Primary *P*: Promotion

Davis used a trade-show exhibit to sell dealers on the popularity of his product, then set up a promotional tour and created merchandise to reinforce the Aunt Jemima brand.

• • • • • • •

SCHLITZ AND BUDWEISER   Lasting Impressions

A good part of making the press work for you is understanding timing and coordinating developments concerning your product with current events. Two different beer companies, Schlitz and Anheuser-Busch, broke into the mainstream due to public relations efforts that verged on being clever stunts. Yet, instead of making the beermeisters look like fools, the stunts made them look like geniuses. And their products broke through from middling (or no) sales to national stories and big-time bucks.

August Krug, an Austrian immigrant, owned a small restaurant in Milwaukee where he brewed his own beer to serve with the knockwurst and sauerbraten his wife Anna prepared. Demand for the beer grew, and Krug sold 150 barrels in 1849. When he died in 1856, his assistant Joseph Schlitz took over. Schlitz married the boss's widow and changed the name of the brewery to his own.

Fifteen years later, Schlitz was struggling to sell 6,000 barrels a year. Then, on October 6, 1871, the Great Chicago Fire burned out most of Chicago's breweries and the city was desperate for water. Schlitz volunteered to increase production and shipped kegs of water and low-cost beer down Lake Michigan to thirsty survivors in Chicago. Beer production soared, and grateful Chicagoans began mentioning Schlitz's generosity at every turn. With no advance planning, Schlitz's heretofore little-known brand became known as "The beer that made Milwaukee famous." The phrase was emblazoned on the beer's label in 1894.

When Admiral Dewey won the Battle of Manila Bay, Schlitz, in a flight of jingoistic fancy, sent 150,000 barrels of beer to his troops, with congratulations and compliments of Schlitz Brewing Company. The feat produced yet another unplanned flurry of publicity for Schlitz when the Women's Christian Temperance Union wrote a letter of protest to Admiral Dewey and asked that the beer be confiscated. The admiral himself declined to comment, but a Schlitz manager answered the ladies by indignantly telling reporters, "Any sensible person would know that beer was very healthful for any person subjected to malarial diseases."

Whether it cured malaria or not, Schlitz beer made Milwaukee famous with the unplanned but now widely accepted notion that if you give away product to the right people at the right time you will get more than you spent on the product in goodwill, good wishes, and good publicity—which will, in turn, sell even more product.

What Schlitz did for Milwaukee, Anheuser-Busch did for St. Louis. In 1855, young Adolphus Busch won the hand of Lilly Anheuser and the chance to run the Bavarian Brewery of St. Louis (which Lilly's father had won in a poker game). Busch had sold brewers' supplies in Germany and had a similar business in St. Louis. After taking over, he enhanced the brewery's reputation by buying showy draft horses and keeping gleaming beer wagons on display, eventually turning the factory into a showplace, with the public invited to drop by and say hello, an amenity no other brewery offered and a brilliant public relations move.

The brewery was somewhat successful when Busch's friend Carl Conrad discovered an exceptional beer in the German village of Budweis. Conrad trademarked the name Budweiser, brought the recipe back to St. Louis, and sold the rights to Busch. The two men worked together on recreating the taste and discovered it resulted from a process called "*kraeusening*," in which fermentation is induced twice to give the beer a very smooth taste.

Given this product difference, Busch knew he had something really special to sell. He invested in a fleet of refrigerated railcars and set up a system of railside ice houses to take his new brand—Budweiser—national. America's first national beer, it was selected as the finest of its time at the 1876 World's Fair and won similar honors in Paris, Amsterdam, and Vienna. By 1901, Anheuser-Busch was the world's largest brewery and was selling a million barrels of beer a year.

Then came Prohibition.

You could tell Adolphus Busch and his son Augustus A. Busch that every cloud has a silver lining, but it's unlikely they would have believed you in 1919. The undisputed leader in their category, they were suddenly denied the right to sell their product. The company began producing bus and truck bodies, got into cars a little bit, diversified into corn products and starch (which it still sells), and even made a malt-based, nonalcoholic beverage called Bevo, which was briefly popular during Prohibition. Mostly the Busches relied on their keen sense of public relations: They kept the picturesque brewery in tip-top condition, invited the public to stop by, and actively lobbied for Repeal.

When Franklin D. Roosevelt was elected President, it became clear that Repeal was inevitable. Yet, in January 1933, Anheuser-Busch found itself in the ridiculous situation of reintroducing what amounted to a new product in a field with seven hundred brands of beer. The very prospect of starting over made the Busch men think back to the good old days when Budweiser was America's number one brand. Remembering those halcyon days, they saw giant Clydesdale horses pulling shiny beer-wagons through the streets of St. Louis.

In a wave of nostalgia, his employees presented August Busch, Sr., with a gleaming beer-wagon and six matched Clydesdales ranging from bay to black in color. When Busch, Sr., saw the horses, he decided to use them to thank New York's Governor Al Smith, who had worked tirelessly for Repeal.

Despite great logistical problems, eight horses and two cases of Budweiser were flown to New Jersey. One account of the event has the Clydesdales passing from New Jersey into New York via the Holland Tunnel . . . on foot. On April 7, 1933, at almost the exact moment that Prohibition died, the high-stepping Clydesdales paraded up

New York's Fifth Avenue, right to the Empire State Building where Smith had his offices, and a jubilant crowd of 10,000 New Yorkers marched right along behind the horses. Budweiser employees presented Smith with the beer, which he acknowledged with a short speech, and the impromptu event created pages of colorful, unplanned publicity for Budweiser.

This public reaction convinced the Busch family to send the Clydesdales on tour throughout the East coast, and the first product publicity tour to feature animals was born. The horses have since toured the U.S. every year except for the war years 1939–45. Three hitches of horses (kept in St. Louis, Valencia, California, and Merrimack, New Hampshire) participate in community events around the country and have created favorable publicity for Anheuser-Busch for more than fifty years, translating public interest and goodwill into sales of beer.

•   •   •   •   •   •   •

PRODUCT   SCHLITZ/BUDWEISER

Pivotal P: Publicity

Schlitz and Budweiser unintentionally created good publicity, but then followed it up, Schlitz with a slogan and Budweiser with the Clydesdale horses.

Primary P: Promotion

The Clydesdales have become a rare example of animals as a living trademark, and they generate goodwill for Budweiser 365 days a year all over the United States.

•   •   •   •   •   •   •

PAPER MATE PENS   Spotted Reputation

Publicity can "make" a brand, as with Budweiser, but sometimes he who lives by the press, dies by the press. The highly promoted ballpoint pen entered the marketplace as an exceptional new product and exited quickly as a dismal failure. It was a case of faulty premises and broken promises, cured only when Paper Mate had the nerve to make friends of the ballpoint's biggest critics.

At 9:30 on the morning of October 29, 1945, 5,000 New Yorkers stormed the gates of Gimbels department store to get their first look at one of the marvels of the postwar era.

Twenty-seven men and women fainted in the frenzied rush, but the rest surged forward through a barricade of fifty extra policemen, clutching wads of dollar bills and pleading to buy—at $12.50 each—a pen.

No ordinary fountain pen, it was instead the first ballpoint to be sold in the United States, and, by extension, a war hero to boot. Bedeviled by fountain pens which leaked at high altitudes, U.S. and British bomber crews had turned to the newly available ballpoints in the thick of aerial combat, a fact noted again and again in the nation's newspapers.

The ballpoint pen had been developed by Laszlo Joszef Biro, a Hungarian refugee living in Buenos Aires, and his chemist brother, George. While other ballpoints had been gravity-fed, Biro spent twenty years experimenting on a ballpoint that would work by capillary action, allowing it to be used in positions other than directly upright. Biro had a working model after twenty years and had also found a way to grind a metal ball so that it would rotate smoothly inside a brass seat.

In 1943, RAF pilots stationed in Argentina began using the pens in combat and showed them off to their American colleagues. One U.S. pilot sent one of Biro's Eterpens (for Eternal Pen) to the Quartermaster General, and the Quartermasters Corps issued a request to U.S. manufacturers for a similar pen, one that would also be unaffected by changes in altitude and climate and that would use ink that dried quickly.

Several U.S. manufacturers were sent specifications, and, eventually, Biro sold the U.S. rights to Eberhard Faber, which, in turn, sold a share of the rights to the Eversharp Pen Company. Eversharp executives turned handsprings over the new product, despite complaints from engineers that the pens sometimes leaked. Sensing a breakthrough product (with appropriate breakthrough margins), Eversharp's top brass funded a $2 million research program and began telling key accounts about the new pen while supplying them to Uncle Sam as a military item.

The pens caught on with flight crews, spread to desk officers, and were used aboard the U.S.S. Missouri to sign the formal truce with Japan ending World War II. Stories about the pen and its wartime role began surfacing in the press, and Eversharp eagerly anticipated a publicity windfall upon the introduction of its new product.

Ballpoints did generate waves of publicity, but, as it turned out, not for Eversharp.

Salesman Milton Reynolds, three times a millionaire and three times bankrupt, saw Biro's Eterpen in Argentina and decided it would make a perfect novelty item for the first postwar Christmas season. After doing some research on ballpoints, he found that an American, John J. Loud, had patented a ballpoint pen in 1888 for writing on leather and other rough surfaces. Even though it had expired without ever being used for writing on paper, the Loud patent narrowed the scope of Biro's invention; Reynolds had only to patent a new gravity-dependent method of feeding ink to the penpoint to avoid infringing on the Biro patent.

While Eversharp was thoughtfully trying to figure out a way to stop its capillary pen from leaking, Reynolds was putting together a crash program on a gravity-fed ballpoint and simultaneously honing his sales pitch. One night, while writing with the pen on a soggy napkin, he got the flashy slogan he needed: "It writes under water."

Gimbels bought the line and the goods and fulfilled Reynolds's wildest dreams with full pages of advertising in New York newspapers. Even making allowances for the time, the copy was extraordinary. Gimbels promised its customers "the most incredible bargain of the century . . . a miraculous fountain pen . . . guaranteed to write for two years without refilling."

But some of the pens literally exploded.

Others splattered ink on shirts and skirts.

Advertised as being able to write equally well under water and at 20,000 feet, the pens had problems on dry paper at ground level. Those few that did put ink on paper without skipping or streaking disappointed their owners eventually, too, because the ink faded when it had fully dried.

Incredibly, such drawbacks didn't dampen consumer enthusiasm in the beginning. Gimbels sold its entire shipment of 10,000 pens in six hours and averaged 6,000 pens a day for four months. Nearby Macy's, not to be totally outdone, began selling Biro's original pen for $19.98, and Eversharp marketed an improved version for $15. Both sold briskly, even at these premium prices; however, by the spring, the Great Ballpoint Bubble had burst. Seven months after the Reynolds pen had been introduced, 104,000 of them had been returned as unsatisfactory. In addition to the problems associated with gravity feeding, the low-quality ink used in all ballpoints contained metal particles that eventually corroded the ink cartridge or ruined the penpoint, causing the pen to leak.

General consumers weren't the only dissatisfied customers. Bankers began fulminating publicly against ballpoints, because (1) the ink faded on checks, endangering their validity, and (2) forgers were carefully lifting ballpoint signatures with moistened thumbs and transferring them onto other pieces of paper. Teachers, too, refused to accept compositions written with ballpoints because they smeared so easily. Given the objections of such highly respected opposition, public opinion solidified against the ballpoint pen. By creating great expectations for a product that had not been fully developed, Reynolds, Gimbels, and others had apparently doomed the ballpoint to an early death.

Fortunately, a Los Angeles chemist named Fran Seech (also Hungarian) had kept experimenting with an ink for ballpoints that wouldn't leak, form the bubbles that led to clogging, or explode. After several months of experimenting with dyes in a tiny lab, he discovered a workable solution—using glycol as a solvent—and told a local ballpoint manufacturer about it. The penmaker borrowed money to hire Seech but, unable to repay it, bartered the company instead to twenty-eight-year-old Patrick Joseph Frawley, Jr., of San Francisco.

The Frawley Pen Company had been selling ballpoints to countries that still considered them "miraculous" and quickly saw the benefits of Seech's formula. Frawley earmarked $35,000 to develop a non-smear ink, and by 1948, Seech had made the ink leakproof. As a further improvement, Frawley suggested making his Paper Mate pen retractable to cut down on any problems associated with leaks.

Unfortunately for Frawley, finding a formula for a nonsmear pen was easier than finding a formula for marketing it. Dealers burned by Reynolds and other ballpoint companies refused to stock Paper Mates because of their unhappy experiences in the past.

Frawley was convinced that the Paper Mate would eventually overcome the ballpoint's bad reputation due to the convenience it offered, but he realized that a few minor improvements wouldn't change the minds of most disappointed users, who considered ballpoints "damaged goods." What he needed was a dramatic way of reversing the pen's negative image with both dealers and consumers. On the theory that there's no bigger booster than a convert, he decided to target his biggest detractors—stationery retailers, bankers, and teachers.

He began cultivating dealers by giving them free pens, offered them a standard push technique (consignment billing), and a persuasive new wrinkle—he paid the dealers their profits in advance. Naturally, this technique ensured that dealers would always reorder and keep Paper Mates on display.

When retailers proved recalcitrant even to easy profits, Frawley created what he called Project Normandy. Salespeople would waltz into retail stores, pin down startled dealers, and begin scribbling on their white shirts. When the retailers flared up, Paper Mate staffers would offer them $15 if the ink didn't wash off quickly. When it did, retailers had dramatic personal proof that—even if the ballpoint did leak—the stain could be removed quickly and easily, preserving the dealer's relations with customers.

After this bold tactical strike, Frawley opened a second front in the Battle of the Ballpoint by mailing free pens to San Francisco teachers and school principals. While the pens were sent without obligation, a month later, Frawley's salespeople followed up with phone calls and interviewed the startled educators, who had never been asked for an opinion on anything other than the three R's. Most agreed that, yes, the Paper Mate had eliminated the objectionable features of earlier ballpoints. Then, with the educators' permission,

Frawley took their oral testimonials and transformed them into print ads for local newspapers headlined "Principals Approve!" or "Teachers Approve!" When Frawley was able to convince two local banks to honor checks written with Paper Mates, his publicity department arranged stories in the Bay Area suggesting that his pen was a superior product and had been "banker-approved."

Frawley's strategy was a great success. By changing the minds of the ballpoint's biggest critics, he reversed public opinion almost overnight. In 1949, the first year of the unusual endorsement campaign, Paper Mate sales came to $300,000; five years later, when the campaign had taken hold nationally, sales reached $30 million. Ten years after Milton Reynolds had given birth to the first boom-and-bust of the ballpoint pen, Patrick Frawley had sold Paper Mate to Gillette for $15.5 million in cash.

His campaign benefited other manufacturers as well. In 1951, $13.4 million worth of ballpoints were sold (at manufacturers' prices) as opposed to $45 million worth of fountain pens. In 1986, according to the Writing Instrument Manufacturers Association, the fountain-pen industry is one-tenth the size of ballpoints, which became nearly a $560 million business.

• • • • • • •

PRODUCT   PAPER MATE PENS

Pivotal *P*: Publicity

Patrick Frawley's campaign silenced his severest critics—educators and bankers—and used their endorsements to reap a publicity bonanza.

Primary *P*'s: Promotion, Perception

Frawley's point-of-sale theatrics convinced dealers that Paper Mate wouldn't offend customers. Turned into allies, they assured clients that the pens were safe to use.

• • • • • • •

BURMA-SHAVE   Stop Signs

When Johnny came marching home from World War I, he brought with him the new safety razor thoughtfully provided by Uncle Sam and King Camp Gillette and considered himself quite the modern dandy.

The truth of the matter was that Johnny had updated only half of his shaving equipment. Like most men in the 1920s, and their fathers and grandfathers before them, he still applied a badger-hair brush to shaving soap to create lather and then rubbed it on his face.

While the ritual was masculine and comforting, the brush wound up wet and smelly; all shaving brushes of the period eventually became mildewed and turned a sickly, greenish color. A British manufacturer had introduced Lloyd's Euxesis brushless shave cream in the United States and trumpeted it as a scientific breakthrough; however, this sales appeal cut no ice with conservative American men and the product bombed.

Clinton Odell, formerly a successful insurance salesman recovering from arthritic rheumatism, heard about Lloyd's when he tried to sell a family remedy, Burma-Vita liniment, which his father had bought from an old sea captain. Odell quickly learned from a wholesale drug company in Minneapolis that liniments were unprofitable, because it took a lot of ailments to use up a whole bottle. On the other hand, the wholesaler respected Odell's marketing ability and in 1925 suggested he try his hand at selling Lloyd's Euxesis, the original brushless shaving cream.

Lloyd's was gummy, sticky stuff and didn't do much of a job in softening the beard. Like its successors, Lloyd's was more like a woman's cold cream than a soap and was packed with fatty acids and alcohols. Warren Schubert, a research chemist with Colgate-Palmolive, speculates that, "Some Englishman probably saw his wife shaving her legs with cold cream and got the idea to make it into a shaving cream for men."

Odell and his sons Leonard and Allan also thought Lloyd's campaign, "the greatest scientific advance in shaving," was offputting to Americans set in their ways about shaving and comfortable with their cup and brush. Changing that long-established ritual was going to take a different kind of appeal, and since Lloyd's was no great shakes, the Odells decided to make their own brand of brushless with the help of chemist Carl Noren. It took Noren nearly three hundred formulas to come up with a brushless that gave the user a comfortable shave with no wet brush to worry about.

The Odells first marketed Burma-Shave with what Allan called his "Jars on Approval program." He gave free Burma-Shave to retailers (as Patrick Frawley, Jr., had done with Paper Mate). Allan Odell promised to come back a week later and do one of two things: retrieve the unused portion for nothing or pocket fifty cents, the purchase price. Seven days later Odell returned and found there was nothing to pocket; the retailers who had seen no future in Lloyd's had just as little confidence in Burma-Shave and hadn't moved a single jar.

Brushless was batting 0-for-2, but before retailers could perform the last rites on it, Allan redeemed himself with a different marketing approach. Driving back from nearby Aurora, he had seen a set of signs spread fifty feet apart advertising a gas station—"Gas/Oil/Restrooms"—followed by a sign pointing to the station itself. He understood instinctively that spacing signs in series could hold a motorist's interest until he or she had seen the last one.

Excited, he told his father about the idea, and Clinton Odell ran it by some advertising nabobs in Chicago, all of whom pooh-poohed it as "too frivolous." This was the age of sound "reason-why" copy, and frivolity of any kind in advertising was frowned upon.

Nevertheless, the Odells believed in the idea enough to scrounge up $200 and make it their sole way of drawing the public's attention to a new product in an unsuccessful category. They bought forty second-hand billboards at a local wrecking company and put up a series of four signs that said:

> Shave the modern way/Fine for the skin
> Druggists have it/Burma-Shave.

Ten sets went up on each of the roads to Albert Lea and Red Wing in the fall of 1925, just before the ground froze. The following January, Burma-Shave got its first reorders—all of them from druggists serving people who traveled those roads.

In a dozen words, Allan Odell had given motorists two good "reasons why" to buy his product—it was modern and didn't hurt the skin—plus the name of the product—Burma-Shave—and the place where it could be purchased—the druggist's. Encouraged with these first results, Clinton Odell sold 49 percent of the Burma-Vita Company to raise money for a national billboard campaign.

> His face was smooth/And cool as ice
> And oh Louise!/He smelled/So nice

The Odells discovered that, at thirty-five miles per hour, the speed at which most cars traveled in those days, it took almost three seconds to proceed from one of five or six signs to the last one, fifteen or eighteen seconds in all. That was far more time and attention than a print advertiser could expect to command in a magazine or newspaper. The signs also established a semihypnotic reading pace and heightened suspense for whatever came next. Furthermore, the eye couldn't race ahead of the car and spoil the effect.

> Said Juliet/To Romeo
> If you won't shave/Go homeo

While some of the jingles promoted traffic safety or pointed out Burma-Shave's advantages over the badger brush, the basic message of the signs was "Boy gets girl—if he uses Burma-Shave." The public quickly caught on and began sending in their own jingles. Later the Odells offered a hundred dollars for the best jingle and advertised the contests heavily. Some campaigns drew more than 50,000 entries.

> If you think/She likes/Your bristles
> Walk bare-footed/Through some thistles

Business picked up tremendously. Signs costing $25,000 translated into sales of $68,000 in 1926, and by 1929, sales had quadrupled. One boost for business was the publicity the signs generated. In the 1930s, every radio star from Jimmy Durante to Fibber McGee had fun with the signs and popularized Burma-Shave. The U.S. Navy asked the company to put up signs at McMurdo Sound in the Antarctic as a morale builder. One of them was:

Dear Lover Boy/Your photo came
But your doggone beard/Won't fit/The frame

The story was picked up by U.P.I. and ran in thousands of newspapers.

Given the publicity boost and goodwill, Burma-Shave prospered during the Depression and was soon grossing more than $3 million a year. Things were going so well by 1936 that the Odells decided to add a truly frivolous set of signs.

Free—Free/A Trip/To Mars
For 900/Empty jars

The tongue-in-cheek challenge was taken up by Arliss French, manager of a Red Owl supermarket in Appleton, Wisconsin. He wired Burma-Shave that he was accepting their offer and asked, "Just where should the jars be shipped?" Allan Odell wired back:

If a trip/To Mars you'd earn
Remember, Friend/There's no return

French replied:

Let's not quibble/Let's not fret
Gather your forces/I'm all set

The Odells capitulated:

Our rockets are ready/We ain't splitting hairs
Just send us the jars/And arrange your affairs

A Red Owl publicist had found a town in Germany named Moers, but pronounced "Mars." He persuaded Burma-Shave to take care of French's plane fare and promised that Red Owl would do the rest. On the appointed day, French showed up in a silvery space suit with a bubble on his head, his wife, and a Brink's truck filled with empty jars. When they landed on "Mars," Red Owl arranged a warm welcome. The contest caused another flood of publicity for Burma-Shave.

"At ease," she said/"Maneuvers begin
When you get/Those whiskers/Off your chin"

Burma-Shave held its own through the war years. The publicity never stopped, and the brand still got laughs in the early days of television. Fred Allen did a sketch called "The Death of the Burma-Shave Poet" on his Texaco Hour, and sales spurted again.

But the signs were clear by the mid-1950s that Burma-Shave was on the way out. Growth began to plateau in 1955, a boom time for products of nearly every other description. With cars routinely traveling at sixty miles an hour, the old measured pace of the jingles was lost, and the signs became anachronisms. The Burma-Vita Company was bought by Philip Morris in 1963, the last year the signs appeared. The signs had prefigured their own end in this 1930 jibe:

> Shaving brushes/You'll soon see 'em
> Way down east/In some/Museum/Burma-Shave

Nevertheless, before they became museum pieces (and collectibles), the Burma-Shave signs had struck a responsive chord with the public and had created a new medium for mass advertising—billboards in series.

•   •   •   •   •   •   •

PRODUCT   BURMA-SHAVE

Pivotal *P*: Publicity

Burma-Shave's serial billboards were innovative and produced scads of publicity when radio comedians and feature writers lampooned their gentle, folksy humor.

•   •   •   •   •   •   •

Chapter Eleven

DON'T LAUNCH A

PRODUCT

WITHOUT A

PROMISE

"PROMISE her anything," said the ad, "but give her Arpege."

That copy line sums up the importance of a promise to marketing. Few products are launched that don't make a concrete promise. Instead, products seem to scream their promises from the shelves, "Buy me, buy me. I'll make you thinner, prettier, sexier, save you time, pain, embarrassment, impress your spouse, your boss, your kids." If the product fulfills its promise, it gets bought again, otherwise. . . .

Using promises, marketers set levels of expectations for their products. By the 1990s, even the most naive consumers know they are being manipulated and have learned to expect disappointment. Nevertheless, we approach products we're trying for the first time expectantly; when the expectations are too high, we feel cheated.

Countries, cities, and theme parks promoting tourism are often guilty of making the most blatant promises, which is why areas that don't do that—like Australia—win friends and influence people. Paul Hogan's good-natured "Put another shrimp on the barbie" showed Americans a country at ease with itself, and therefore inviting. On the other hand, Busch Gardens promises "Europe right here at home," a promise guaranteed to appeal only to accidental tourists who'd rather stay home in the first place.

Moving Images   Advertisers haven't used words to promise us "washday miracles" or romance created by using the right toothpaste for some time. They've learned that words are too specific, too direct, too easy a yardstick against which to judge their products' performance. Instead, they show the promise of the product indirectly through slick, quick-cut images. The promise of Seagram's Golden Wine Cooler, for instance, is that the drink sparks young dancers and musicians, and it suggests that if you want to be chic and kicky like them, "Buy our booze."

Broken Promises   It's great to be first in the marketplace with a seductive new promise like this, but what happens to the people who come along after that promise is broken, the way Milton Reynolds temporarily killed the market for ballpoint pens? Not much. No one holds parades for the men and women who merely correct the marketing mistakes made by their predecessors. They just clean up the mess and hope that they can dominate their chosen fields for years like other latecomers—Singer sewing machines, Postum, and Paper Mate. One company entering a field where broken promises was the rule shook things up with a new marketing technique and wound up not only covering the problem but covering the earth.

SHERWIN-WILLIAMS   Paint Job

"Unscrupulous manufacturers of, or dealers in, paint have . . . induced the gullible to buy the most worthless stuff which is guaranteed in the strongest terms."

The writer is Henry Alden Sherwin, cofounder of Sherwin-Williams Company. He was fulminating against the many manufacturers of so-called "patent" paints who made claims for their wares that bore as much relation to the truth as the flummery used to sell patent medicines. As a result, when Sherwin entered the marketplace, he had more than a perception problem on his hands. He had to find an instant way to gain public acceptance for his product, or he was dead in the water.

Producers of patent paints claimed their wares covered huge surfaces, never ran, were of uniform color, and required no expertise to apply. Such claims were impossible to support in the 1870s, because no manufacturer had yet developed a satisfactory way to suspend pigments in a liquid that would stay suspended in a can.

Paint had to be stirred by hand constantly to prevent the pigment from sinking to the bottom, and it had to be used immediately, otherwise it would dry out and become unusable. In the absence of containers to prevent hardening, there was no way to ship paint more than a few miles. Finally, patent paints nearly always streaked, meaning the surface to which they were applied remained unfinished and had to be painted again.

Prepared house paint had been tried first in 1842 but had failed almost immediately for the reasons outlined. Twenty years later, most paint manufacturers still offered only "makings"—oil, pigments, and putty, which consumers had to mix together themselves to make paint. One step up from the do-it-yourselfers were the barrels of popular paint that local entrepreneurs created in the rush of the spring painting season; they would laboriously mix barrel-sized batches of the latest colors by grinding oily pigments into an ointment, stirring in more oil, and adding thinners and driers. The barrels were sold as is or smaller portions would be transferred into whatever containers happened to be at hand.

In July 1867, D. R. Averill, of Newburg, Ohio, was awarded the first patent for a prepared paint and the first trademark for an American product. At the time, Sherwin was a partner in a paint business and viewed Averill's invention as something less than a godsend. He wrote, "Averill thought he had made a great discovery and that a fortune was in his grasp . . . after seeing the materials he used, I came away content to vigorously oppose 'Patent' paint."

Sherwin had plenty of opposing to do, because Averill spawned a clutch of imitators, the more unscrupulous of whom applied themselves to figuring out ingenious ways to increase their profits at the public's expense. Some weighted their paint cans with crushed stone. Others diluted their oil with water or "extended" white paint by adding chalk which mixed in with pigment and couldn't be detected before being purchased; it was only after the job was completed that consumers saw white streaks and realized they had been bilked.

Fortune would later comment, "The quick-profit boys began cashing in on Averill-type paints, and in so doing they gave prepared paints a bad name." In a reaction to this attitude of "Chalk and water, and let the public beware," many people still bought their own makings and made their own paint. The obvious drawback was that mixing paint from scratch made it extremely difficult to come up with the same formula again if more paint was needed later on.

A meticulous man with a rare appreciation of quality, Sherwin was initially put off by the idea of manufacturing "patent" paint, because Averill and his imitators used cheap limestone and calcium carbonate, which doomed every painting job with white streaks. Sherwin prided himself on the purity of his ingredients and did nicely selling makings to consumers and house painters. Nevertheless, he saw that a reliable brand of premixed paint could be a gold mine, because people could do their own painting with complete confidence and save money.

Even without precise measuring and repeatable formulas, paint was a $20 million business in 1870. However, Sherwin's original partners were equally certain that the future lay not in paint but in linseed oil, because "People have always mixed their own paint so that they know what color they're getting." Sherwin decided to dissolve the partnership, giving up the linseed part of the business and keeping the paint for himself.

Needing a new partner, he found an apt one in Edward Porter Williams, a Phi Beta Kappa graduate of Western Reserve University, who shared his convictions about machine-made paint. Where Sherwin was precise and studious, Williams was a born salesman—jovial and congenial, the kind of man who greeted everyone by first name, made friends and influenced people.

In 1870, Sherwin-Williams & Company was formally organized and originally distributed makings like paste paints, oil colors, and putty. In preparation for the day they could offer their own premixed paint, the partners began developing their own lead and zinc mines, smelters, linseed-oil mills, chemical units, color-making facilities, and canning plants so that they could control quality every step of the way. By 1873, the firm was marketing its own products for direct sale to the public, and Sherwin was developing a paint-making formula that would obviate the problems associated with ready-made paint.

The key was being able to grind pigment fine enough so that it would remain suspended in oil, making the paint reliable and the formula repeatable. In 1876, Sherwin created a mill to achieve that purpose and overcame a second hurdle in 1877, when he patented a reclosable paint can, which reduced waste and guaranteed that tomorrow's coat of paint would look like today's. These refinements led the partners to test a line of paint in 1878, eight years after they had gone into business.

Rather than gamble with the Sherwin-Williams name, they called it Osborn Family Paint in honor of A. T. Osborn, a short-lived partner of theirs. After two years of test marketing, however, it became apparent that the public, conditioned to inferior patent paints, wouldn't take a chance on another, presumably unreliable, brand of machine-made paint.

To his credit, the logical, punctilious Sherwin was able to understand that what was holding customers back wasn't a concern about physical matters like paint, oil, or pigment at all; rather, Sherwin and Williams had to hurdle an emotional barrier and find an ironclad way to make ready-made paint respectable. They came up with a plan that not only destroyed the notion of unreliability but also offered "do-it-yourself" painters a unique benefit in the form of an insurance policy.

Where other manufacturers had backed up their paints with worthless promises, Sherwin put his money where his mouth was; he created the first national, iron-clad, money-back guarantee.

In 1880, Sherwin-Williams offered its new SWP brand paint with this notice:

> Since some of the most worthless paints in the market are guaranteed in the strongest terms, it is humiliating to us to feel

obliged in any way to conform to a custom so much abused
. . . we would not do so were it not that our paint is constantly being introduced to people who have not known the
character and standing of this company. . . . But to satisfy
strangers and doubters, the following guarantee is used on the
labels:

"We guarantee that this paint, when properly used, will
not crack, flake, or chalk off, and will cover more surface,
work better, wear longer, and permanently look better
than other paints, including Pure White Lead and Oil. We
hereby agree to forfeit the value of the paint and the cost of
applying it if in any instance it is not found as above
represented."

There were some exceptions. Sherwin-Williams refused to reim-
burse the user for paint used on wet, knotted, sappy or unseasoned
lumber, paint applied to uneven surfaces, or paint "doped, thinned, or
mixed with anything which we could not approve of as reliable paint
material." But the big news was the guarantee itself as well as the
promise of reimbursement for labor costs. The company was saying, in
plain words, "There is no way you can make a mistake using this
paint. We couldn't afford to make such an outlandish promise unless
we were absolutely sure about our product."

Sherwin-Williams was now not only selling paint, they were selling something far more important: a promise, a guaranteed promise of
reliability.

In a sense, Sherwin-Williams had defused the whole question
of the reliability of prepared paint merely by offering such an all-
encompassing guarantee to potential customers. Sherwin's idea was
straightforward:

- *Add value*—Paint that was protected by a money-back guarantee was clearly more valuable than paint backed up by
  mere words. People buying SWP could do so without fear
  that their house or barn would turn streaky a day later.
- *Remove the irritant*—Armed with the guarantee, consumers
  didn't have to worry about the paint not working out, be-

cause they won either way. If the paint worked, they got the job done; if not, they got their money back and could try again without losing anything.

- *Create a climate of acceptance*—Sherwin-Williams's confidence in its own product and the acceptance of financial responsibility inevitably rubbed off on dealers and consumers. Sherwin later commented, "We studiously tried to mix confidence with our paints and colors."

The paint justified Sherwin's confidence, and customers began buying Sherwin-Williams paint in large quantities, allowing the partners to leave retailing and devote their full attention to wholesaling prepared paint in volume. The company was soon supplying custom-made paint for dozens of industrial uses and added color after color confidently, because each new color depended on a repeatable chemical formula.

To make the point that it offered paint in many colors, Sherwin-Williams adopted a chameleon as its logo, but the public thought the reptile was a snake and sales slumped momentarily. Fortunately, George W. Ford, Sherwin-Williams's advertising manager, had an interest in a cleaning compound called Eureka whose logo featured earnest little brownies scrubbing a globe. When it went out of business, Ford acquired the logo and adapted it for Sherwin-Williams's use. The "Cover the Earth" logo is recognized instantly around the world.

Given its head start in manufacturing technology, Sherwin-Williams developed the paint roller and the first modern latex paint and grew to become a $2.7 billion company.

•   •   •   •   •   •   •

PRODUCT   PREMIXED PAINT

Pivotal *P*: Promise

Sherwin-Williams had to give premixed paint extra value to combat its bad reputation. They added security to their paint by offering the first money-back guarantee.

•   •   •   •   •   •   •

COLEMAN LANTERNS   Blurred Vision

Twenty years after Thomas Edison had invented the electric light (in 1879), most Americans still used gasoline lanterns for artificial illumination.

Although Edison was an innovator in many respects, he was hidebound and intractable in others. In particular, Edison politicked against George Westinghouse's invention of alternating current and insisted that his bulbs run only on direct current because AC was "dangerous and commercially unfeasible." Since direct current can only travel limited distances, a mere 8 percent of the U.S. had electricity by 1907, the first year such information was gathered for *Historical Statistics of the United States.*

Over and above Edison's jealousy, there were other reasons for the use of gasoline lanterns. The electrical circuitry of the day was limited to metropolitan areas and what there was was unreliable, leading to frequent blackouts; moreover, the illumination produced by gasoline lanterns was twenty times as powerful as that produced by the carbon-filament bulb then in use. Even though some gasoline lanterns varied in quality—particularly those fed by gravity—they were cheaper to operate and more accessible than electricity.

To sum up the situation, electric light was not viewed as a final solution to the problem of artificial illumination. As a direct result of its failings, patents for no fewer than 2,400 lighting devices were issued between 1892 and 1900. Although kerosene was available everywhere, gas vapor made from petroleum burned more brightly and was cheap, since gasoline sold for 14 to 20 cents a gallon.

As lighter crude oil became more plentiful, more inventors began creating gasoline lamps fed by gravity which could be mounted on poles and used to light streets and barns. The lamps gave off strong light, but particles of carbon and other impurities tended to collect in the generator, which made for frequent cleaning or replacement.

Other inventors worked with liquid fuel, too; however, rather than burn it directly, they fed it, under air pressure, into a small tube which forced the fuel into the generator. The generator could then be heated with a small alcohol torch, vaporizing the fuel; as the gas vapor escaped through a tiny opening in the generator, it entered a burner where it mixed with air and ignited. This method of "force feeding" eliminated the problems of impurities clogging the supply line, because any particles reaching the generator were trapped inside a porous wick. Moreover, the intense heat produced by the vapor method caused the lamp to glow dazzlingly.

One winter night in 1899, the brilliant light of such a pressurized gasoline lamp in a drugstore attracted the attention of William Coffin Coleman, an aspiring law student, who was selling typewriters in Brockton, Alabama. Since Coleman only had 25 percent vision in one eye and 50 percent vision in the other, his parents had had to read his schoolbooks to him. This pressurized gas lamp was the first artificial light that he could really see by at night; consequently, seeing it became "the most important moment" of his life.

He had originally sold typewriters to generate money for law books; all that changed when he saw the light and became excited about the lantern's commercial possibilities.

Coleman tried to locate the salesman who had hung the lantern in the drugstore, but didn't catch up with him until they met a month later in Caruthersville, Missouri. As it turned out, the long-awaited meeting was a bust; the salesman was selling exclusive territories to agents for the Irby-Gilliland Company of Memphis, Tennessee, at wildly inflated prices and promised Coleman $25,000 if the two of them could sell $100,000 worth of territories within a year.

He wrestled with his conscience all night and told the *Saturday Evening Post*, "I kept remembering in the Bible when the devil took Christ upon a mountain and showed him all the kingdoms of the world and said, 'All this power will I give thee. . . . If thou therefore wilt worship me.'"

The next morning Coleman turned him down; two days later, Coleman got a telegram from the lamp's manufacturers offering him the salesman's job. It turned out that the salesman had been selling territories to farmers with no sales experience while Coleman was already an experienced manufacturer's rep. That experience was a plus, because manufacturers William Irby and Forrest Gilliland were in the crockery business full time, and Irby had only patented his hydro-carbon vapor lamp as a sideline. Offered the sales territory of his choice, Coleman settled on Kingfisher, an up-and-coming town in the Oklahoma Territory that fancied itself a potential state capitol once the territory achieved statehood.

He came to Kingfisher on the first day of a new century, January 1, 1900, and saw a thriving town full of stores that stayed open until 10 P.M., but were lit dimly with oil-wick lamps. Rubbing his hands in anticipation, he went to work selling lamps, and one week and sixty sales calls later, he'd sold only two.

Coleman had expected to sell between eight and ten lamps a day and couldn't figure out why people in Kingfisher were so dead set against them. Sam Lowry, the owner of the town's largest saloon, enlightened him by walking to the back of his storeroom and showing Coleman a collection of thirty slightly used gasoline lamps hanging on a pole. Another salesman had sold dozens of gravity-fed gasoline lanterns in Kingfisher, but after he'd left town, the lanterns had become clogged with carbon and no longer worked. Lowry told Coleman, "We got bit once, but we won't get bit twice."

Trying to explain to Lowry that his lamp was technically superior to the gravity lamps served no purpose. Obviously, gasoline lanterns were damaged goods in Kingfisher, because the hit-and-run salesman hadn't backed up his sales with service.

Coleman had to figure out a way to sell a product considered completely unreliable in Kingfisher, knowing that consumers weren't interested in mere technical advances. After some thought, he realized that consumers were buying not the lantern itself but rather the illumination it provided. Coleman later told the editor of a company publication, "I saw that I wasn't selling a product at all; I was providing a service."

Quite obviously, the key to that service was reliability. Knowing that it would be nearly impossible to sell lanterns in the atmosphere of distrust that pervaded Kingfisher, Coleman decided to try to rent them to local businesspeople with a clear need for reliable illumination.

Renting the lamps for a dollar a week and guaranteeing the results rather than selling them for $15 apiece enabled Coleman to offer customers a unique promise—a small cash outlay for a product that was regarded with suspicion. Moreover, this technique made for good public relations. The original salesman had gouged every possible penny out of Kingfisher; by reducing the initial cost of his lamp, Coleman was positioning himself as a businessman with the long-term interests of the community at heart, not as merely another drummer out to make a quick buck.

If the "illumination-service" idea didn't immediately create a climate of acceptance for the gasoline lamp, at least it helped remove the stigma attached to lamps that had cost $15 and didn't work. Coleman removed the irritant—a lantern that didn't work—by following Sherwin's example and making every sale dependent on performance. If the device didn't work, he reasoned, his lessees shouldn't have to pay for it. If his lamps became clogged, like those his predecessor had sold, the storeowners wouldn't owe him a penny; however, if the lamps functioned correctly, he would earn one dollar per store per week under what was the nation's first service contract.

A service contract is a promise.

He walked into the first store early one morning and told the proprietor, "I worked my head off here last week trying to sell you some lamps, but now I'm glad you didn't buy. There has been a complete change in the policy of our company. We've got something too good to sell. Now all we are selling is our service. The other stores are going to be lighted by our service, and you can't afford to go on trying to sell in the dark."

Coleman's inspired salesmanship was quickly rewarded. Four days after he'd started using the service-contract idea, the former law student had leased all twelve of his demonstration lanterns. Since Irby-Gilliland had yet to get its money back on the first lanterns, the company refused to give Coleman more lanterns without some payment.

Based on his success with the service contract, Coleman borrowed $1,000 from his farmer brother-in-law and later called it "the greatest sale I ever made." He bought several hundred lamps and formed the Hydro-Carbon Light Company; a year later, he was able to buy all the stock and patent rights to the lantern for $3,000 and expanded to Wichita, Kansas (which remains company headquarters), Oklahoma City, San Diego, Albuquerque, and Las Vegas.

Of course, Las Vegas now glows with electrified light, which became widespread after Edison lost the fight for direct current. But long before cities had become totally electrified, Coleman had retargeted his sales efforts from institutions to outdoorsy men and women who loved to hunt, fish, climb, or camp out, with gratifying results. Sales run nearly half a billion dollars a year, and the stock with which William Coleman repaid his brother-in-law's $1,000 loan is now worth about $500,000.

The Coleman Company is run by William Coleman's grandson, Clarence Coleman, Jr., and it still sells more than a million of the original pressurized gasoline lamps every year. Coleman is the last gasoline-lantern manufacturer left in North America, but its lanterns and other outdoor products—sleeping bags, hot tubs, target bows, canoes, catamarans, and camping trailers—are available worldwide.

● ● ● ● ● ● ●

PRODUCT   COLEMAN LANTERNS

Pivotal P: Promise

Faced with selling a problem product, William Coleman created a variation on the money-back guarantee by leasing lamps under the first service contract.

● ● ● ● ● ● ●

TONI HOME PERMANENTS   Hair Dues

When bobbed hair became the rage, permanent waves followed, but home permanent products fizzled until Toni's manufacturers found a way to make promises the company could keep.

The first "permanent" waves were created by British hairdresser Charles Nessler in 1906, using borax solutions and electrically heated irons. Nessler introduced the new wave to America in 1915, and hair waving became firmly established in the 1920s.

By 1937, 100,000 beauty parlors in the United States offered hair waves to women, despite three annoying factors. Even though the treatments were described as "permanent," they only lasted as long as it took new hair fiber to grow. Second, they cost between $7.50 and $10, which was beyond the reach of most women during a crippling Depression. Finally, women resented the amount of time it took getting a permanent, which could be as long as six hours. Given such conditions, half of America's 72 million women had never had a permanent by the end of the 1930s, even though waves made up 25 percent of beauty-parlor business.

While there were drawbacks to the waves themselves, the beauty products business began booming toward the end of the Depression.

Shortly after graduating from Yale in 1937, a young St. Paul man with an odd nickname borrowed $5,000 from his father to buy a moribund beauty company with an even odder name. Richard "Wishbone" Harris (nicknamed for his fondness for that part of a chicken) bought Noma, Inc. (named for its products, which curled hair with *no machine*). Noma sold chemically activated curling pads and wave lotions to the trade. Permanents became more popular after America entered World War II; by 1943 the enterprising Harris had built Noma into a $500,000 business.

After he became more familiar with beauty-parlor permanents, Harris thought he saw an opportunity to make Noma an even greater success. He reasoned that he could package the ingredients the company already sold in a home-permanent-wave kit, which would require only curlers, made of fiber rather than plastic, curling solution, and a set of instructions. Such a kit could save women large amounts of time and money.

Harris was no innovator, because three other "home perms" were already available in retail drugstores for ten dollars apiece, but they weren't selling because they took about eight hours to work and used foul-smelling sulfites to curl the hair. Since no brand had sold well, manufacturers had great difficulty getting retailers to stock any more.

Deciding to build demand for his product directly with consumers, Harris invested $20,000 in developing it as a mail-order product. "Rol-Wav" packaged together curlers, powdered ammonium nitrite (which, when mixed with water, curled the hair) and a set of instructions—all of which originally sold for twenty-five cents.

He spent an additional $5,600 on national advertising and told his mailman, "Wait 'til Monday morning, you'll be snowed under." He told *Life*, in 1948, "I figured we'd have trucks backing up to the door. Well, Monday came around and we got six letters." He later admitted, "When women have been buying something for ten bucks and you come along and say you've got the same thing for a quarter, they just won't believe it's any good."

It wasn't.

First, the wave itself wasn't satisfactory, which turned off potential customers before the product had any appreciable distribution. Second, enclosing powdered chemicals to be put into solution with water was a mistake because it left too much margin for error. Finally, ammonium nitrite was too harsh a curling agent and actually damaged some women's hair.

Harris had placed too little emphasis on R & D and had brought an unsuccessful product in an unsuccessful category to market prematurely. To his credit, Harris hired research chemists to come up with a new formula versatile enough to wave any normal hair without injury; these efforts proved successful when a liquid curling solution using ammonium thioglycolate was substituted for the powdered nitrite.

At that moment, the infamous "New-Improved" slogan was born, a technique that would rescue Harris, and many others who followed in his footsteps. When a product comes back into the marketplace with an improved stance, it begs the public for a second chance. And Americans are just romantic enough to believe that everyone deserves a second chance.

Harris studied hair care a lot and was eventually able to write a foolproof set of instructions. Then, while driving a Noma distributor to Detroit, he found a good name for his product. The distributor told Harris, "What you need is a tony name—one with class." Harris says, "That word 'tony' stuck in my mind. I worked it around a lot, changing the spelling to an 'i' instead of a 'y' and using a small 't.' It looked good. As it turned out, it was the perfect name—short, clear, wonderful for printing, good for radio."

Convinced he had all the elements together at last, Harris started the Toni Company in 1944 with $1,000. This time, he priced his product at $1.25, when most perms were running $10. "That wasn't too high, and it wasn't too low. . . . I wasn't going to make the mistake of cheapening the product again."

Instead of continuing with mail order, he switched back to retail distribution in an attempt to lose the stigma of a "cheap mail-order product." To his chagrin, owner after owner showed him shelves full of home permanents that weren't selling. There had been too many broken promises and failed dreams.

Finally, in desperation, Harris told one Minneapolis store owner, "If you'll put $54 worth of Toni kits on your shelves, I'll take out $54 worth of advertising and run it under your name. If they don't sell, I'm out 54 bucks. If they do, I'll get my money back and you'll have your profits. Either way, you can't lose. How about it?"

The promise was to the dealer and it spelled M-O-N-E-Y.

Harris got a yes, bought space in the Minneapolis and St. Paul newspapers, and offered free demonstrations to the saleswomen in the drugstore, using promotion as a means of parlaying his promise into reality. When customers asked the saleswomen about Toni, they could point to their own hair and say, "I've got one myself."

By giving that first retailer advertising support and allowing him to pay on consignment, Harris was able to overcome the stigma that home permanents wouldn't sell. Given just this little push, Toni became a success throughout Minneapolis; six months later, Harris used a similar approach with drugstores in Iowa, Wisconsin, and Illinois and achieved similar results. The improved version of Toni sold itself to consumers once retailers stocked it.

When sales passed the $1 million mark, Harris asked his brother Irving to help him fill the orders. Irving filled orders, but he also created one of the great advertising slogans. He photographed twins with identical hairdos, one done in a salon, the other with a Toni kit, and asked consumers to decide, "Which twin has the Toni?"

The phrase was picked up by teen-agers, disk jockeys, and comedians. Beauticians and their lobbyists felt compelled to counterattack. Florida's State Board of Beauty Culture declared it a crime to do beauty work outside a beauty parlor, and the Kentucky Hairdressers' Association tried to have housewives arrested for "operating a beauty shop without a license." The housewives retaliated by forming Toni Clubs, where they could make curling their hair a social occasion.

At the start of 1948, Toni was selling 85 percent of all the home-wave kits used in the U.S., and that June, a mere five years after he'd started the company, Harris sold Toni to Gillette for $20 million. Never at a loss for a quip, Harris looked at his first check—for $6 million—and exclaimed, "What a dilemma! All my assets are tied up in cash."

As Russell Adams points out in his book *King C. Gillette*, the Harrises didn't take the money and run. They were elected to Gillette's board, moved from St. Paul to Chicago, where the new Toni headquarters took root, and ran Toni even more successfully than before. In the first year of joint ownership sales rose from $59.5 million to $85.9 million.

●　　●　　●　　●　　●　　●　　●

PRODUCT   TONI

Pivotal P: Promise

Slow-selling home perms forced Toni to get off the ground store by store. Free advertising and free perms made retailers' pitches for Toni more promising.

Primary P's: Price, Perception

Toni needed a price hike to become credible. Women thought cheap perms would hurt their hair and refused to buy until the price met expectations for a quality product.

●　　●　　●　　●　　●　　●　　●

Chapter Twelve

SOMETIMES the only thing a marketer can do to make the product work is to keep on keeping on.

If you've checked and double-checked your other *P*'s and still believe in your product, then you have only one choice—Persevere.

There's a Place for Us For one thing, although your precious product may bomb with its original target market, it may eventually score somewhere else if you persevere. In 1963, Dupont's Corfam was going to "revolutionize the shoe business"; instead, it was a disaster in the U.S. The shoes didn't breathe like leather, which was a serious detriment in a fashion shoe; however, offered to Polish workmen as a durable shoe, Corfam has been a steady seller for twenty years. And don't forget that Marlboro was first a woman's cigarette, 7-Up was a cure for infant dyspepsia, and Kleenex was a beauty product before all three found wider acceptance.

In one of the most spectacular cases of this kind, a food broker created a dog food in the 1930s and named it Balto after the Huskie who delivered serum in a blizzard to save Nome, Alaska, from a diphtheria epidemic. Broker Sam Hornstein had pulled out all the stops and was selling 50,000 cases a year. Then he began getting angry letters from disappointed consumers whose dogs were experiencing digestive problems. It turned out that fish was far too rich for the average dog's diet and could only be used as a supplement every two weeks. Fortunately for Hornstein, cats had been attracted by the fishy odor and had been eating Balto for more than a year. Hornstein renamed his dog food Puss'n Boots and later sold his dog food turned cat food to Quaker Oats for $6 million.

Reinventing the Wheel   When a marketing plan for a new product is bombing, onlookers often chide the manufacturer for "reinventing the wheel." In fact, the wheel has been reinvented any number of times: What are the Frisbee, the long-playing record, the computer diskette, and the circular space satellite if not updated versions of the wheel?

Hang On Sloopy   Of course, product innovation is not for everyone. Innovators must have the courage of their convictions, because reinventing the wheel involves flying in the face of conventional wisdom. It also means hanging in there, even when no one seems to believe but you. It can mean selling out, or buying in.

It means assailing the unassailable by starting a third hamburger chain when McDonald's and Burger King have the market sewn up (Wendy's), using the legal system to tilt the playing field against the world's largest company (MCI), networking a local television station (WTBS), or coming up with a four-color national newspaper when "newspapers are dying" (USA Today).

The Road Not Taken   It means walking the plank, going out on a limb, zigging when everyone else is zagging. It means having guts. When Seagram's decided in the mid-1950s that the world needed yet another premium Scotch (Dewar's), its advertising agency was not immediately ecstatic; however, after researching the way others advertised various brands of Scotch, they saw an opening that, in turn, led to a strategy.

All the other agencies did the bulk of their advertising in the fall and winter and used newspapers to remind forgetful Christmas gift buyers about their clients. Seagram's avoided newspapers altogether and in the summer months ran "image" ads in upscale magazines like

Fortune and the *New Yorker*. In an uncrowded advertising environment, Dewar's had all the Scotch consumer's attention and capitalized on the opportunity by developing a quality image, which ultimately led to larger margins and higher profits.

First Impressions   Being first with a revolutionary product is, by itself, no guarantee of success, particularly with high-tech products. Few people remember that the first videocassette machine was perfected by Ampex, that the first pocket calculator was a Bowmar Brain, or that the first digital watch was a Hamilton Pulsar.

Cott was the first company to market sugar-free soft drinks in the 1940s, and still survives although that attempt failed. Next, Kirsch introduced No-Cal soda for diabetics and was pleased to attract weight-conscious nondiabetics as well. That tipped off Royal Crown, whose Diet Rite Cola established the mass market and led directly to the introduction of Tab and Patio Cola. The latter was an immediate dud, and Tab is a flagging brand, but their successors, Diet Pepsi and Diet Coke, now dominate the field.

Long Green   Thankfully, there's a silver lining to this dark cloud. Despite all the cautionary tales, despite the fact that most new products die aborning, despite the high costs involved, innovation can be very very good business, because it can be immediately profitable and can lead to market dominance over a long period of time. How long? A 1923 survey of leaders in twenty-five product categories was updated in 1983. Sixty years later, twenty of them were still number one, four were in second place, and the other was fourth. Being first and being able to crack the distribution problem puts you in line for a bigger share of the pie—if the public proves ready to eat your pie.

Yes. It's a fact. Pioneers that do their jobs right sell to a larger potential audience than that available to latecomers. A paper on pioneering brands published by the Massachusetts Institute of Technology in 1984 states, "Second entrants obtain on the average only about three-quarters of the market share of the pioneer, and later entrants are able to capture progressively smaller shares."

So, take heart and take a spin at reinventing the wheel. A naturalist did it and created a great way to preserve food. So what if he didn't turn a profit for seventeen years.

BIRDS EYE FOODS   Frozen Assets

Clarence "Bob" Birdseye once said, prophetically, "Only through curiosity can we discover opportunities, and only by gambling can we take advantage of them."

He should have added persevering, since Birdseye had faith in freezing foods and maintained that faith during all the years his firm bled red ink.

The idea of preserving food by freezing it had been around for centuries. Emperor Nero made sure the imperial wine collection stayed fresh by storing jugs of it on oxcarts piled high with ice deep in the catacombs of Rome. In 1626, Sir Francis Bacon had frozen a chicken by killing it and then stuffing its carcass with snow. (He died shortly thereafter from exposure.)

Food was stored on top of blocks of ice until 1890, when a mild winter prompted food processors to try "cold storage." Fruit, fish, and poultry were packed in boxes and kept in rooms lined with pipes into which volatile liquids like ammonia were fed. The gas was compressed, then allowed to expand suddenly through a nozzle; it cooled off quickly, and the boxes of food froze solid at plus fourteen degrees Fahrenheit.

From his knowledge of cells and the speed with which they deteriorated unless frozen, Birdseye knew cold storage couldn't be fully effective. When food is frozen slowly, as in cold storage, tissues freeze slowly and form ice crystals, which are relatively large. When they thaw, these cell walls are ruptured, making the food taste bad.

Birdseye, a naturalist who had trapped frogs for the Bronx Zoo, later worked as a surveyor for the U.S. government in Labrador. There he was exposed to another method of freezing food—the Eskimo method of quick-freezing fish by pulling them out of the ice and letting them air dry until they were frozen solid. The fish could then be thawed and eaten months later with no loss of flavor.

With $7 worth of brine, ice, and an electric fan, Birdseye experimented with quick-freezing fish, meat, and a variety of vegetables by exposing them to a circulating mist of brine at forty-five degrees below zero Fahrenheit. He perfected a process for mechanical quick-freezing, received a patent for it in 1921, and launched Birdseye Seafoods, Inc., in New York City two years later.

The idea proved unpopular in the food world. Butchers wailed that individual cuts of frozen meat would ruin their livelihood, and restaurants, fearful of losing trade because people could eat more cheaply at home, claimed that frozen foods were unhealthy. One New York chain even attached a card to its menu that read, "No frozen food deception here. Your doctor will tell you frozen foods can't give you all the fresh food vitamins." Shortly thereafter, the American Medical Association endorsed frozen fruits and vegetables, and the restaurant's management apologized.

Turning around consumer attitudes wasn't quite so easy, because the American public instinctively distrusted any mechanical process related to food and didn't see any difference between Birdseye's "frosted foods," as they were known then, and cold-storage products. Cold-storage foods were usually of such doubtful quality that many states required markets stocking them to post signs warning consumers that "We sell cold storage foods."

Consumers also had first-hand experience with "icing" food in their own homes. The icebox, or icehouse, was refilled by icemen who cameth daily to refill the box. Food could keep for just a day, then the ice would melt. It was difficult to see how anyone could keep fish (the second-most-perishable protein after milk) fresh. Unable to change long-standing consumer attitudes, Birdseye's company soon went bankrupt.

In 1924, he persuaded three new backers to stake him to $60,000 and started General Seafoods Corporation in Gloucester, Massachusetts (even though the company also sold meat and vegetables). Continuing research convinced him that the secret of thawing consumer attitudes about frozen foods lay in even more rapid freezing. By placing packages of fish between two metal surfaces chilled to subzero temperatures, he was able to achieve the results he wanted and ultimately developed this "belt froster" into a forty-foot high, twenty-ton "Quick Freeze" machine; he also organized the original General Foods Company to control all his patents on the freezing process.

Unfortunately, this sophisticated freezing method caused even greater problems with retailers, who were loath to invest large sums of money in the refrigeration equipment needed to store frozen food. More to the point, housewives weren't showing enough interest to change the retailers' minds. As the winter of 1928 approached, most of the 1.6 million pounds of fish Birdseye had frozen and warehoused the previous summer remained unsold; he desperately needed capital and ways to increase distribution.

Every food processor he approached turned him down until he called on the Postum Cereal Company (see Chapter 3). Postum officials saw tremendous potential in frozen foods and already had a well-established system of distributing food through grocery stores and food brokers. In June 1929, Postum, together with Goldman-Sachs Trading Corporation, purchased Birdseye's assets and patents and the Birds Eye trademark and rechristened itself General Foods Corporation.

In an effort to test the depth of consumer resistance to frosted foods, General Foods put together a forty-week sales effort in Springfield, Massachusetts, that was ambitious, even by today's standards. General Foods home economists and salespeople:

- interviewed hundreds of women to determine what they knew about frozen foods;
- offered home economics classes, women's clubs, and church groups the chance to discuss frozen foods with nutritionists;
- paid for and installed the first refrigerated cases ($1,500 apiece) in eighteen Springfield grocery stores and billed the grocers for frozen foods on a consignment basis;
- sent teams of demonstrators to the grocery stores to encourage shoppers to sample frozen chicken, steak, and strawberries.

Amid great anticipation, the introduction was set for March 6, 1930, and it was a partial success. Housewives who had been approached individually bought the frozen loganberries, steaks, and bluepoint oysters; on the other hand, there was no huge demand for frozen foods. Moreover, it had taken General Foods six months to stockpile 600,000 pounds of food for the Springfield experiment and only 75,000 pounds were sold.

General Foods increased spending on other freezing plants,

super-insulated railroad cars, and customized fishing trawlers; however, these expenditures produced little change in consumer attitudes or acceptance among retailers. By 1933, Birdseye's firm had sold nearly 23 million pounds of frozen food, but was selling it in only 516 retail outlets, nearly all of them in New England.

The time had come for drastic changes, and General Foods made two important ones. The company developed a new, relatively inexpensive, freezer case, which it was able to offer to retailers at a reasonable monthly rental fee—$10 or $12.50, depending on the size of the store. Retailers were willing to try the new equipment on a short-term rental basis, where they had flat out refused to buy freezers before.

But the key change came in marketing direction. Rather than continuing to sell individual consumers one by one, the new strategy promoted bulk sales to institutions—hospitals, schools, hotels, restaurants, even prisons. The target prospect was no longer an individual housewife, but a large hotel, restaurant, hospital, or steamship.

The idea of targeting institutional markets offered several advantages:

1. Institutional buyers purchased in large quantities, which could staunch the sixteen-year flow of red ink at Birds Eye. Where a grocer might buy a dozen packages at a time, a hospital might buy five hundred.
2. Institutions were grateful for the convenience of preparation and time savings that frozen foods offered; there was no more sorting, no more chopping, and there was easy storage of odd-shaped vegetables like broccoli.
3. Large numbers of consumers would be introduced to frozen foods with no fanfare. Some executives had contended that all the hoopla in Springfield had put consumers on their guard and had increased their natural sales resistance to frozen foods.
4. There was positive "rub-off" from having hospitals and schools use frozen foods and, by extension, endorse them and lend their own good names to the process of educating consumers about the healthfulness of frozen food.

The process of knocking on institutional doors was entrusted to George L. Mentley, who decided to call on the toughest customers outside New England first and set up shop in New York City. (He figured if he could make it there, he could make it anywhere.) After some turndowns, he made a sale to the Childs restaurant chain and then made a deal with the Chase National Bank to supply its employee and executive lunch rooms. Finally, he sold the world-famous Waldorf-Astoria Hotel, leading to a publicity windfall and an immediate promotion to general sales manager.

When General Foods got similar results in Syracuse, New York, favorable word of mouth began filtering into grocery stores. Six months later, Birds Eye's sales volume in New York state had tripled. With strong institutional sales, General Foods was able to go back to grocery and supermarket owners and report a tangible change in consumer attitudes concerning frozen foods. A national city-by-city roll-out followed, and by 1937, Birds Eye began to show a profit for the first time in its history.

But Birds Eye would require a world war to reach its full potential. As American women became increasingly involved in wartime mobilization, they had less and less time to prepare food and increasingly turned to their grocers' frozen food cases to save time in preparing meals. Birds Eye was finally able to achieve full national distribution just around the time that one out of every four American housewives became a defense worker.

Convenience foods had come of age, but Birds Eye had one last obstacle to overcome. After the Japanese attack on Pearl Harbor, food processors of all kinds were threatened by the U.S. government with production cutbacks, since they were considered "nonessential" industry. Executives from General Foods were able to convince the government that freezing food in paper packages was infinitely more economical than canning it, since canning 20 million pounds of vegetables required 2,600 tons of vital steel. The argument proved so persuasive that quick-frozen foods were eventually listed on the Office of Price Administration charts of available foods posted in food stores everywhere.

After the war, the frozen-food industry expanded dramatically, and 450 packers were involved in quick-freezing a billion pounds of food. Before his retirement in 1948, Clarence Birdseye went on to patent 250 other products, from infrared heaters to recoilless harpoon guns. Asked his secret of success, he said, "go around asking a lot of damfool questions and taking chances."

• • • • • • •

PRODUCT   BIRDS EYE FOODS

Pivotal *P*: Perseverance

Birdseye tried to popularize frozen food one-on-one. By focusing on the institutional market, General Foods found a larger audience with a greater need for preserved food.

Primary *P*'s: Position, Perception

Since institutions need reliability in food purchasing, their endorsement made frozen foods "safe" in the public's mind and gave frozen food a big push toward acceptance.

• • • • • • •

PAMPERS   Bottom Liner

Vic Mills, a director of Procter & Gamble's development division, didn't fully understand the limitations of cloth diapers until he babysat for his first grandchild in 1956.

After several unhappy experiences, he brought the matter up in several product-development meetings. P & G had just bought the Charmin Paper Company, which had already done some R & D work on disposable diapers. The company did extensive market research and learned that a dozen cloth diapers a day had to be rinsed, soaked, washed, dried, and folded.

To add insult to all this drudgery, most consumers were, like Vic Mills, not very pleased with the diapers' performance. Although cloth diapers were universally accepted, they had several drawbacks.

- They bunched up when wet, making babies unhappy.
- They weren't absorbent enough to keep babies dry.
- They trapped wetness, which irritated tender skin.
- They required either tedious rewashing at home or employing a diaper service, which made them expensive in time and money and a nuisance to store when soiled.

Disposable paper diapers had drawbacks, too. Mothers considered them even less effective in controlling wetness; most were bought by traveling parents as a stopgap. The existing brands, Chux and Drypers, were considered pricey and were used in less than 1 percent of the 15 billion annual diaper changes in America.

To sum it up, like strained baby food in the 1920s, disposable diapers were regarded as a "specialty product," all right for traveling but not as good as cloth for everyday use. Taking into consideration the drawbacks of cloth diapers, their own expertise in making absorbent disposable products like Bounty paper towels, and the immense size of the market, P & G saw an opportunity and decided to get into the disposable-diaper market late in 1957.

P & G's first idea was to develop a highly absorbent, pleated pad that could be inserted into a specially designed plastic panty similar to a diaper being sold successfully in Scandinavia. Six months later, smiling P & G marketers delivered pads and panties door-to-door to parents in Dallas. The offer of free diapers was accepted, but, with the thermometer hovering around 93 degrees, test results were overwhelmingly negative. The diaper was absorbent and shaped comfortably, but it made babies too hot and caused diaper rash even more frequently than the plastic pants associated with cloth diapers.

Despite this unhappy beginning, P & G remained committed to creating a marketable disposable diaper and spent another six months and $175,000 in raw materials redesigning the product. Eventually, company engineers came up with a way to get rid of the plastic pants entirely by using a thin sheet of plastic that kept moisture in but allowed greater air circulation to beat the heat problem.

A second innovation—a porous sheet between the baby and the absorbent material—allowed fluid to pass through but kept it from coming back, keeping the babies drier and more comfortable. When the final design was approved, 37,000 hand-assembled diapers were given to parents in Rochester, New York, for a second test, and nearly two-thirds thought the product was as good as or better than cloth diapers.

With this encouraging feedback, P & G set out to produce in quantity what was an entirely new product. An engineer told Oscar Schisgall, author of *Eyes on Tomorrow*, "There was no standard equipment. It seemed like a simple task to take three sheets of material—plastic back sheet, absorbent wadding, and water-repellent top sheet—fold them in a zigzag pattern, and glue them together. But glue applicators dripped glue. The wadding generated dust. Together, they formed sticky balls which fouled the equipment." Although P & G had filed a patent for the first multifold disposable diaper on July 17, 1961, it would take another whole year for engineers to design and build a small production line.

All the problems weren't encountered on the production side, either. For one thing, competition was heating up in what had been a sleepy category. Chux were a Consumers Union Best Buy in 1961, and mass merchandisers were making their presence felt in disposables—Montgomery Ward with Tiny World and Sears, Roebuck & Company with Honeysuckle. These brands were square, like the cloth diapers mothers were used to dealing with; Pampers were rounded, and some women stretched them beyond their breaking point, causing the diapers to leak.

This problem was corrected by putting specific instructions on the first packages of machine-made diapers, but more serious problems remained. Some women equated the time they spent on their babies with the amount of love the babies received. These women resisted the idea of disposables, feeling guilty and unworthy (according to P & G research) because they were devoting fewer hours to their babies' welfare and weren't taking care of them in the accepted way, an attitude that Gerber had also had to deal with.

P & G dealt with this brilliantly when it came time to name the diapers. Serious contenders included Dri-Wees, Tads, Solos, Larks, Winks, and Zephyrs, but P & G chose a name that suggested directly that disposable diapers were even better for baby than cloth diapers; they named the disposables Pampers. The name eloquently suggested that the Pampers user was just as concerned about her baby's well-being as mothers who used the more traditional, but less effective, cloth variety.

In December 1961, Pampers was first test marketed as a mass-production line item in Peoria, Illinois, and was heralded as a convenience item. "No more washing diapers," crowed the local *Star-Journal*. Some glitches appeared immediately, however. The diapers, which were advertised as flushable, often stuck in pipes, making plumbers happy but mothers furious. In addition, the diapers cost about ten cents a diaper, only slightly less than the cost of cloth diapers and diaper service. Since Pampers hadn't been accepted as a mainstream product, consumers thought the price was "too much to pay." And finally, perhaps most important, the convenience argument didn't seem to be making much of a dent with mothers, perhaps due to disappointments with earlier disposables. The company admits, "The Peoria test was a major disappointment."

Pampers had laid an egg.

Just when P & G might have thrown in the towel, new demographic studies showed that the U.S. was about to experience what would turn out to be a second baby boom mirroring the post–World War II boom. This meant that the figure of 15 billion diaper changes reported in 1957 was seriously outdated and would become nearly 20 billion by 1962. With the potential market growing by a third, disposable diapers could still become immensely profitable, given some economies of scale to be achieved through a combination of production and promotion.

As is often the case, the key to reducing production costs lay in simplifying the package—cutting back from three- to two-color printing, reducing the costs of certain raw materials, and speeding up the assembly lines. But the more important change was made in television commercials and print ads. Instead of promoting Pampers as a convenience item for mothers, the whole focus was changed to babies, stressing that Pampers kept babies dry and happy.

The main benefit for consumers was changed from convenience to peace of mind, a more compelling argument, particularly to mothers using what was still considered a slightly unconventional product. Now, assured that their babies were drier and more comfortable, Pampers users could justify switching to disposables, particularly when the price was nearly a third less than that of cloth diapers. A second test in Sacramento featured Pampers for about eight cents a diaper, and consumer response was enthusiastic. More important, there were repeat purchases, meaning that disposables were now perceived as an everyday item, not a specialty bought just when the family took a trip.

As reorders began pouring in, new plants were built to produce Pampers in Pennsylvania, Missouri, California, and Georgia. With increased sales, the price kept dropping, and eventually P & G was able to meet its target of six cents a diaper. By 1976, half the babies in the U.S. wore Pampers.

Ironically, the price issue, which had seemed so daunting in 1961, became irrelevant once disposables were accepted. In 1987 the price per diaper was twenty-eight cents—three times what a diaper service charges to pick up soiled diapers and leave clean ones. Nevertheless, nearly 75 percent of all babies regularly wear disposables, which now sport improvements like refastenable tapes, elasticized leg gathers, and superabsorbent material that interrupts the formation of diaper rash.

Once disposables became accepted, P & G's legendary patience was rewarded with a soaring sales curve and the lion's share of a $5 billion international market. These days, the focus is not on selling Pampers, but in finding ecologically sound ways of disposing of them.

• • • • • • •

PRODUCT PAMPERS

Pivotal *P*: Perseverance

Procter & Gamble stuck with Pampers through production problems, high prices, and consumer resistance and made them better than cloth diapers by using baby's point of view.

Priority *P*'s: Positioning, Pitch, Price

The name Pampers undercut the notion that mothers who didn't handwash diapers didn't love their babies. Eventually, Pampers' popularity brought the price down, too.

• • • • • • •

In every other chapter of this book, the stories are told in chronological order; however, I have made an exception to make the story of Gail Borden the last one. His story is so poignant and such an example of tenacity that I wanted to end with the story of a man who learned—a bit late—that, for thirteen years, he'd been trying to sell the wrong part of the cow.

BORDEN'S MILK   Bum Steer

Gail Borden helped write Texas's first constitution, edited the *Telegraph and Texas Land Register*, and printed in it the words that became Texas's declaration of independence—"Remember the Alamo."

Borden had become interested in health matters early in life when a persistent hacking cough plagued him in the 1830s. The cough was eliminated by a family move from Norwich, New York, to Amite County, Mississippi, where he taught school before moving to Texas. When Texas won its independence from Mexico, Borden became a tax collector in Galveston, laid out most of the city streets, and sold real estate to support his family.

Aware that many deaths of the period were traceable to tainted food, he foresaw that settlers would eventually be forced to find a method of food storage beyond eating fresh-killed meat. One of the most promising methods was dehydrating meat to condense it. When a yellow-fever epidemic claimed his wife and four-year-old son in 1844, he redoubled his efforts and was soon boiling 120 pounds of beef down to 10 pounds. When gold was discovered at Sutter's Mill in 1848, thousands of would-be miners flocked to California. Borden saw a second market for a condensed, nutritious, nonspoiling meat product like pemmican, the Indians' dried beef.

He learned to retard spoilage in raw meat by blending it with flour, pressing it into two-pound loaves, and drying it in the sun. Gold miners bought six hundred pounds of these "meat biscuits" over a two-year period, and explorer Dr. Elisha Kent Kane used them on an expedition to the Arctic Circle. In 1851 Queen Victoria awarded his biscuits the Great Council Medal at London's International Exhibition, and he and his brother Tom built a large meat-condensing plant in Galveston.

Unfortunately, there was no volume market for condensed meat.

When Borden tried to sell his wares to the U.S. government as army rations, the Quartermasters Corps was put off by the biscuit's pungent taste. Managers of hotels, railroads, and hospitals had similar opinions. Finally, to make matters worse, mining had lost much of its appeal in the intervening three years—the California Gold Rush was almost over.

In 1852, Borden lost his plant in a bankruptcy proceeding, but he still retained his optimism. He bragged to a friend, "Don't infer that I have given up, for I know that the meat biscuit is one of the discoveries of the age." Convinced of the value of condensation, he continued, "I mean to put a potato into a pillbox, a pumpkin into a tablespoon, the biggest sort of watermelon into a saucer."

Several years later, his tone had changed. With his resources exhausted, he wrote another friend, "Every piece of property I own is mortgaged. I labor fifteen hours a day." Clearly, Borden had overestimated the market for condensed meat, so he began searching for another way to retain his hard-won knowledge of the condensation process and transfer it to another product.

He thought back to an incident that had occurred aboard ship on the way back from London. A herd of cows supposed to supply infants on board with fresh milk took sick, and as a result, four babies died of impure milk. Borden knew that Nicholas Appert, the father of the glass bottle, had condensed small amounts of milk in bottles for Napoleon's soldiers. He decided that supplying babies with condensed milk was a way to cater to a far larger market than selling meat biscuits to miners.

He initially tried boiling the milk; those experiments added a few more hours of freshness but gave the milk a burnt taste. Recalling how the Shakers used vacuum pans to condense sugar and fruit juices, Borden switched to vacuum equipment; vacuum cans avoided the burnt taste by permitting evaporation with less heat and also retarded spoilage by eliminating air during evaporation. By greasing the Shaker pans, he could prevent milk from souring for as long as three days.

Nevertheless, his first patent application was denied, because the patent commissioner couldn't "conclude that this exclusion of air is important." Fortunately, Robert McFarlane, editor of *Scientific American*, and Dr. John H. Currie, the head of a New York laboratory, tested Borden's claims and concluded that the vacuum pan was indeed a new and important discovery. Borden was granted a patent in August 1856, and two months later the world's first condensed milk factory opened in Wolcottville, Connecticut.

It proved to be yet another financial disaster for Borden.

Farmers and grocery stores mounted effective campaigns against the unnatural "canned milk," and Borden became so discouraged that he sold half the rights to his patent. In the spring of 1857, just when the nation was entering a recession, he decided to try one more time in Burrville, Connecticut, and would probably have failed again because of undercapitalization had not chance intervened.

Riding on a train one day, Borden happened to meet Jeremiah Milbank, a wholesale grocer and banker. Intrigued with the idea of supplying condensed milk for babies, Milbank agreed to bankroll Borden. In May 1857 the New York Condensed Milk Company came into being, and forty-quart cans of Borden's condensed milk were carted through New York streets. Condensed milk got a boost when *Leslie's*

Illustrated Weekly praised Borden's for its purity; however, that publicity didn't translate immediately into sales, and, according to company literature, the company "hoed a hard row until the Civil War."

Ironically, the federal government, which had turned thumbs down on Borden's meat biscuit and fought his patent application for three years, was later the source of his salvation when the Civil War broke out. The Union army placed a huge order for its field ration; when Mary Todd Lincoln patriotically served condensed milk at a White House dinner, civilian sales got a boost as well.

In 1864, Borden decided to sell the milk in small individual cans to reduce the price and to facilitate storage. Naming the little cans of condensed milk Eagle (after our national symbol) enabled Borden to show a $145,000 profit over the course of two years, and they're still on the market, more than 120 years later.

Borden used his remaining ten years working on other condensation projects, including the abandoned meat-preservation experiment. He never did find the solution, though, and he died in 1874. Borden is buried beneath a huge granite-shaped milk can in New York City's Woodlawn Cemetery, and his epitaph reads, "I tried and failed, I tried again and again, and succeeded."

•   •   •   •   •   •   •

PRODUCT   BORDEN'S MILK

Pivotal *P*: Perseverance

Gail Borden never gave up on condensing food. When he switched from meat to milk and miners to mothers, he appealed to a far larger audience.

Primary *P*'s: Pitch

Condensed milk gave moms low cost and retarded spoilage plus a key emotional pitch—peace of mind. (Michelin recently used babies in a similar way to sell tires.)

•   •   •   •   •   •   •

· · · · · · ·

EPILOGUE

· · · · · · ·

I FEEL a special kinship with the people whose stories make up this book—Clarence Birdseye and C. W. Post, "Boss" Hoover and Gail Borden, Ed Noble and Walter Mack. Like them, I too had to stumble and fall, pick myself up, and start all over again—with this book.

It was completely rewritten on three separate occasions and started with another publishing house. My editor tried to clone a successful book called *Intrapreneuring* and told me to rewrite mine, using it as a template; I "lost" it before I had even left the building, wrote the publisher asking for the rights back, and salved my wounded pride while the book sat in a drawer for three years.

Before I was ready to dig it out again and face the possibility of writing it again (and failing again), I read Peter Drucker's book *Innovation and Entrepreneurship*. In discussing failures, Drucker wrote:

> A good many failures are, of course, nothing but mistakes, the results of greed, stupidity, thoughtless bandwagon-climbing, or incompetence whether in design or execution. Yet, if something fails despite being carefully planned, carefully designed, and

conscientiously executed, that failure often bespeaks underlying change and, with it, opportunity.

I got the message. While it may be difficult to see at first, failure *can* be the road to opportunity, the road to a second chance. The first version of the book rambled in spots; it wasn't clear. I tried again, reworking it in two large sections—new products and failed categories (like grain-based coffee). That version was, if anything, even worse. It was preachy, pedantic; it was boring. The book went back into the drawer.

In August 1989, my wife Suzy suggested I take another look while I was reading *The Heart of the Order* by Thomas Boswell, who writes as thoughtfully about baseball as Drucker does about business. Talking about the 1980s, Boswell says:

> If baseball in the eighties . . . has taught us one distinction, it's
> the difference between success and excellence. . . . There's no
> substitute for excellence—not even success. Success is tricky,
> perishable, and often outside our control; the pursuit of success
> makes a poor cornerstone. Excellence is dependable, lasting,
> and largely an issue within our own control.

To paraphrase, pursuing excellence is more important, more reliable, and more easily attainable than courting fickle success. The notion sank in, and I started to think about responsibility and the products in this book. When things go awry technically, television tells us, "We regret that we cannot bring you the program originally scheduled due to circumstances beyond our control." The lesson I belatedly learned from Borden and William Coleman and Henry Crowell and Patrick Frawley was that absolutely nothing was beyond their control. They researched, worked with, and approved or changed every aspect of their products.

If some brands of ballpoint pens had leaked, Frawley must have said, "Well, gee, that's too bad, but, hey, I think I can do it better." If consumers didn't buy gasoline lanterns or strained baby food or caffeine-free coffee, the Colemans and the Gerbers and the Posts saw that they had their reasons and worked hard to overcome the obstacles others had put in their way.

There is no one formula for success, but in evaluating the people behind the stories in this book, it's safe to say that, as a group, they:

- took total responsibility for their products, because only by controlling the variables that had tripped up their predecessors could they improve them.
- were committed to doing the job right—no matter how long it took or what it entailed.
- looked on failures as part of the process and learned something from each one.

When I began this book, one of the first sources I explored was Thomas Berg's book on *Mismarketing*, and I reread a section of it while writing this epilogue. In my favorite passage, Berg tells of the advice IBM's Thomas Watson (once, William Patterson's right-hand man at NCR) gave to another struggling writer named Arthur Gordon:

You're making a common mistake. . . . You're thinking of failure as the enemy of success. Every one of those manuscripts was rejected for a reason. Have you pulled them to pieces looking for a reason? That's what I have to do when an idea backfires. You've got to put failure to work for you . . . go ahead and make mistakes. Make all you can. Because, remember, that's where you'll find success. On the far side of failure.

· · · · · · ·

SELECTED

BIBLIOGRAPHY

· · · · · · ·

NEWSPAPER AND MAGAZINE ARTICLES

"The Ad Biz Gloms on to 'Global.'" *Fortune*, November 12, 1984, p. 77.

"The Battle of the Brands." *Forbes*, February 9, 1987.

"Breakfast of Champions, Inspiration for Millions." *Los Angeles Times*, March 15, 1985, Sec. III, p. 1.

"Cheap, But Still Rich." *Forbes*, February 24, 1986.

"Cleaning Up." *Corporate Report Minnesota*, February 1986.

"The Cola War." *Newsweek*, August 30, 1976, p. 67.

"The Company That Should Have Gone Broke." *Saturday Evening Post*, September 24, 1949, p. 26.

"Dannon's Culture Coup." *Marketing & Media Decisions*, November 1986.

"The Day Smirnoff Came to Heublein." *Heublein Today*, July/August, 1975.

"The Frawley Phenomenon." *Fortune*, June 22, 1981, p. 104.

"Gas From Gasoline." *Coleman Co.*, July 1982.

"Glue's Failure Backs 3M's Biggest Success." *Los Angeles Times*, December 14, 1985, Sec. IV, p. 1.

"Has-Been Brands Go Back to Work." *Fortune*, April 28, 1986.

"Here's One Tough Cowboy." *Forbes*, February 9, 1987.

"High Stakes at the High Chair." *Marketing & Media Decisions*, October 1986.

"The History of Writing Instruments." Paper by Connie Brinker, presented at Wade Seminar, August 2, 1985.

"How to Save an Aging Product." *New York Times*, January 24, 1982, Sec. VI, p. 6.

"History of Jell-O." *Leroy Gazette-News*, January 12, 1939, p. 1.

"Increasing Sales by Breaking Merchandising Precedent." *Printer's Ink*, February 13, 1930 (reprint).

"Industry Feature: Seven-Up." *Madison Avenue*, March 1975, p. 20.

"Isaac Singer and His Wonderful Sewing Machine." *American Heritage*, March 1967.

"Jell-O Deal Sewed Up." *Advertising Age*, January 5, 1987, p. 22.

"Kleenex." *Modern Packaging*, April 1950.

"L'eggs Gilds Lily, Peps Up Sales." *Package Engineering*, March 1971.

"L'eggs Products, Inc." *Harvard Business School Study*, 1975.

"Living with the Limits of Marlboro Magic." *Fortune*, March 18, 1985.

"The Lures and Limits of Innovation." *Fortune*, October 20, 1980, p. 84.

"Minnetonka's Hard Sell for Softsoap." *Sales & Marketing Management*, January 12, 1981, p. 27.

"Minnetonka's Struggle to Stay One Step Ahead." *New York Times*, December 28, 1966, p. 8.

"Mister Chesebrough's Wonderful Jelly." *Reader's Digest*, May 1954, p. 123.

"Mixing Confidence With Paint," *The Chameleon* (Sherwin-Williams Company), April 26, 1893, p. 1.

"More Bounce to the Ounce." *The New Yorker*, July 1, 1950, p. 32.

"A New-Found Pep at P & G." *New York Times*, February 3, 1985, Sec. F, p. 4.

"New Filter Marlboro's Bid for Top Spot." *Printer's Ink*, January 25, 1955, p. 73.

"New Payoff From Old Brand Names." *Dun's Business Month*, April 1985, p. 42.

"Now They Write on Paper, Too." *Pageant*, April 1962, p. 125.

"Our L'eggs Fit Your Legs." *Business Week*, March 25, 1972, p. 96.

"Pepsi-Cola's Walter Mack." *Fortune*, November 1947, p. 127.

"Preservation of Perishable Food By New Quick-Freezing Methods." *Journal of the Franklin Institute*, April 1933.

"Quaker State Expects Sales Gains with New Packaging System." *Marketing News*, February 3, 1984, p. 154.

"Question: Just What Is Welch's?" *Madison Avenue*, June 1985.

"Seven-Up Bids for Youth with a Negative Pitch." *Business Week*, February 15, 1969, p. 48.

"Seven-Up Seeks Uncola As Its Trademark." *Chicago Tribune*, July 18, 1973.

"Sherwin-Williams." *Fortune*, August 1935, p. 6.

"Striking It Out: How 3M Almost Scotched Its Best-Selling Product." *Corporate Report*, July 1984.

"Tough Times for P & G." *Dun's Business Month*, August 1984, p. 53.

"Tupperware." *Time*, September 8, 1947, p. 90.

"Turning Up the Heat on Frozen Novelties." *GF News* (General Foods Corp.), April/June 1986.

"Welch Foods' Fruitful New Products." *Prepared Foods*, August 1985.

"What's New in Corporate Contests." *New York Times*, July 7, 1985, Sec. 8, p. 11.

"Wheaties' 'Big Boys' Tune Is Jingle of Note." *Advertising Age*, July 26, 1984, p. 3.

"When Entering Growth Markets, Are Pioneers Better Than Poachers?" *Business Horizons*, March/April 1986.

"Why Products Fail." *Inc.*, May 1984, p. 98

BOOKS

Adams, Russell. *King C. Gillette*. Boston: Little, Brown, 1978.

Allen, Margaret. *Selling Dreams*. New York: Simon & Schuster, 1981.

Allyn, Stanley C. *My Half Century with NCR*. New York: McGraw-Hill, 1967.

Arnold, Oren. *What's in a Name*. New York: Julian Messner, 1979.

Atwan, Robert, McQuade, Donald, and Wright, John M. *Edsels, Luckies, & Frigidaires*. New York: Delta, 1977.

Berg, Thomas L. *Mismarketing*. New York: Anchor, 1971.

Bernardo, Stephanie. *The Ethnic Almanac*. New York: Dolphin, 1979.

Brandon, Ruth. *A Capitalist Romance*. Philadelphia: Lippincott, 1977.

Broekel, Ray. *The Great American Candy Bar Book*. Boston: Houghton Mifflin, 1982.

Campbell, Hannah. *Why Did They Name It . . . ?* New York: Fleet Press, 1964.

Carson, Gerald. *Cornflake Crusade*. New York: Holt, Rinehart, 1957.

_____ *The Old Country Store*. New York: Oxford University Press, 1954.

Chesebrough Pond's. *The Story of Chesebrough Pond's*. Greenwich, CT: 1965.

Cleary, David Powers. *Great American Brands*. New York: Fairchild, 1981.

Colmer, Michael. *The Great Vending Machine Book*. Chicago: Contemporary Books, 1977.

Day, Richard Ellsworth. *Breakfast Table Autocrat*. Chicago: Moody Press, 1946.

Deford, Frank. *Lite Reading*. New York: Penguin, 1984.

Dietz, Lawrence. *Soda Pop*. New York: Simon & Schuster, 1973.

Dixie Cup Co. *Is It True What They Say About Dixie?* Norwalk, CT: 1953.

Eberhart, Douglas E. "William Henry Hoover." Undergraduate thesis, Princeton University, 1985.

Felton, Bruce, and Fowler, Mark. *Famous Americans You Never Knew Existed*. Briarcliff Manor, NY: Stein and Day, 1979.

Fleming, Thomas. *The Smirnoff Story*. Farmington, CT: 1975.

Freeman, William. *The Big Name*. New York: Printer's Ink, 1957.

Fryburger, Vernon, ed. *The New World of Advertising*. Lincolnwood, IL: Crain, 1975.

Fucini, Joseph and Suzy. *Entrepreneurs*. Boston: Hall, 1985.

Furst, Sidney, and Sherman, Milton. *Business Decisions That Changed Our Lives*. New York: Random House, 1964.

Gerber Co. *Fifty Years of Caring*. 1978.

Glatzer, Robert. *The New Advertising*. Secaucus, NJ: Citadel Press, 1970.

Green Giant Co. *Memories of a Giant*. 1978.

Grocery Manufacturers of America. *To Market, To Market*. 1983.

Gunther, John. *Taken at the Flood*. New York: Harper, 1960.

Hartley, Robert. *Management Mistakes*. Columbus, OH: Grid Publishing, 1983.

_____ *Marketing Successes*. New York: Wiley, 1985.

Hendrickson, Robert. *The Grand Emporiums*. New York: Scarborough, 1980.

_____ *The Great American Chewing Gum Book*. Radnor, PA: Chilton, 1976.

Hintz, Don. *The People of Culligan*. Canton, OH: Culligan, 1986.

Hoover, Frank. *The Fabulous Dustpan*. New York: World, 1955.

Hopkins, Claude. *My Life in Advertising*. New York: Harper, 1927.

Huck, Virginia. *Brand of the Tartan*. East Norwalk, CT: Appleton Century-Crofts, 1955.

Hyams, Jay, and Smith, Kathy. *The Complete Book of American Trivia*. New York: Rutledge Books, 1983.

Johnson, Laurence. *Over the Counter and On the Shelf*. Rutland, VT: Tuttle, 1970.

Johnson, Richard. *American Fads*. New York: Beech Tree, 1985.

Johnston, Ross. *Marion Harper*. Lincolnwood, IL: Crain, 1982.

Kahn, E. J., Jr. *The Big Drink*. New York: Random House, 1960.

Kaye, Marvin. *A Toy Is Born*. Briarcliff Manor, NY: Stein & Day, 1973.

Kimberly-Clark Corp. *Four Men and a Machine*. 1947.

———— A History of Kotex. 1966.

———— The Story of Kleenex. 1968.

Lois, George, and Pitts, Bill. *George, Be Careful*. New York: Saturday Review Press, 1972.

3M Co. *Our Story So Far*. 1977.

McGrath, Molly Wade. *Top Sellers, U.S.A.* New York: Harper & Row, 1958.

Mack, Walter. *No Time Lost*. New York: Atheneum, 1982.

Marchand, Roland. *Advertising the American Dream*. Berkeley: University of California Press, 1985.

Marquette, Arthur. *Brands, Trade Marks and Good Will*. New York: McGraw-Hill, 1967.

Martin, Milward W. *Twelve Full Ounces*. New York: Holt, Rinehart, 1962.

Mayer, Martin. *Madison Avenue U.S.A.* New York: Harper & Row, 1958.

Miller Brewing Co. *Lite Beer Fact Sheet*. 1986.

Moch, Cheryl, and Varga, Vincent. *Deals*. New York: Ballantine, 1984.

Morgan, Hal. *Symbols of America*. New York: Viking, 1986.

Moskowitz, Milton; Katz, Richael; and Levering, Robert. *Everybody's Business*. New York: Harper & Row, 1978.

Nabisco Brands. *History and Details of Life Savers Candy*. 1985.

Nance, John. *Splash of Colors*. New York: Morrow, 1984.

Nelson, Walter Henry. *Small Wonder*. Boston: Little, Brown, 1965.

National Cash Register. *NCR Primer*. January 1916.

Powell, Horace. *The Original Has This Signature: W. K. Kellogg*. Englewood Cliffs, NJ: Prentice-Hall, 1956.

Procter & Gamble. *Pampers, a New Product, Comes to Market*. 1974.

Ries, Al, and Trout, Jack. *Positioning*. New York: Warner Books, 1981.

———— *Marketing Warfare*. New York: McGraw-Hill, 1986.

Riley, John. *A History of the American Soft Drink Industry*. New York: Arno Press, 1972.

Room, Adrian. *Dictionary of Trade Name Origins*. Boston: Routledge and Kegan Paul, 1982.

Rowsome, Frank, Jr. *The Verse by the Side of the Road*. Lexington, MA: Stephen Greene Press, 1965.

_____ *They Laughed When I Sat Down*. New York: Bonanza, 1959.

_____ *Think Small*, Lexington, MA: Stephen Greene Press, 1970.

Schisgall, Oscar. *Eyes on Tomorrow*. New York: Doubleday, 1981.

Schulz, Don, and Robinson, William. *Sales Promotion Essentials*. Lincolnwood, IL: Crain, 1982.

Sherwin-Williams Co. *The Story of Sherwin-Williams*. 1955.

Shook, Robert. *Why Didn't I Think of That!* New York: Signet, 1982.

Sigafoos, Robert. *Absolutely Positively Overnight!* Memphis, TN: St. Luke's Press, 1983.

Thornton, Harrison. *The History of the Quaker Oats Company*. Chicago: University of Chicago Press, 1933.

Ward, Baldwin. *The Fifty Great Pioneers of American Industry*. Englewood, NJ: Year, Inc./C. S. Hammond, Inc., 1964.

Watkins, Julius Lewis. *The 100 Greatest Advertisements*. New York: William Morrow, 1978.

INDEX